Mud Creek

For Valerie
from
Dent Olive

Mud Creek

The story of the town of
WOLFVILLE
Nova Scotia

Edited by
James Doyle Davison

A New Horizons Project of the Wolfville
Historical Society
1985

ISBN 0-9691719-0-0

Typeset by Irene Melanson and the Acadia University Student
Union, Inc., and by John Woods Ltd., Printing Shop, Halifax,
N.S.

Production Consultant Steven Slipp

Printed and Bound by W.R. Davis, and the Sentinel Printing,
Ltd., Yarmouth, N.S., and Bound by Campbell's Bookbinding
Service, Halifax.

Published and Distributed by Wolfville Historical Society,
P.O. Box 38, Wolfville, N.S. B0P 1X0

Price - softcover, $12.50 postpaid
        hardcover, $17.50 postpaid

CONTENTS

An artist's view of Grand Pre and the Basin of Minas

DEDICATION

To Those Unreported In The History, and Personified by

John Hardwick, Laborer

In Randall House Museum hangs the photo of John Hardwick, Wolfville, described on the picture as "Familiar Figure circa 1890." In the Register of Deeds of 1881 he was recorded as selling property to Leonard P. Johnson. Mrs. Mary Forbes (aged 92 in 1980) immediately recognized him and recalled that he worked as a woodcutter, earning fifty cents per cord. Edgar DeWolfe remembered Hardwick working for his father Dr. H.T. DeWolfe, recalling that John whistled while he labored and kept time to music. When it was suggested that he work to "Yankee Doodle," the saw rushed across the long logs at great speed. John Hardwick, and others like him, warrant the dedication. They gave life and color to the community.

CONTRIBUTIONS

In Appreciation Of

Karl W. and Amy (Wambolt) Borden
by James H. and Catherine (Borden)
McLellan

Marianne (Bishop) Brotz
by Mr. and Mrs. Lovett G. Bishop

Clarence A. Brown
by J. Vernon Brown

E. Percy Brown
by Bryce S.H. Hatfield

Curtis Holmes Chipman
by Donald A. and Carol Ann
(Chipman) Buckley

Dr. and Mrs. C.E. Avery DeWitt
by Dr. Clarence K. and Esmonde
(DeWitt) Morehouse

Paul Ratchford DeWolf
by Mrs. Beryl (DeWolf) Gordon

Dr. and Mrs. Frank H. Eaton
by Keith E. Eaton

Clara (Chisholm) Eaton
by Clara (Nowlan) Jefferson

Dr. Malcolm R. Elliott
by Robbins and Shirley Elliott

Mrs. Madge Forsythe-Smith
by The Forsythe-Smith Family

Major and Mrs. W. Kenneth Fraser
by Mrs. Muriel D. (Fraser) Kerr

Dr. and Mrs. Alexander Gibson
by Dr. M. Allen Gibson

R.E. and J.D. Harris
by Mrs. Gwladys (Babs Harris)
Murray

John Frederic and Minnie Rounsefell
(Simson) Herbin
by J. Robert and Gwendolyn (Kitchen)
Herbin

Mrs. Vesta (Pick) Ilsley
by Mrs. Dorothy M. (Ilsley) Tarr

Mr. and Mrs. J.A. Ingraham
by Ethel C. Ingraham

Mr. and Mrs. R.A. Jodrey
by Dean S. and Jean (Jodrey) Hennigar

Ronald McN. and Margaret B.
(Stackhouse) Keirstead
by Mary Glen (Keirstead) Routliffe
and Peggy (Keirstead) Scammell

Prof. George T. and Emma (Longard)
Kennedy
by Clarence and Norma (Stewart)
Burton

Miss Maud P. Kennedy
by Clarence and Norma (Stewart)
Burton

William and Olive (West) MacIntosh
by Eva (MacIntosh) Urban

Hon. George C. and Miriam (Chisholm)
Nowlan
by J. Patrick Nowlan

Charles A. and Sarah C. Patriquin
by J. Graham and Jessica W. Patriquin

Dr. Frederic W. and Minnie (Johnson)
Patterson
by James D. and Enid (Patterson)
Davison

Harold R. Phinney
by Tom and Gertrude (Phinney) Beattie

Horton W. and Florence (Purdy) Phinney
by Norm Phinney and Bernice
(Phinney) Frizzle

Orville Rex Porter
by Dr. Everett and Ruth (Ingraham
Porter) Linton

Hazel I. Rathbone
by David M. and Althea G. (Rathbone)
Woods

The Ruffee Family
by Jeannette Ruffee

Leon M. Shaw
by Arnold M. Tedford

Dr. Alexander Sutherland
by Allen D. Nickerson

Thomas R. and Winnifred Manning
(Longley) Wallace
by Mrs. Marion (Wallace) Dawes

Mrs. Mary J. (Ma) Warren
by F. Keith Warren

Mr. and Mrs. Aubrey M. Wheaton
by Bryce S.H. Hatfield

Donald Edward Williams
by Horace and Maxine (Williams)
Hughson

Mr. and Mrs. John W. Williams
by Ralph and Betty (Williams)
Chapman

W.D. Withrow, Q.C.
by Mrs. Edna J. (Melvin) Withrow

DIRECTORS

Wolfville Historical Society Directors of the New Horizons Program. Top row: Esther Wright, Glen Hancock, Ian Macdonald, Roy Comeau (New Horizons Field Representative), Allen Nickerson, Harold Stultz; bottom row: Harold Dewis, James Davison (chairman), Marion Grant, Dalton MacKinnon, Marie LeBlanc (secretary, absent).

BOOK STAFF

Editor — James Doyle Davison

Directors — James Doyle Davison (chairman), Edwin Harold Dewis, Marion Elder Grant, Glen Nelson Hancock, Marie Chiasson LeBlanc (secretary), Ian Ranald Macdonald, Dalton Russell MacKinnon, Allen Douglas Nickerson, Harold Thorne Stultz, Esther Clark Wright.

Writers — Helen Dorothy Beals, Mary Elouise Black, Linda Levy Cann, Margaret Slauenwhite Conrad, James Doyle Davison, Jeannette O'Brien Denton, Joan Tyler Easton, Clark Russell Elliott, Sydney Thomas Flecknell, Agatha Palmer Ganong, Glen Nelson Hancock, Eileen MacKay Hiltz, Raymond Kenneth Jefferson, Ruth Ingraham Porter Linton, Margaret Godfrey McCarthy, Austin Donald MacPherson, Barry Morris Moody, Douglas Oscar Snow, Frances Baker Snow, George Richard Stevens, Harold Thorne Stultz, Laurabel Bigelow Taylor, Claudia Lutes Tugwell, Esther Clark Wright.

Readers — Enid Patterson Davison, James Doyle Davison, George Lorimer Moody, Marjorie Allison Wickwire, Edith MacKay Haliburton.

Cover Artist — Helen Dorothy Beals.

PREFACE

The town of Wolfville had no written history in 1980, and realization of the need led the Wolfville Historical Society to provide one. In 1966 the town had commissioned Dr. Watson Kirkconnell, Dr. B.C. Silver, and Mrs. Elsie Findlay to procure information about century-old houses in the community. Drs. Kirkconnell and Silver compiled the material, and a booklet on *Historic Homes* was published in 1967. Dr. Kirkconnell also wrote *The Streets of Wolfville, 1650-1970*. The town recognized this contribution and in 1977 published for the Historical Society a revised edition incorporating both accounts.

The Society agreed in 1979 to consider publishing a pictorial record of Wolfville, and appointed Patricia Townsend and James D. Davison who learned that Lois Hill, recent Acadia graduate, had received a Canada Works Program grant for a similar project. Hill, Heather Leigh, and James Tillotson researched and wrote for a year. Their work was then passed in 1980 to Davison who had been preparing stories about Wolfville after he became Chairman of the "Mud Creek Days" celebration program. Previously, a summary of the Town Council minutes had been prepared through a three-month Winter Works/Municipal Employment Project of late 1977 and early 1978. Those employed by the town were: Gary Hartlen, Martha MacLeod, Judith Swift, and Dawn Russell.

During the Anniversary Celebration the Program Chairman decided to produce a History of Wolfville. He solicited co-operation for the Town Council and the Historical Society, resulting in a town grant to the Society, and the members agreed to help write, publish and distribute the books. They arranged with New Horizons Program for a preliminary grant towards preparing the book, and later the Society received further financial assistance towards the cost of printing *Mud Creek*.

For a more complete story this history should be read along with the 1978 Commemorative Issue of *Wolfville's Historic Homes* and *The Streets of Wolfville*. Also turn to the microfilm collection of the *Acadian* newspaper at Acadia University Library to read B.O. Davidson's "Wolfville of 1869" series, beginning November 1945, and to the issue of mid-August 1930. The town's largest industry, Acadia College/University, has received little attention in this account. That story warrants separate treatment, which it will for Acadia's 150th Anniversary Celebration in 1988. *Mud Creek* covers the period from "Before History" to the end of 1980.

At the suggestion of the New Horizons Directors the local School students (Primary to IX) volunteered a title for the history. The Directors selected that proposed by Richard Anthony Stirling and thank Principal Carson MacDonald and his staff for their co-operation.

Several people have helped to produce *Mud Creek*. The Society engaged Boyd MacLean to assist the Editor in selecting items from the *Acadian*. The staff and facilities of the University Library-Archives have made much easier the collection of data. Through the kindness of Mrs. Herbert Morine, her record of burials at Willow Bank Cemetery was used extensively.

The Directors are indebted to Helen Beals for her cover painting. The Chairman thanks the writers, and the readers of the typescript and galley proofs, and is grateful to the Directors who met regularly to produce and publish the book. The word processor of the Acadia Student Union office was used to prepare the book pages, and the Society appreciates this typesetting service. The Directors also commend Dr. George R. Stevens, of the Geology Department of Acadia University, for his account of "History Before History."

The Federal Department of Health and Welfare wishes that it be clearly understood that the views and conclusions stated in *Mud Creek* are not necessarily those of the Department. The Society highly values the grants provided through the New Horizons Program and completely releases the Department of all responsibility for the contents of *Mud Creek*.

Housing west from Earnscliffe.

FOREWORD

Our family moved to Wolfville when I was six years of age and there my parents lived out their days. So, although I cannot count myself among those who were born there, Wolfville always has been home.

Much of my education was acquired there. Within hours of our arrival, I was a kindergarten pupil in the old MacKay school. At the end of the term, I was given a prize for most improvement. It was a copy of Stevenson's "A Child's Garden of Verses" and was presented by the Sir Robert Borden Chapter of the Imperial Order Daughters of the Empire. The little volume is still on my bookshelves, a reminder of those early days in Wolfville.

It was our great privilege to grow up in Wolfville during the years between the wars. Much of that period was difficult for our parents because the country was in the grip of a severe economic depression. In spite of that, Wolfville did its very best for its young people. When I think of my contemporaries, it is to realize that many extremely fine and able individuals came from the Wolfville of my generation.

The names of a multitude echo through my memories. One does not forget such teachers as Principal B.C. Silver who not only taught what was prescribed in the curriculum but who also worked tirelessly to produce adults of grace and quality.

The town was fortunate, too, in the number of men and women who took time to work with the young. Prominent among them was E. Percy Brown, the scoutmaster. His own life governed by high principles, he expected the same of those to whom he offered leadership.

The presence in our midst of Acadia University provided innumerable opportunities for cultural enrichment and athletic diversions. A growing boy did not always appreciate what was available but, inevitably, his life was touched and enhanced.

What a marvellous kaleidoscope of memories are mine — ball games on the school grounds — magazines at Val Rand's — school friendships — ice cream at The Palms — skating on the duck pond — watching the trains come and go — hiking to White Rock — swimming at Evangeline Beach — Post Office, busy mail time — church on Sunday — Scouts on Friday night — and ...!

Behind all those events and involved in them were the people of Wolfville, beautiful, honest, hard-working people! With folk like that, it had to be the fine town of which I cherish every memory.

All of which is part of an ongoing event, a chapter in the story of Wolfville. I am glad that the tale now is being more fully told. This book is a valuable addition to the archives of the province and to the records of the town. It represents the work of many individuals to whom the rest of us are indebted for their efforts.

It is pleasing to read of that which took place before our time. It freshens precious memories as we are reminded of our own days. And, in years to come, there will be this record for our children that they may read of the Wolfville we know so well. Perhaps, as they read, they will understand why we love the place so dearly.

M. Allen Gibson

I.

IN PRAISE OF WOLFVILLE

A community is judged on first viewing. The evaluation may lead to love at first sight or can be decidedly negative. Newcomers have passed judgement on Wolfville in the past, indicating a favorable opinion. When brochures gave approval, the result has been high praise. These views have extolled the physical attractions of the village and town and its environs. The inhabitants accept that favorable portrayal, and particularly welcome the descriptions that follow.

Wolfville and the surrounding area contain much of the province's most memorable history and legend. The visitor is in the land of the apple, the amethyst, Evangeline, Glooscap, the world's highest tides, dykes that keep out the mighty waters of the Minas Basin. Furthermore, Wolfville has been depicted as the smallest registered harbour in the world.

Four times daily in the Bay of Fundy millions of tons of water pour between the outer walls of Blomidon and Parrsboro shores, creating a gigantic "rapids," lowering and raising water levels in the Minas Basin by fifty and sixty feet. The tides of Wolfville go to thirty feet.

Joseph Howe travelled through Nova Scotia in 1829 and he glowed with praise of the passing scene.

> We ride on through Horton, and a prettier scene no man need desire — now you catch a glance at the Basin, and Blomidon and the Cornwallis River, to your right; and then in a moment more, some huge hill shuts out all these; and to your left, a stretch of marsh, and a sweet little cottage, with patches of corn, and oats, and wheat, to say nothing of the garden and orchard, open upon your view, and make you sigh for the possession of the little Paradise, and almost forswear mingling with the City again.

Wolfville greatly impressed young students who came to Horton Academy, and G.E. Day reported to the *Acadian* his recollections of 1851.

> We are apt to think that the sky was bluer, the grass greener and the water purer near the home where our youth was reclined and our childhood played, than elsewhere. But as I looked over Wolfville for the first time under the bright full moon, and through the clear autumn air which seems to bring objects nearer, I thought this was the most paradisical spot I had ever seen.

Albert Coldwell graduated from the College in 1869 but had previously won a prize for an essay in which he pictured Wolfville.

> The site of the College is one of the finest in North America. It combines natural beauty with a heartfulness in a remarkable degree. Fogs and malaria are unknown, and extremes of temperature are rarely experienced. The lover of natural scenery will find here landscapes of rare attractiveness. The eye can never tire of the beautiful panorama spread out before it of mountain, river, valley, sea and sky. These scenes linger in the memory of the graduate long after he has entered upon the business of life, leading him often to look back yearningly upon the pleasant happy days when, as a student, he opened his

1

heart to the healthful influences of Nature, and allows his eyes to drink in with deep delight the enchanting scenery that stretches from bold Blomidon to the beautiful valley of the Gaspereau.

The Halifax *Herald* of 1888 described Wolfville and its surroundings:

In the middle distance ten miles away rises bold Blomidon, always majestic in his simple grandeur, but varying in beauty as the light and shadows alternate upon his changeful brow; sometimes he is capped with a fleecy cloud-covering, at others standing out in bold relief, the guardian of the inland water; while as the seasons roll by, the soft blue of summer in which he arrays himself gradually changes to the sombre gray of winter. Beyond Blomidon, in the remote background, stretches the long range of the Cobequids, the highest land in Nova Scotia.

In the rear of Wolfville lies the Ridge, a span of the South Mountain, from the summit of which are obtained some of the loveliest views in the province. On the one side the view embraces Minas Basin with all its beautiful surroundings and the valley with its four tidal rivers looking like silver threads in the distance; while on the south we can look down on the beautiful Gaspereau Valley, lovely beyond description.

Gaspereau Valley from "The Stile," N.S.

The view from the South Mountain, the "Ridge".

Charles S.A. Ritchie was a Canadian diplomat, Ambassador, United Nations representative, and was the High Commissioner to London before his retirement. He wrote his recollections in four volumes. From *Diplomatic Passport* are taken a few quotations which reflect his thoughts of Wolfville of 1951 and 1952. He walked on Main Street.

The post office was empty — people collected their mail at the bustling hour of twelve after the Halifax train has come in ... Sundry old ladies are resting — resting their rheumatism, their weak hearts, their jangled nerves. In and out of the sunny main street too blows the town's gossip — blowing like pollen from house to house, from garden to garden.

Wolfville is charming even pretty, the houses painted in spotless white, the gardens tended, trees surrounding the colonial houses. The little town seems like a place met with at the very beginning of a fairy story, before out-of-the way things start happening — a jumping off place and a place to which one is not sorry to return, to see its lights cheerfully glowing after an excursion into strange terrain...

Charles Ritchie's great-great-grandmother, Harriet Sophia DeWolf, was a granddaughter of Simeon DeWolf. Wolfville has beauty of setting, an influence upon the DeWolfs and upon all the fortunate residents of the locality.

A popular scenic view.

II.

HISTORY BEFORE HISTORY

Before the people, and just before history, the glacier had finished its work of re-sculpturing the valley and its flanking ridges. For a million years Nova Scotia had lain asleep beneath a mile-thick blanket of ice. The slow but persistent advance of the ice towards the sea scoured away the forests and the soil, scraped, ground, and polished the bedrock. The land was being prepared for a new birth beneath a new sky. About 12,000 years ago, a warming climate had succeeded in melting all but a few last remnants of the ice. Its removal gradually laid bare a bleak and barren landscape of smoothed hills, torrential streams, and valley choked with thick deposits of sand and gravel from meltwater outwash. On the highlands, patchy mounds of glacial till filled hollows and dammed the drainage channels to create thousands of lakes and marshes. As the ice disappeared and the new land was exposed, the dark green carpet of spruce, fir, and pine began to appear, and with the new forests came its many animals: caribou, musk-oxen, moose, deer, bear and a host of the smaller creatures. And soon came people, and then villages, and Wolfville among them, in its very special place.

Wolfville is located at the eastern gateway to the Annapolis-Cornwallis Valley, and its widest part, (about 9 miles) between North Mountain and Wolfville Ridge. Early settlers, whether native Canadians, Acadian French, or New England Planters, chose wisely to establish at the Valley's mouth, on the gentle slope of the slate ridge. The land about is fertile, and well watered by the many brooks and streams which drain into the Cornwallis River, for the most part following ancient post-glacial drainage ways. The tiny harbour on the Cornwallis River gave ready access to the fishery of the Minas Basin, to other villages on its shores and to the entire world beyond. The remarkable alignment of the North Mountain Ridge somehow blocks and diverts the severe weathers of the Bay of Fundy, and shields the Valley itself like a great bulwark. Sweeping the length of the Valley, the prevailing westerlies bring ideal summers of unusual warmth, sunshine, and just enough rainfall to sustain the water table set by the preceding winter's meltwaters. Nature seems to be in ideal balance here.

There are geological reasons which clarify our understanding of this good fortune. They explain the existence of the two major ridges which flank, and define the valley itself, and explain the more recent topographic changes which have led to the landscape of today. Reaching only a short way back into Earth's own history, two hundred million years, we perceive that our region went through a succession of extraordinary geological settings. These include vast desert conditions and wide-spread volcanic eruption as North America began to split apart from Europe and Africa. Much more recently, the region was Arctic, and lay covered beneath the eastern edge of the great North American-

ERA	PERIOD	EPOCH	START OF, MILLIONS OF YEARS AGO	MAIN EVENTS IN NOVA SCOTIA
CENOZOIC	QUATERNARY	RECENT	0.01	
		PLEISTOCENE	1.6	------ Glacial Age
	TERTIARY	PLIOCENE	5.3	
		MIOCENE	23.7	
		OLIGOCENE	36.6	
		EOCENE	57.8	
		PALEOCENE	66.4	
MESOZOIC	CRETACEOUS		144	
	JURASSIC		208	North Mountain / Vulcanism (Basalt)
	TRIASSIC		245	Blomidon & Wolfville Red Shales & Sands. Start of "Continental Drift".
PALEOZOIC	PERMIAN		286	
	PENNSYLVANIAN		320	Coal Beds
	MISSISSIPPIAN		360	Limestone, Gypsum, Salt.
	DEVONIAN		408	Granite Intruded.
	SILURIAN		438	Slates, Quartzites, Volcanics.
	ORDOVICIAN		505	Slates of Halifax Formation.
	CAMBRIAN		570	Marine Sandstone (Goldenville)

PRECAMBRIAN: Includes most of the Earth's history, back to the time of solidification of the Earth's crust, about 4 to 5 billion years ago.

(Geologic Time Scale Since the Precambrian).

Greenland ice-sheet. Deserts, volcanoes, and glaciers have all done their work here, and left their marks. Before these, Nova Scotia lay beneath the sea for half a billion years.

The rocks reveal their own history. While it may require the expertise of a geologist to interpret the details, anyone sensitive to nature can perceive the clear differences between the soft, stratified red shales of the Valley and Cape Blomidon, the hard dark basalt lava sheet on the crest of North Mountain, and the slates of Wolfville Ridge. Perception leads inevitably to questions of meaning and to a desire to understand the geologic history reflected by such diverse bedrock types.

If we are to understand any history, whether that of an empire or that of the Earth itself, we must put events in proper sequence and establish a calendar of sorts. The calendar of the Earth is very long but no less sequential than any other, and certainly no less understandable. On the basis of two centuries of careful work, geologists have established an accurate earth-calendar covering the time and events since the Earth first developed a hard crust, a space of over four billion years. Since that time mountain systems have risen and fallen, continents have slowly drifted apart and collided, living things have appeared in the seas and on the land, have evolved, proliferated and diversified. Some species have disappeared. The geological calendar accurately records all such events and places our dynamically evolving planet into a time framework we can all appreciate and understand.

(see Table I - The Geological Calendar)

The geologic history of the Wolfville region in Nova Scotia is included within the most recent one-eighth of the Earth's entire history, or since Cambrian time. Primitive living animals had by then developed hard protective outer shells and could thus be preserved or fossilized in the muds which enclosed them upon death.

The bedrock exposed on South (Gaspereau) Mountain consists of slate, quartzite ("sandstone"), and granite. The oldest of these three rock units is the Goldenville Quartzite, originally deposited as a thick blanket of marine sandstones in Cambrian time. It is exposed near Black River Lake along the canal, where it is in contact with the granite of South Mountain. These layers of sand were deposited on what was then the offshore continental slope and at the base of the slope, in strata whose total thickness exceeds four miles. This unit is exposed throughout mainland Nova Scotia and is well known for its gold-bearing veins in some places. In the Wolfville area the rock has been baked by the heat of the granite which intruded into all of the older bedrock units in Devonian time.

Much more common in the Wolfville area is the "Halifax" slate, which is well exposed on Wolfville Ridge and in the Deep Hollow at Greenwich. This rock was deposited in Ordovician time in the deep sea as black mud, with thin laminae of silt, and ultimately attained a thickness of about two miles. Like the Goldenville formation, the Halifax slates occur throughout Mainland Nova Scotia. In places both of these rock units have yielded gold from quartz veins. A good, typical exposure of the slate in Wolfville itself can be seen at the crest of Gaspereau Avenue beneath the highway overpass. The slate there is gently arched into an anticlinal fold and is strongly cleaved in nearly vertical planes.

In the nearby Deep Hollow, beds of the "White Rock Quartzite" are exposed. This rock provided much of the building stone for Wolfville, where several buildings are made from it, as well as stone walls about properties. The old Gymnasium and Horton House of Acadia University, and the stone wall fronting the President's house on Main Street are good examples. The rock is still being quarried today but for use as rubble and erosion protection on the dikes.

The White Rock formation was deposited in Silurian time as blankets of clean white sand above the black muds of the Halifax formation. Like it, metamorphism has changed the sandstone into a totally recrystallized, very hard white quartzite. The pink and brown colours seen in the buildings made from it are due to faint staining by weathered iron-bearing minerals. This formation is rather thin in the Wolfville area, where it attains a thickness of less than 600 feet, but towards the southwest it is much thicker. At Yarmouth the White Rock formation is over a mile thick and includes several volcanic layers along with the quartzite.

The sequence of marine deposits noted above provided continuous sedimentation from Cambrian through Devonian time, for over 200 million years. The unusual episode of deposition which formed the White Rock strata was only a brief interruption in an otherwise continuous sequence, for after the White Rock sands were laid down marine muds were deposited again. These are the "Kentville" slates, and though younger than the the "Halifax" slates, resemble them closely. They can be seen in outcrops along Highway 101 in several places west of Wolfville. Though both slate units are typically dark gray, each has brick-red varieties in this area.

Through later Silurian and into Devonian time, marine conditions and sedimentation prevailed, but the rock units are not exposed near Wolfville. Towards the end of this period, however, a most dramatic event began, one which affected the rock of all of Eastern North America, and parts of the Old World as well.

For millions of years the ocean which separated what are now North America and Europe had been narrowing, due to tectonic movement of the continental plates. Thus "continental drift" eventually brought the two continents into slow, grinding, crushing collision which caused the rock strata to become faulted and folded, like an accordion closing. The high pressures, heat, and deep burial caused metamorphism of the rocks into the conditions we see today. Mudstone and shale changed to slate, sandstone to quartzite, and limestone to marble. Mountains of Alpine scale rose on the surface, the first Appalachians.

Meanwhile, deep underground, immense volumes of liquid rock were being generated, pooled, and intruded into now-folded rock layers. This liquid rock, or magma, solidified to form granite, and it too suffered from the compressive forces of continental collision which were still going on.

Today, the granite occurs as a great mass which occupies a large part of the South Mountain Highlands. Exposures near Wolfville can be seen at Black River Lake.

With the union of the great continents and closure of the "Iapetus" sea which formerly separated them, only shallow, scattered marine basins remained. These became increasingly saline as water evaporated from them in the warm climate, causing precipitation of salt, gypsum and lime muds. Near Windsor, and at many other places in Nova Scotia, these shallow marine deposits have become important economic resources.

The same conditions gave rise to broad marshy woodlands throughout much of the future Nova Scotia, and the buildup of organic material from these eventually formed the many coal strata of the Province. Nature, through cataclysm, was preparing a bright economic future for those who would eventually live here.

Whatever the forces that brought the continents together, creating the Appalachian and Caledonian Mountain systems in the collision process, these forces waned, stopped, then strangely reversed direction. Two hundred million years ago (Triassic time), great cracks began to appear along the eastern side of the earlier suture zone. The land became stretched across a line which today can be traced from Nova Scotia to Florida, and began to break by block-faulting into basins and uplands. One of these fault-basins would become the Bay of Fundy and Annapolis-Cornwallis Valley, filled with reddish sediments washed in from adjacent highlands.

Lizard-like reptiles, the ancestors of the great dinosaurs yet to appear, wandered about the mud-flats and dunes of a desert landscape. Their prints, trackways, and even their bones can today be found in the strata at places about the Minas Basin, not far from Wolfville.

Along a great fracture zone that is now the medial line of the Atlantic Ocean, the great continental mass began to split slowly apart, and the Atlantic Ocean was born by seawater flooding into the ever-widening rift. Volcanic lava poured from the many cracks, both on the sea floor, and on the land. Foraging dinosaurs in the still unformed Annapolis-Cornwallis Valley region must often have been sent into stampedes of terror as earthquakes shook the land, the great rifts opened up, and volcanic eruptions of fiery lava fountained from the earth. Eventually, the entire landscape became buried beneath scores of basaltic lava flows, totalling nearly a thousand feet thick.

Today these basaltic lava flows constitute the bulk of North Mountain, which is a seaward-tilted table-land, or cuesta, extending 125 miles from Cape Blomidon to Brier Island. The caprock of the cuesta is a sheet of hard, resistant basalt which rests on the softer red shales and sands seen prominently at Cape Blomidon. The lavas also make up parts of the floor of the Bay of Fundy.

By now (Jurassic time) the Appalachian Mountain Range had already seen most of its evolution, with peaks of Alpine size. Continental rifting, block-faulting, and vulcanism were features of the Nova Scotia part of the continental shelf. For the next 180 million years, however, this region became essentially quiescent. The land persisted above sea-level, so that erosion was the dominant geological process. The great peaks became worn down, the topography subdued, and though cataclysmic events were taking place elsewhere, the Atlantic seaboard was essentially inactive, geologically at peace. The Alps, Rockies, Andes, and Himalayas all came into being during this quiet time for Eastern North America, where erosion and deposition in balance were creating the vast Atlantic Coastal Plain. Today these sedimentary rock strata of Mesozoic and Cenozoic age, particularly on the offshore continental shelf, are rich sources of oil and natural gas.

The most recent major geologic event to affect this region began only two million years ago (geologically a very short time), with cooling of the climate. Eventually, the winter snowfall would not completely melt in the brief, cool summer, and the permanent snow-ice buildup gradually blanketed much of North America. This glaciation greatly modified the landscape, eroding, scraping, rounding and subduing the bedrock and depositing vast quantities of meltwater outwash sands, gravels, and glacial till everywhere.

Due to the melting of the vast glacier, sea-level rose conspicuously, worldwide. Locally, the rising sea filled the Bay of Fundy and Minas Basin, though the land itself has also tended to elevate slowly, due to "rebound" from the missing weight of the glacier.

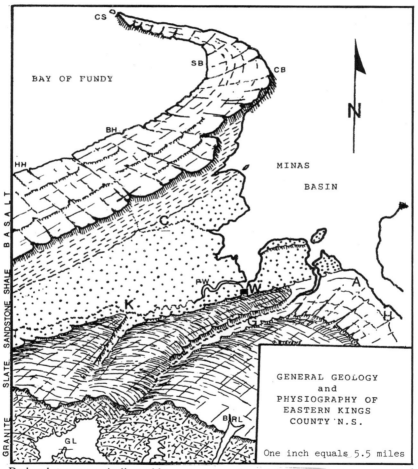

Bedrock types are indicated by patterns, and are labelled on left margin. Key to place-names: A, Avonport; BH, Baxters Harbor; BRL, Black River Lake; C, Canning; CB, Cape Blomidon; CS, Cape Split; G, Gaspereau; GL, Gaspereau Lake; H, Hantsport; HH, Hall's Harbor; K, Kentville; PW, Port Williams; SB Scotts Bay.

9

The lower part of Wolfville is sited above tide on a platform of glacial outwash sands and gravels, themselves deposited on bedrock slate and sandstone. The high porosity and permeability of these glacial sediments permit storage of large quantities of groundwater, and Wolfville draws a major part of its water supply from these glacial sands. The upper part of the town is built on slate bedrock, a notably poor aquifer. Thus, water-supply and quality have largely guided the early settlement and development of the town.

Today the Wolfville-Cornwallis Valley area is geologically quiescent. The faults and volcanoes have risen and then worn away, and the glacier come and gone. All the evidence of these events is clearly stored within the bedrock of the region, a region whose present peaceful, pastoral landscape belies its dramatic, cataclysmic history.

Bluffs of red shale of the Blomidon formation, west shore Minas Basin.

III.

EARLY SETTLEMENTS

1. The First Inhabitants

From 14,000 B.C. to A.D. 1,000 successive waves of Indian bands of the Clovis, Laurentian, Bear River and Shields Archaic type would gather in this part of the valley to catch and cure the spring run of salmon and shad in the Gaspereau River or to make agate spearheads and arrows at Cape Blomidon. As early as 5,000 B.C., hunters camped at Melanson, and various other tribes came and went until A.D. 700 when the Micmac Indians arrived and drove out the other tribes. The conquerors belonged to the Algonquin tribe, were known as "the people of the dawn." It seems that small bands of Micmacs first came about A.D. 1,400 from the Great Lakes region and were kinfolk of the Ojibwas. Like their predecessors, they were seasonally migratory in life style, leading a nomadic existence.

The Micmacs were distinctive. In winter hunting they were the first to use dogs to hunt deer, and the first to have webbed snowshoes. One of their fishing stations was the Melanson site where the Tusket people had smoked fish, where the cemetery now stands. The Micmacs were the first to appreciate the wealth of semi-precious stones available on the beaches of Blomidon. Their arrowheads were chipped from jasper, chalcedony, agate, quartz, and even amethysts. Always they used local stones for the arrowheads they constantly needed; chips and arrowheads of North Mountain stone began to appear over the whole province.

When the French landed at Port Royal they found these nomads sought only sufficient food for their present needs and were not accustomed to accumulate reserves. The weather determined their success and their continued existence, and sometimes its ravages did not permit survival. The men were more rugged and enduring than were the women and children. There were then about 3,000 Micmacs in what are now the Maritime Provinces when the French came.

The Micmacs habitually returned to favoured locations, generally for food, a little of which they stored in trees. Sometimes they would head for Segepenegatig, the area of the present Kings County, and here they met the Acadians who ultimately changed the Indian culture, because the stronger force and superior claims of the whites altered their thinking and living. The missionaries, who tried to convert the Indians, and the traders, who exploited them, generally came before the settlers, who often used the Micmacs to strengthen their fighting forces, and to procure food, but destroyed their self-assurance, convinced them of their inferior place in the white man's society, and removed the red man's claim to the land.

According to tradition, the knoll above the beach at Avonport was an Indian chapel and burying ground, and French settlement was thereby delayed.

The erection of the Grand Pre church made the Avonport chapel unnecessary, and a house was built later on the site. The digging of the foundation unearthed beads and knives beside it. The articles probably had been obtained through trade with the French but may have been useless to the Micmacs. It was thought that the grave was that of a local chief.

The Treaty of Utrecht supposedly gave control of the Nova Scotia area, but did not for long settle the differences between the British and French. Both sides looked upon the Indians as tools and weapons to assist in conquest or defence. Although the Indians in the Melanson area had contact with a priest who spoke the Micmac language, most of them retained their beliefs in nature spirits and their traditional patterns of behaviour. The French authorities did not encourage the Micmacs to associate with those who spoke French, but preferred that they be unlearned and free of the danger of new forms of sin.

The British demand for allegiance to the British King across the waters drew the Indians and French together for a united resistance against this new power. Indian groups attacked the British, but a peaceful agreement was reached in 1720. The French and Indian forces increased in power and numbers, and the British brought in New Englanders to help in upholding the Crown's authority. The New Englanders established a fort at Minas, where they located nearly 500 troops. The Micmacs continued to take the side of the French, who lost out in the end. After the expulsion of the Acadians in 1755, the Micmacs began to lose interest in these squabbles between nations. In 1761 they ceased fighting the English, though the enmity and distrust continued for another twenty years and the Indians occasionally threatened to attack the colonists. Meanwhile the British attempted to gain the support of the Indians, and continued to present gifts to the tribesmen.

In the 1770s the New England colonists in Nova Scotia won predominant positions through their numbers and leadership. When the Revolutionary War came the Micmacs decided to ignore the American pleas for support, but not until 1779 did they last fight with the British. By the time the war ended in 1782 the Indians played no important part for or against either side in the conflict, and they ceased to be a significant segment of the population. By 1830, when Wolfville received its new name, the Indians had settled in areas throughout the province, and those who had formerly encamped near Wolfville ceased to come. In 1838 there were 1,425 Indians in the province: by 1841, when they had been placed on reserves, their numbers had fallen to 1,166.

2. The Acadians

The Acadians, the first Europeans to settle in the Horton area, began moving from Port Royal up the Bay of Fundy and into the Minas Basin, perhaps as early as 1650, certainly in large numbers from 1670 to 1682. Most of those moved to Minas were younger sons and daughters of Port Royal settlers, and were influenced strongly by the traditions brought with them from their original home province of Brittany. By settling further up the Bay, they hoped to achieve greater safety from English raiders and more freedom from the seigneurial control in Port Royal. The Minas settlement became the most important of the Acadian farmlands, and the population grew rapidly from fifty-seven people in 1682 to 350 in 1693. When Acadia was ceded to the British by the Treaty of Utrecht in 1713 the Acadians were reluctant to leave their productive soil. The Minas Basin settlement was retained, and its population increased by other Acadians from the now British-dominated Annapolis Royal. By 1731, 168 families lived in Grand Pre and Canard (Les Mines).

The Acadians built dykes on the rivers flowing into the Minas Basin and grew their crops and grazed their cattle on the dyked land. They produced their own homespun cloth and milled their lumber by windmill, watermills in brooks, and tidal-powered sawmills. They had sufficient produce and livestock to create a surplus for trade. From the New England traders who plied their way up and down the coast of Nova Scotia and Newfoundland they got the goods that they could not produce. This trade was illegal, but, as the French government at Quebec was unable to supply the colonists with these luxury goods, it was permitted. As peasant farmers, successful enough to have a surplus for trade, the Minas settlers were tolerant of other Europeans and satisfied with co-existence with the Indians.

Unfortunately for the Acadians, they were not allowed to continue their quiet life as peasant farmers under British suzerainty, because the authorities at Quebec and in France saw the Acadians as a valuable fifth column and a means of regaining their lost colony. Politically minded priests, who were certain of the return of French domination, informed the Acadians in no uncertain terms where their loyalties should lie and would not let them take oaths of allegiance which the English governors of Annapolis Royal were trying to get. When war broke out between Britain and France in 1744, the turbulent situation at Louisburg and Port Royal threatened the British sovereignty in Acadia, and that alarmed the colonists to the south, who had suffered much from French and Indian raids. Late in 1747 they established a force of near-

The old willow trees in Grand Pre Park.

13

ly five hundred around Grand Pre and housed them in the homes of Acadians who wanted to be neutral. Early in the morning of a snowy day, February 12, 1748, a surprise attack was made by the Quebec Canadians, with two Indian detachments of sixty, and a number of Acadians as guides. Colonel Arthur Noble was killed in what was called the "Grand Pre Massacre," also two sentries and about one hundred of the Americans. The French claimed they killed 140. Peace was agreed upon, and the Americans troops withdrew to Port Royal.

The British fears about the uncertainties of the situation led to establishment of a small permanent force at Grand Pre from 1749 to 1753. Orders were sent from England to the King's governors in America to drive the French from their territories by force so that Britain could have supremacy in the colonies. Meanwhile, the Acadians wished only to be left alone and allowed to remain neutral.

Although the war had ended, both sides in Acadia geared up for the next round. By this time the British authorities in Nova Scotia were firmly convinced of the perfidy of the Acadians. Indians and Acadians had become allies against the British. The Acadians asked for retraction of the order to disarm. In reply, the British demanded complete allegiance. The French refused. A determined Governor Lawrence took quick action to achieve what had long been a British objective — the expulsion of the Acadians. Chief Justice Belcher approved the action but it was not communicated to the home authorities before action was taken.

The task was carried out by Colonel John Winslow and his force of New Englanders with all the cruelty and severity of the eighteenth century. The men were summoned to the church where they were held captive until the transports arrived. In September 1755 the British transport came to carry the people into exile. For twenty-nine days, after making their tragic trek to the embarkation place near Horton Landing, the Acadians waited to board the ship. Some 2,182 persons from Grand Pre were transported. After the last vessel, "The Dove," sailed on October 10, the torch was set to Grand Pre, and only one building was left.

The sudden uprooting of the Acadian population from a land in which they had lived for a century, the loss of lands, homes, personal belongings, and the transportation to distant countries were severe blows, compounded by the separation of the men from their families. By no means all the Acadians had been removed from Nova Scotia, for many had escaped into the woods and managed to survive somehow. One group seized the vessel on which they were being transported and came back; others journeyed overland from their alien surroundings. By 1764 a few of the Acadians were willing to take the oath of allegiance the British required, and by 1793 they were ready to volunteer for military service.

3. New England Settlers

The New England settlers were the founders and developers of Wolfville. It was considered essential by the British authorities to fill up the lands left vacant by the removal of the Acadians, and to open up other sections of the Minas Basin area, partly because the sovereignty of the new world was still in doubt, and partly because Halifax and other Nova Scotia garrisons needed supplies from farms. The British government suggested sending English soldiers and their families, but Governor Lawrence, aware that funding from England had been reduced, due to the cost of the continuing war with France, ruled out that possibility. He suggested that New England settlers, acquainted with life in the new world, could more quickly become self-sufficient. It was not until 1758, however, that he issued in the *Boston Gazette* of October 12 a proclamation that lands along the shore of the Bay of Fundy, and at Liverpool, Barrington, and Yarmouth, were now available.

Prospective settlers showed considerable interest, but raised a number of questions about Nova Scotia. A second proclamation, in January 1759 cleared up many of the matters not clearly stated in the earlier one, and stressed that a great expanse of cultivable land was available to newcomers. It also emphasized that all would be given freedom of religous worship and beliefs, a matter that had become important in New England. The Puritans, who had left England more than a century before because of their desire for freedom of worship, had in their turn become intolerant, and a number of individuals and families had left Massachusetts in search of religious freedom. There was also a need for expansion, which at the time seemed impossible westward because of the Alleghanies and the frequent raids by Indians on settlements on the western fringe.

In May 1759 five scouts or agents for New England groups, Major Dennison, John Harris, Joseph Otis, James Fuller from Connecticut, John Hicks from Rhode Island, proposed to settle a township of Minas, "joining the river Gaspereau, including the great marshes, so called: which township to consist of 100,000 acres, to 200 families." Charles Morris, the Chief Land Surveyor of Nova Scotia, had accompanied the group, and during the next months, army engineers surveyed the planned Township of Horton for the largest settlement. Morris chose Vieux Logis (where the old fort used to be) as the centre of Horton Township. Each grantee was entitled to 500 acres with a town lot, dyke lot, three classes of farm lots, an island lot, and others. The town lot was one half acre of a rectangular piece of Town Plot where a house and barn were to be erected. Each grantee was also entitled to half share for a grown son, Horton Township, named for Lord Halifax's home in Northampton, Horton Hall, was the area south of the Cornwallis, extending from the Pisiquid and Halfway rivers at Hantsport to Berwick, or possibly as far as Aylesford Bog. Johnson Bishop said that the first and second tiers of lots extended from the covered bridge at Horton Landing to the meeting-house at New Minas. Lots between the Cornwallis and Gaspereau rivers, labelled A and B indicated the Upper Horton area. Baseline A (later Pleasant Street) was laid out between the A or river front lots, and the first tier of B lots, the ridge lots, and Baseline B (later Ridge Road) was laid out between the two tiers of B lots. The island lots, which were intended to give the settlers access to fishing in the bay, were four to six acres on Long Island, Oak Island or Boat Island.

The terms of the settlement were agreed upon with the agents. The grants would be fee simple, subject to the proposed quit rent. Blockhouses were to be built and garrisoned for the defence of the settlers. Fifty families of the number were to have from government an allowance of corn, one bushel per month to each person, or an equivalent in other grain, for one year, and

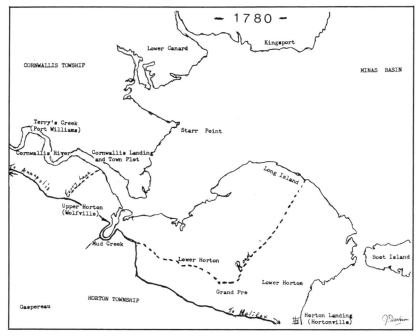

(The Minas Basin Area).

arms and ammunition for defence. The people, with their moveables, stock and equipment, were to be transported at the expense of the government. On May 27, 1759, several hundred persons of Connecticut received grants of land on the Basin of Minas. The Acadian settlements of Canard and Mines were renamed Cornwallis and Horton. A few months later large areas on both sides of the Pisiquid River and its estuary, which became known as Falmouth and Newport, were laid out for the Rhode Island settlers. These, too, were in the King's County which the authorities of Nova Scotia had laid out in 1749 and which included most of the present Hants County, a corner of Lunenburg, more than a third of Colchester, a large portion of Cumberland, as well as the present King's County.

Most of the settlers for Horton and Cornwallis came from the eastern counties of Connecticut on the snow *Halifax,* and province brig *Montague,* and fourteen transports. There may have been an advance landing of forty families in May, but the main body of the settlers were delayed until June and July 1760, because of the threat of Indian raids.

Since Elizabethan times, the term Planter had been used for the people who planted colonies. The New Englanders who came up to settle the Nova Scotia townships were referred to as the New England Planters, and the name stuck, particularly to those who came to Horton and Cornwallis. It was the Horton Planters who were most closely associated with the beginnings of Wolfville, and it is their progress that is of most concern to historians of Wolfville.

16

IV.

HORTON PLANTERS

1. Land Grants

The arrival of the Planters in June 1760 took place at Horton Landing, on the south side of the Gaspereau River where the Town Plot had been laid out. Presumably erection of temporary shelters was the first duty. The next was to draw lots. Two barrels had been fitted with cranks, with the names of the applicants in one barrel, and the numbered lots in the other. Two blindfolded women drew out the slips, and the barrels were rolled for each drawing. After the names and numbers had been matched, the results went to the government records. Each settler drew his lots, and he was then assessed for quality and quantity, with additional small parcels of land granted in compensation for unusually small or infertile lots. After the initial granting, many land transactions took place as settlers tried to consolidate their holdings. The Town Plots were often sold and claims to farmland tracts retained.

Because of the lateness of their arrival, the settlers were unable to raise any crops that year. The next winter was severe and caused much distress. In addition, a great gale which had increased the height of the tides by ten feet, had broken down the Acadian dykes in November 1759. Although there were meadows and uplands which richly rewarded the industrious newcomers, the lands reclaimed from the tides by the ingenious dykes of the Acadians were flooded. Soon the Planters were employing Acadians to repair the dykes, but it was considered by later critics that the New Englanders did not make good use of the dyked land, as they used it chiefly for hay and pasture. Neither did they plough in the fall, which would have enabled them to plant earlier in the spring.

The 1762 census of Horton Township showed 900 persons in 150 families; in 1763, there were 154 families, with 5,000 marshland acres, 3,000 acres of cleared land, and 92,000 woodland acres. The 1770 census recorded 117 family names and the numbers in the households:

The following list indicates the names of the adult settlers and their households: Stephen Amsbury (5), John Allen (7), John Allen, Jr. (5), John Atwell (8), James Anderson (8), Robert Avery (7), Benjamin Beckwith (7), Benjamin, Jr. (3), Obed Benjamin (7), Caleb Bennet (7), Zadok Bennet (6), Elijah Bent (6), John Bishop (3), John Bishop, Jr. (8), Timothy Bishop (6), William Bishop (8), Noah Bowman (Bowan) (6), Thenchas Brooks (3), Darius Brown (6), Jacob Brown (1), Jacob Burnham (2), John Caldwell (5), Jonathan Caldwell (2), William Caldwell (5), Eleazar Chappel (4), John Chappel (2), Benjamin Cleaveland (1), Ezekiel Comstock (3), John Copp (9), Silas Crane (3), Andrew Curry (5), Jonathan Darrow (1), Andrew Davison (8), Cyprian Davison (4), Andrew Denison (8), D. Sherman Denison (8), Samuel Denison (4), Nathan DeWolf (4), Jehiel DeWolf (8), Simeon DeWolf (7), Charles

Dickson (10), Charles Dickson, Jr. (1), John Dickson (1), William Dickson (8), David Dodge (8), Thomas Dunlap (9), Laurence Eagell (4), Mary Elderkin (6), Noah Fuller (8), Jonathan Graves (7), Jonathan Graves, Jr. (3), Samuel Griffin (3), Joseph Hacket (6), Joseph Hacket, Jr. (4), Marshall Hackley (Harkley) (1), George Haliburton (5), John Hall (5), John Hamilton (5), Samuel Hamilton (1), Jonathan Hamilton (9), Abraham Harding (6), Israel Harding (7), Lemuel Harding (6), Stephen Harding (4), Thomas Harding (5), Daniel Harris (6), James Harris (6), Jonathan Harris (5), Lebbaeus Harris (11), Lebbaeus Harris, Jr. (2), John Hatch (1), Enoch Hovey (1), Thomas Hovey (1), Gamaliel Hunt (11), Thomas Jackson (4), Jeremiah Jordan (2), Elisha Lathrop (8), Andrew Lisk (5), James Lockhart (7), James Markham (8), Philip Mathers (8), Martha Miner (3), James Miner (3), Sylvanus Miner, Jr. (3), Miner (8), James Murdock (5), Philip Murdock (Mosher) (1), James Newton (5), Benjamin Peck (5), Cyrus Peck (1), Silas Peck (8), Henry Pelton (4), Pierce & Fillis (8), Thomas Pousson (3), Oliver Pencie (1), William Pride (7), Amos Rathbun (8), Duncan Reed (2), Samuel Reed, Jr. (5), Rolin Rogers (9), Stephen Rogers (5), Joseph Scott (4), John Turner (9), Samuel Turner (5), John Vinlisson (3), Daniel Whipple (2), Zebadiah Wickwire (4), Joseph Williams (2), Anna Witter (7), Joseph Woodworth (6).

2. Customs

A few names seem to have been omitted in the 1770 census: Palmeter, Schofield or Scovill, Stewart, Townsend, and Welch, although there are references to the presence of persons of these names both before and after 1770.

The 1766 census had reported four grist mills, two saw mills, seven fishing boats, and one schooner or sloop. Some of the settlers in the new township apparently preferred hunting and fishing to agriculture. The export of wheat had been forbidden, and manufacturing was discouraged lest it interfere with the home trade. The settlers had little money, but they raised most of what they needed and had a surplus for trade. There was plenty of wood for cooking and for heating the homes in winter; they raised their own grain, and cattle and sheep for meat; they made their own sugar and molasses from the sap of the maple trees, and cider from their apples. They made their cloth from the wool of their sheep, linen thread from their flax, candles and soap from the fat of their animals. A brick oven in the chimney was used for roasting meat and for baking bread and pies. There were no friction matches, but sulphuric matches, flint and steel, or a "burning glass' were used to start a fire. Sometimes also they used the spark or flame emitted by a flint lock gun when a small quantity of black powder was exploded by the hammer of the gun. The fireplace provided light, except for special celebrations or important guests, when candles were brought out.

There were few clocks in the settlements until the Yankee pedlars came. Evening gatherings were held at early candle light. The bell ringer would call out the time of the night: "Eight o'clock and all is well"; "Eleven o'clock and all is well; sleep in peace, oh ye honest citizens."; an hour later his cry would be, "Midnight, and all is well. A new day doth come to us all." As well as clocks, the Yankee pedlars brought shoes, scythes, rum, rice, sugar, and spices.

In the early 1800s blacksmith forges, carpenter shops, and cider presses were working to provide for the needs of the people. The ingenious blacksmith not only shoed horses, but manufactured small articles and made repairs. Metal came from New England. Agricultural implements of the period were heavy and clumsily constructed.

Often the early settlers lived at a considerable distance from their nearest neighbours, and there was special enjoyment of visits when the women could chat about their dairies, their dye pots, spinning wheels, homespun cloth, and their many household duties. The men would talk about their stock and the prices they fetched, or about hunting adventures. After a substantial meal, chess, draughts, whist, or other games might be enjoyed, but many of the settlers frowned upon such levity. With a Puritan background, the former New Englanders applied strong measure of discipline and the law frowned upon "neglect of worship and services on the Lord's Day, blasphemy, swearing, profanation of the Sabbath, public gaming houses, playing cards, dice, or any game whatsoever, either in public or private houses."

There were many picnics, frolics, or "bees'" when a house or a barn was raised, when ships were launched, or when families joined to harvest the crops. The women would have paring parties when they were preparing apples for drying or for apple butter. The young folk of the villages had fulling parties to shape the newly woven cloth. Sometimes the cloth was placed on the floor between two rows of young people who pounded it with their bare feet. At other times the well washed and soaped cloth was placed on a long table, on each side of which girls sat on straw bags, and twisted and turned and pounded the cloth, perhaps to the tune of a popular folk song. This process thickened the cloth and helped it to wear for years. Hay rides and sleigh rides in winter were special treats for the young folk, and a wedding might sometimes call for a dance, but that might be frowned upon. When Joseph Howe was visiting the Valley in 1828, he was dissuaded from walking on a Sunday from Windsor to Kentville, lest he create a scandal in the eyes of the church goers.

3. Housing and Apparel

From their homes in New England, many of the settlers brought frames and lumber for their houses in old-fashioned fishermen's vessels. Occasionally, bits of building material could be gleaned from the ruins of Acadian settlements. Some of the farmers' dwelllings were rude and roughly built, without plastered walls or window casings. The uprights and boardings of walls, the timbers of the upper floors would be in view, unfinished. Huge chimneys were built and cavern-like fireplaces. Occasionally, in the first settlements, people lived in rude log houses. Very little paint was used, but the houses of the more ambitious were white-washed. Each community boasted a few larger and more impressive houses. The DeWolfs and Charles Randall, for instance, had two-story buildings. A few houses were built in the manorial style, with household servants and tenants gathered around.

Generally the houses were built square, with a large chimney in the centre to carry off smoke from all the fireplaces. The bricks for the chimneys were laboriously and expensively made. The settlers built with post and pan, and when the house was about nine feet high the dimensions were reduced slightly. When the house was about six feet higher, the builder set the chamber windows and above them their roofs. Occasionally a third story was added. After the house was boarded, it appeared neat and complete. Clapboards covered the outside up to the shingled roof. The better houses had glass, brought from New England, in the window sashes. Each house had a cellar, an important part of the economy, where vegetables, salted, pickled meat, and fruit could be stored, where milk kept cool, and crocks of butter, and home-made cheeses were set apart.

The better houses had a convenient kitchen, a chamber, the "Borning room", and a parlour, which was papered and contained two closets. The furniture of the house might include a pine table, some plain chairs, perhaps a few three-legged stools, and a bench near the fireplace. Sets of rough crockery lined the shelves. The furniture was mainly simple, often made of rock maple or black birch, with lighter articles of pine, spruce, cherry, or walnut. In the better homes, some furnishings were made locally, and others were brought from New England. Manufactured articles were few and carefully guarded. A few straight-backed chairs were to be found, but benches and stools were more numerous. Some people slept on pallets on the floor or on low platforms or in corded bunks. Spinning wheels, looms, dairy and table utensils, tools, and lanterns were made of wood or horn.

The Planter women generally refused to work outdoors, but they made butter, cheese, starch, yeast, cider, spruce beer, apple butter. They made woolen and linen cloth. The wool was carded by hand, then spun, and woven, and part of it coloured blue in the indigo dye pot, which every family had. For improved cloth for Sunday clothes, the cloth was sent to the fuller, who shrank and pressed it for a better surface. It is not surprising that the women sought domestic help to assist them in their many duties.

The Planters are depicted as arriving in long black broadcloth frock coats and trousers to match, with a dickey and large black stock or cravat, and beaver or silk hats. If true, it must have made quite an impression on Horton Landing! When at work they wore homespun, with checked shirts. In summer the trousers were long, reaching down to the bare feet; in winter, breeches, woolen stockings, boots, and linsey-woolsey shirts were used. On Sundays they dressed in their finest cloth and linen, sometimes ruffled shirts, and beaver or silk hats, if they had them.

The women also wore homespun, products of their own spinning wheels and looms. Their leather shoes were made by travelling shoemakers who brought their tools and supplies with them and stayed in the house while fitting out the family — "shipping the cat" it was called. Except on Sundays and special occasions, the women wore woolseys, both for petticoats and aprons. Because stays, imported from New or Old England, were too expensive, the women wore loose jackets. In summer, the women, like the men, generally went without shoes and stockings, and many without caps. They took much pains with their hair, which was coiled at the top of the head. On Sundays, the women wore silk or calico dresses, if they could possibly afford them, for it took a great many eggs or pounds of butter to pay for silk and calico. At church or meetinghouse, all women, whatever their social standing, carried fans.

4. The Planters and the Government

Before the summer of 1760 was over, each township had its small palisade fort, capable of holding all the settlers, and a few troops for protection from Indians and Acadians. During the summer of 1762 a landing in Nova Scotia by the French was feared, and several King's County men were called for military duty. Colonel Denison, head of the King's County Militia, gave orders that 130 Acadians were to be delivered to Halifax, because a French vessel had been sighted off Newfoundland. However, the warship failed to appear off Nova Scotia, and the settlers were allowed to return to their homes. Taxes were levied to support the militia.

The New Englanders were used to organized town government, which was a new concept to the authorities at Halifax, who had brought from England the idea of autocratic rule by the governing class. In 1763 the people of King's County wrote to the Board of Trade to complain about the discontinuance of aid by provision of seed, about absentee ownership, about the local office behaviour of Henry Denny Denson's Isaac Deschamp, and about the military obligations laid on them during the panic of 1763. They asked for their own town government. This strong request was signed by sixty-three New England settlers in King's County, but did not reach the Board of Trade. It may, however, have had some effect on the Halifax authorities who found it wise to resort to methods of persuasion in dealing with the remote settlements. In 1764 the township agreed to assess themselves for poor relief. In 1765 the Assembly determined the form of township government, authorized collecting of revenues and levying of charges on absentee landlords.

One of the first acts of the King's County Session was to erect a pillory, stock, bolts and shackles. There the guilty would stand with head and hands through the wooden walls, with spectators enjoying the victim's discomfort. In 1796 a forger was penalized by standing in the pillory for an hour, and by having an ear cut off. The whipping post was also used. In 1807 for stealing three yards of cloth, an individual was ordered thirty-nine lashes on neck and back. Penalties for offences against the law were publicly advertised: a fine of one shilling for sheep that broke loose; five shillings for a horse that broke loose. In 1806, Thomas Jackson paid forty shillings for refusing to serve as a grand constable.

King's county was entitled to two members in the Assembly at Halifax. In 1761 Colonel Robert Denison and Charles Morris, Jr., were the representatives, and William Welch and Lebbaeus Harris attended for the Township of Horton. Denison was replaced by Winckworth, and, in 1765 the member for Horton was William Welch. Charles Dickson later was the member for Horton Township and was succeeded by Joseph Pierce, who resigned in 1778 because of age and infirmities. He was replaced by Thomas Caldwell, merchant.

When revolt threatened in the colonies to the south, the government of Halifax received orders from England that all inhabitants of Nova Scotia take the oath of allegiance. When war broke out, two companies of troops from King's County were called up for the defence of Nova Scotia. The sloop of war, the *Vulture,* was stationed in the Bay of Fundy for protection of Fundy settlements. The attacks by American privateers tended to alienate the Minas Basin settlers from their former communities in New England.

5. The Decline of Horton Landing

Life for the Planters in Horton Township had its difficulties. The land had been left uncultivated for five years, and many of the dykes had been cut. Since it required about three years to leach the salt from newly dyked land, the settlers found their prize lands not immediately arable. Fortunately, they had large quantities of cattle. Six transports had brought cattle to Windsor, and some had been driven overland, through forest trails, from Windsor to Horton. In Falmouth, Jonathan Davison was elected herdsman to tend the animals and prevent them from destroying the crops. As has been noted, owners had to pay a fine if animals escaped from their yards at night. Horton settlers gathered 1,000 tons of hay by the end of 1760, but they had to depend upon supplies for their own use from Halifax for the first two or three years. All the settlements around the Bay of Fundy had to depend on New England traders for other necessities and luxuries such as tobacco, sugar, spices and calico. The profits went to New England, or perhaps to Halifax, and were a serious drain on the economy of the settlements.

Town meetings generally ceased after 1770 because of conflict with the central authority at Halifax, but Horton Landing remained the nominal centre of the township. The Court House, the remains of which are on the Denny farm in Hortonville, was located in the Town Plot. Until the house was burned, the Supreme Court sat there, but later was held in Upper Horton for a time. The first jail was located on the property of George Johnson (now owned by Harlan Fuller). In the early 1800s, twenty houses were reported at Town Plot, one or two stores and three mills, although only one of the mills was actually in Town Plot, and the others were east and west of Crane's corner, at the top of the hill. One of the township taverns and a hotel were at Grand Pre corner, as well as Howard Fuller's machine shop.

Geography played a cruel trick on the aspiring little community of Horton Landing. Because of the wish to maintain overland contact, especially if necessity should call for movement of troops, roads were needed to extend farther down the Valley. Since the land around Horton Landing was low and marshy, an alternative route was taken, the one later known as the Old Post Road. This ran from Upper Falmouth, across Gray Mountain and the South Mountain, down the Harding Brook to Melanson, then up the gentle slope which leads by Maple Avenue into Wolfville. Lower Horton (Hortonvillle) was completely by-passed by the road.

6. Upper Horton Settlement

From the beginning of Horton Township, many settlers had been reluctant to live in the Town Plot, even though there would be a fort, a school and a meetinghouse, but had preferred to live on their farms. The shipyards at Mud Creek had attracted a few, and the building of the road brought further advantages to Upper Horton. It developed naturally into a resting place for travellers. It was on "the road," and a trip to Upper Horton from the outlying settlements was going to "the road."

Because of its location, hotels, inns, and livery stables appeared at Upper Horton. Farmers and villagers made use of the harbour for shipping their produce and for importing the commodities unavailable locally. Mercantile enterprises were enlarged, and wharves were needed for the shipping. There was a demand for houses for the owners of new businesses, and for workers. The increase in population required more farms to provide food for the merchants and skilled craftsmen.

By the turn of the century, Upper Horton had been well established, and became the judicial centre when the burning of the original Court House at Horton Landing resulted in the holding of court at the Baptist meetinghouse. In 1817, Lord Dalhousie described the Court House as "on the confines of the township of Horton and Cornwallis and had gathered some houses together into a sort of village." In 1829 court and jail were moved to Kentville, when that town assumed the function of administrative centre for Horton Township.

Upper Horton, or "the road," or Horton Road was centered around Mud Creek and its shipping facitilies, and the village was often referred to as Mud Creek.

Covered bridge at Avonport

V.

AGRICULTURE

1. In the Beginning

When John Robinson and Thomas Rispin of England visited Nova Scotia in 1774, they made an unfavourable comment about this new land. Between Falmouth and Horton they passed only two houses. They wrote well of the rye, Indian corn, pumpkins, and potatoes, but the people "are as bad managers in this township as any we came amongst. They value their marsh land at two pounds an acre, their cleared upland at one pound an acre, and their woodland at sixpence."

By that time, the Horton Planters were specializing in livestock as their principal commodity. There was a market in Halifax for cattle, and competition from cheap American flour and grain had reinforced the tendency to concentrate on livestock. They did grow wheat, maize, rye, peas, barley, oats, beans, pumpkins, hemp, flax, potatoes, turnips, and carrots. Furthermore, they followed the Acadian precedent of extensive fruit and berry culture. Farmers put down a pig or two in sweet pickle to supply ham and bacon, and a barrel of corned beef for the winter. Lamb was available in season, fowls and occasionally moose or deer meat, and fish. In the early days the farmers took their corn (wheat) to the grist mill on College Brook, just south of the present maintenance building. Later the trip to Obed Benjamin's mill in the Gaspereau Valley with several kinds of grain for grinding, was a part of farm life.

The New England custom of sharing a common pasture was continued for many years. Where there were sufficient numbers, the settlers organized to learn improved methods of planting and harvesting, and of raised stock.

When the Johnsons came in 1773, George and his cousin Joseph and son-in-law Jephtha Elderkin, Wolfville was all farms. They purchased land at the west end of the present town. Jephtha Elderkin's land began with the Scott Stephen's farm, adjacent to J. W. Bigelow's line, and his house was on the boundary between Charles and Albert Elderkin's property of later days. The George Johnson farm extended from Bigelow's west line to Ferry Lane. Elisha DeWolf's farm came next and went to the brook on what was later the Charles Fitch property. Joseph Johnson's farm extended from the brook to the present University Avenue. Daniel Whipple's farm ran from University Avenue to the present Highland Avenue, and his house was occupied by T. L. Hutchinson in 1918. Daniel Whipple either sold or gave his farm to his son-in-law, Johnathan Graham, who divided it between his sons, James and George. James sold his share to Acadia College; George kept his until he sold it to John L. Brown in 1849.

The next farm was that of Elijah Fowler, which extended from Highland Avenue to Gaspereau Avenue, and his house was built where the Post Office

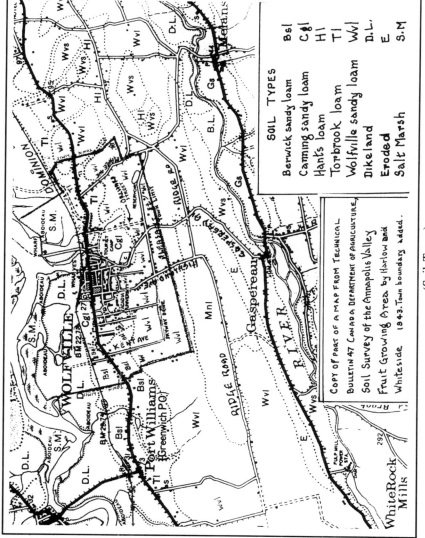

SOIL TYPES

Berwick sandy loam	Bsl
Canning sandy loam	Cgl
Hants loam	Hl
Torbrook loam	Tl
Wolfville sandy loam	Wvl
Dikeland	D.L.
Eroded	E
Salt Marsh	S.M.

COPY OF PART OF A MAP FROM TECHNICAL
BULLETIN 47 CANADA DEPARTMENT OF AGRICULTURE,
Soil Survey of the Annapolis Valley
Fruit Growing Area by Harlow and
Whiteside   1943. Town boundary added.

(Soil Types).

25

now stands. Elijah Fowler might have been the first farmer to dream of a village, and he encouraged the development of one by selling parts of his farm from time to time. In 1811, he sold the southwest corner to the Baptists for a church; he sold land to the Presbyterians for a church and a house near the eastern end of what is now Pleasant Street to Arthur Murphy.

East of Elijah Fowler, Stephen DeWolf's farm extended from Gaspereau Avenue to the east line of the Gould place, west of Mud Creek. The Charles Randall farm was next, and went to the east side of the S. D. Morris property. Rowland Rogers' land was next, near the C. H. Borden house on the present Orchard Avenue. C. R. Johnson's farm then extended to the foot of English Church Hill. Other farms in the community were those of Dwight DeWolf, J. F. Herbin, Owen DeWolf, James Woodman (later owned by Charles Patriquin), John Rounsefell on the east side of Wickwire Dyke, where the old road was, Dr. Johnston, Owen Evans, and Dyer Wickwire.

The distance between the west and east boundaries of the town is approximately two miles. After the 101 Highway was built, the north boundary of its right-of-way was adopted as a more easily recognized south boundary for the town. The town limits enclose about 2,000 acres of land, of which 389 acres is classified as "agriculture" at present. This includes 251 acres of Beckwith and Wickwire dyked lands.

2. Fruit-growing Brings Prosperity

About 1843 John Young, who wrote in the *Acadian Recorder* under the name of "Agricola," recommended improvements in the apple business, and when he became Secretary of Agriculture, organized the modernization he had advocated. In 1863 a modest and informal meeting of the Nova Scotia Fruit Growing Association was held in Halifax to consider growing and shipping methods that would improve the crops and their sale. Three years later the N.S. Fruit Growers Association was formed, and the growers started shipping apples to England. The economy was unpromising in the mid-1860s, and some people questioned the enterprise. The English market improved, and C. R. H. Starr effectively represented the province at an Agricultural Exhibition in London. A report of the Association from 1863 to 1886 named Prof. D. F. Higgins, J. Hea, R. B. Witter, and George V. Rand as Honorary members from Wolfville.

A Berwick apple grower wrote in the *Family Herald and Weekly Star* that the first export of apples occurred in 1870, when a few barrels were sent to London in a sailing vessel on top of a cargo of lumber. Improved transportation throughout the Valley encouraged marketing by vessels, and the coming of the railway meant safe carriage of fruit to Halifax and abroad. Exhibitions attracted prospective buyers, and sales to England increased. In 1881 the steamship *Neptune* carried 6,800 barrels of apples to London, but the average for the five-year period was only 30,000 barrels. This increased to more than a quarter of a million barrels from 1895 to 1899.

In 1880 duties imposed by the United States had closed the market there, although W. H. Chase is reported to have shipped 1,800 barrels to New York in 1886. The duty on apples, and one imposed in 1886 by the United States on potatoes from Nova Scotia, induced farmers to develop trade in apples with Great Britain.

Most of the upland of Wolfville is eminently suitable for the growing of fruit trees, especially apples. At the beginning of the last quarter of the 19th century, the orchards of Wolfville were being planted on a large scale. The land was also suitable for grain, hay, and vegetables, as well as for pasturage. The fenced fields of the past were an indication of the agricultural activities of the area. The King's County newspapers carried information about agricultural matters: in December, 1879 the King's County Agricultural Society began at Horton; at Wolfville in 1883 D. W. Patterson shipped sixty bushels of plums weekly; in 1884 W. H. Chase established at Port Williams the first warehouse for grading and storing apples. C.R.H. Starr and other members of the Agricultural Society presented new ideas, and advertising boosted trade. Wolfville prospered as farmers on fertile land sold their produce to nearby and distant localities.

An Annapolis Valley Small Fruit Growers Association had been formed, and met in Berwick in 1885. In 1886 Wolfville items concerned King of Tomkins apples sold by A. DeWolfe, Esq., the best in his forty years of orcharding; onions and beans grown by J. L. Brown, and large quantities of onions by Charles Patriquin and J. E. DeWolfe; the purchase of the Harris orchard by John Dodd. In 1887 the Small Fruit Growers Association considered joining the N.S. F.G.A. There were references to the fine orchard of Major Cusack, who had come to Halifax and then to Wolfville after retiring from the King's Own Regiment of Liverpool, England.

Between 1863 and 1890 the Nova Scotia Fruit Growers Association held most of its meetings and numerous exhibitions at Wolfville, all of which helped to affect the economy of the community. For some years Wolfville was the major point of departure for small schooners carrying apples to the railhead at Windsor.

In 1891 the Wolfville Fruit and Land Improvement Company was founded by William Charles Archibald, and incorporated with a capital of $48,000. It helped lay out streets, residential blocks, and fruit gardens. The Company bought the J. B. Hemmeon property, the block of land adjoining it, and the portion south of the Earnscliffe Gardens. The new Company aimed to make a residential town out of Wolfville. One hundred acres close to the University grounds was purchased and cut into building and garden lots, known as Wolfville Heights.

W. C. Archibald began operating the Earnscliffe Gardens Nursery about 1890, and the *Acadian* of October 1891 noted that the Nursery advertised for wholesale business. The October *Novascotian* described Wolfville as "almost one large orchard." Earnscliffe Gardens had 2,500 plums, 500 apples, and 200 peaches, and the proprietor kept experimenting with his trees. He lived where E. K. M. Hospital now stands, and the Fitch farm which Frank Welch later bought for an orchard.

In 1892 the Land Improvement Company advertised in Halifax, St. John, in England and the United States. Two acres of land, they believed, with properly cultivated fruit, would yield sufficient income to support the average family. A visitor described Wolfville as best seen from the Ridge. He saw prosperity and promise of great growth on all sides; apple orchards and grape vines in abundance foretold of a future of plenty. Earnscliffe Gardens was a beautiful place, and the garden of C. A. Patriquin was worthy of a visit.

Early in 1894 W. C. Archibald sold about one-quarter of his interests in Earnscliffe Gardens for $3,400, and shortly afterwards severed his connections with the Wolfville Fruit and Land Company. The Dwight DeWolfe orchard, partly owned by Major Cusack, was the largest in Wolfville around 1898, and frequently referred to in the *Acadian,* but Bigelow's orchard and Earnscliffe Gardens were also extensive.

In March 1902 W. C. Archibald, apparently still of Earnscliffe Gardens, sold a large order of 6,000 trees to R. W. Kinsman of Canning. Archibald and C. R. H. Starr received diploma-awards from the Glasgow International Exhibition for their fruit display. The Gardens enlarged, adding many acres of orchards within the next two years. A provincial nursery of thousands of trees was placed between the orchard rows. The Gardens also led in producing plums.

The Nova Scotia Horticulture School was established in 1894, with E. E. Flavelle as principal. The school used the university buildings. In 1898 an attempt was made to get a School of Agriculture established at Wolfville, with possible financial assistance from neighbouring communities, and with association with the Horticulture School. The council offered an inducement of $5,000.

The Horticulture School was controlled by the N.S.F.G.A. and was aided by the provincial government. Sixty-seven students attended in 1899-1900. The founding of the Provincial Agricultural College at Truro made the Wolfville school unnecessary.

3. More Recent Developments

Wolfville was becoming a centre of agricultural developments. In May 1902 Freeman's Nursery began to advertise flowers and plants for sale, and in November 1904, before the Experimental Farm opened in 1910, Freeman experimented with plant genetics and propagation. The Chrysanthemum Show in November drew many visitors. G. M. Peck advertized in 1908 the sale of plants and trees at his nursery, and in 1912 he and his son Henry bought fifty-eight acres on Highland Avenue from Ernest Porter. The business closed at the end of the Great War.

In 1918 the Wolfville Fruit Company, a co-operative of local apple growers, with Henry Peck as the first manager, began packing apples in boxes instead of in barrels. H. F. Davidson gave instruction at the warehouse on the most efficient method of packing. The Wolfville Evaporator, owned by W. H. Chase, R. A. Jodrey, and Dexter Forsythe, burned in October 1919, a great blow to the apple industry, especially at the beginning of the processing season.

Though admittedly incomplete, the following is a description of some of the farming done within or touching on the town limits. First is Zebediah Wickwire, born in 1730 and settled in 1760 at Upper Horton, his farm probably on the south side of the main street. The farm was sold in 1843; eighteen acres of it is now owned by Dr. and Mrs. Herman C. Olsen.

William Kenny, Junior, operates about fifty-five acres, thirty-six of those in the town limits and including the Olsen orchard. The trees are apple, pear, peach, plum, and cherry. He also raises 4,000 day-old chicks and has an attractive sales centre for fruits and vegetables.

Charles Nowlan came from Havelock, Digby County, to Wolfville in 1919, and bought property earlier owned by Andrew and George Johnson. This included the big house built by a previous owner of the Andrew Johnson part of the property. In addition, Nowlan acquired the George Johnson half of the Johnson property south of Main Street, as well as over nine acres of dyked land. He died in 1922. His son Karl set up his canteen in 1947, an enlargement of the one started in 1934. He later sold land for twelve co-operative home builders as the canteen took all of his time.

When R. W. DeWolfe returned from overseas after World War I he was associated first with R. A. Jodrey in the apple industry, and then packed apples for the British-Canadian Fruit Association. Later he bought most of their warehouses. He associated with R. A. Jodrey in the building and operating of an apple dehydration plant until 1968, when it became part of the storage and packing facilities which the R. W. DeWolfe Company now operates. This Company still owns and operates thirty acres of dyked land for hay and pasturage.

Mr. and Mrs. LeRoy Forsythe, Highland Avenue, bought their property in 1941, raised poultry on a large scale on their land, and by renting from Fred Salsman a hen house they kept 14,000 laying hens. Forsythe later built a hen house of similar size on his property. In 1979 A.C.A. (Atlantic Co-operative Association) rented their large house, installed new equipment to raise laying hens which would provide chicks to become broilers.

Fred Salsman, who came to Wolfville about 1922, managed seventy acres of orchard for R. A. Jodrey, ten of which were in town behind the Jodrey house on Main Street. W. H. Chase also operated orchards on land between the railway tracks and the house along the north side of Main Street, and extending from Cherry Lane to west of the old Acadia gymnasium.

Robert Stirling operated orchards north of Pleasant Street, between Gaspereau Avenue and close to Highland Avenue — about twenty acres. They were sold recently to Donald Wallace, and an apartment complex was placed on Gaspereau Avenue. Stirling Fruit Farms still operates about forty acres of orchard on the J. W. Bigelow farm south of Main Street at the west end of the town.

Frank Welch bought the former Charles William Fitch property from Carl Freeman. In 1942 he planted twenty-four acres of orchard, from his Main Street house to the brow of the hill, almost to the present Skyway Drive. He raised pigs on the property for a few years, and later he erected two buildings for cold storage and warehouse space. He added acreage to his orchard by buying adjoining lands formerly owned by Karl Borden and by planting a substantial new orchard south of the first one. Altogether, he eventually owned seventy-five acres of orchards in Wolfville. His original orchard was one of the most attractive and best-managed in the Annapolis Valley.

In 1965 Welch began transforming his Wolfville acreage to housing subdivisions. Most of the lots have been sold and have houses on them. Frank Welch was with the Wolfville Fruit Company for thirty-six years, beginning in 1921. He retired as manager in 1958, and the grocery store was rented from 1969 to Dominion Stores.

VI.

MUD CREEK AND THE DEWOLFS

1. Mud Creek

A little brook making its way down that spur of South Mountain which has become known as Wolfville Ridge found itself dropping into low, marshy ground where the muddy tidal waters from Cornwallis River twice a day poured in and then drained away. The Micmacs had described the lower part of the creek as "Mtaban" or "Mud Bridge," which meant "mud-catfish-catching-ground." The early settlers called it Mud Creek. To get around it, they had to turn up past the tidal pools and construct a bridge where the brook was small.

There were high banks on both sides of the creek where occasionally through the years a small vessel would be built. The incoming ships drew up to the south bank, their bowsprits extending over the narrow road that circled around before making its way along the main highway. After the railway went through, two wharves later stood in the outside harbour, at each side of the creek which wound itself through the dyked land until it emptied into the Cornwallis River.

It is recorded in the Registry of Deeds for King's County, that in 1767 John Lockhart sold to Joseph Gray "a certain tract or Parcel of Dyke Land Situate lying near a place called Mud Creek." Three years later Daniel Hovey sold to Joseph Elderkin fifty acres of land, a part of Mud Creek farm. In 1795 there was a reference to Mud Bridge as the western boundary of a house and land sold by Noah Gale to Abraham Seaman. There was also, in a deed of 1784, a reference to lots bounded by Little Discharge Creek. A Wolfville resident of the nineteenth century wrote that about four miles west of the Town Plot, near where Horton Railway Station was located, Little Discharge Creek emptied into Minas Basin at the mouth of the Cornwallis River, and that farm lots A5 of the Second Division touched on that creek. D. G. Whidden suggested that the settlement at Little Discharge Creek became Mud Creek.

In the *Acadian Orchardist* of May 1900 James R. DeWolf stated that the Horton community was known as Mud Creek and that the centre of the village was Mud Bridge. D. G. Whidden claimed that the early settlers did not give the name to the entire community. Letters of the period, however, show that Mud Creek and Mud Bridge were commonly used. The names lacked dignity, and they were changed. Whidden said that the Horton post office became the Wolfville post office in 1828. The account of Wolfville streets and houses by Dr. Watson Kirkconnell and Dr. B. C. Silver dated the renaming at 1829. I. B. Oakes gave 1830 as the date.

There are two stories relating to the change of name. In 1829 a mail carrier, who probably travelled in a cart, is purported to have asked Postmaster Elisha DeWolf, Jr., what name to call the new Way Office. The postmaster had the choice of Horton, Upper Horton, Horton Way, Horton Road, and either Office or Way Office. Finally, he said, "Oh, call it Wolfville, there are so many DeWolfs here."

The more interesting and more popular explanation for the change of name is connected with two nieces of Elisha DeWolf, Jr., who asked for a better-sounding name for their community. Maria and Mary Starr Woodward (Woodworth) might have attended a boarding school, possibly at St. John, and were embarrassed when their friends asked where they came from and they had to say "Mud Creek," or they had to send their letters to Mud Creek. Their uncle called a family council, it is said, and the name of Wolfville was proposed in compliment to Elisha DeWolf, who was the leading person in the community, and the head of a family group that was large and important. It seems that every other house in the village was occupied by a DeWolf by name or by family connection. The Postmaster-General of Nova Scotia consented, and on August 13, 1830, the names of Mud Creek and Upper Horton gave way to Wolfville.

The official use of the name of Wolfville was delayed for many years, but it slipped into the House of Assembly record of December 1830 when William Johnson and others petitioned for a grant to repair Mud Bridge (so called) at Wolfville in Horton.

But who were the DeWolfs that their names should be given to the community?

2. The DeWolf Family

The three DeWolf cousins who came to Horton in 1761 were descendants of Balthasar, one of several DeWolfs who came from the Low Countries to New Netherlands on the east coast of North America. When the English captured New Amsterdam, the capital, in 1664, and renamed it New York, the other DeWolfs returned to Europe, but Balthasar remained and removed to Connecticut. Simeon, from Lyme, Connecticut, and Jehiel, from Killingworth, were second cousins. Nathan, from Saybrook, was a first cousin once removed of Simeon, and a second cousin once removed of Jehiel, and Nathan and Simeon were brothers-in-law, they having married Kirtland sisters.

The DeWolfs settled first in Grand Pre, where they received grants of 500 acres each. Grantees were required to settle a family, furnish each farm with stock and materials for improvements not later than August 31, 1766. A quit rent of one shilling for every fifty acres was to be paid yearly, and each owner was required to plant two acres of hemp. The DeWolfs disposed of nine-tenths of their allotments, but retained the most valuable part, near the Cornwallis River, where the town of Wolfville eventually grew up. Although they came a year later than their fellow Planters from Connecticut, they soon became recognized as leaders in the community. As their signatures showed, all three had had a good education: Nathan had graduated from Yale College in 1743, and had practised law and conveying. As Registrar of Deeds and Probate, he wrote most of the early deeds of King's County. By 1767 Nathan was senior Justice of the Peace, and he served also as Assessor and County Treasurer. Simeon was Pound Keeper, Surveyor of Highways and Surveyor of the Poor.

The 1770 census returns showed the DeWolfs well established and prosperous. Nathan at that time had a household of five, Simeon had seven, and Jehiel eight. A story concerning Jehiel has been passed down. When an Indian's dog took some of his geese, he shot the dog, and then savagely attacked the Indian when the latter came to complain about the loss of his dog. A serious situation might have developed, if tactful negotiators had not intervened and brought about an acknowledgement of the offence, so that peace was restored.

Nathan's second son, Elisha, held public office from 1784 until his death in 1837. He was High Sheriff of King's County from 1784 to 1789, and was elected to the provincial legislature in 1793, 1799, and again in 1819. He was Postmaster (at his residence), Collector of Excise, and Justice of the Peace. Since Justices of the Peace at that time presided over local courts, Elisha was known as Judge DeWolf. He had a big farm, and apparently operated a large general store.

Elisha DeWolf married Margaret Ratchford, daughter of Thomas and Desiah or Desire Gore, a Cornwallis settler. Her brother, James Ratchford, was an important entrepreneur in the Parrsborough area, and close contact was maintained with the Ratchfords. Elisha's son, Thomas Andrew Strange DeWolf, married James Ratchford's daughter, Nancy, and the enterprising and dominating spirit of the Ratchfords continued to be a factor in the descendants of Elisha.

Nancy Ratchford DeWolf certainly dominated the recollections of the grandson, Pierson DeWolf Crane, who came to live with his grandparents in 1875, at the age of three, in the house near the wharf, which for a few years was the Wolfville Museum. Pierson was brought from Connecticut by a clergyman, and soon learned that silence and obedience in his grandmother's house were required virtues. His grandmother had four servants, and old Martha McCharles, who looked after him, became his rescuer and refuge when he suffered his grandmother's discipline. The boy missed his mother, Caroline Amelia DeWolf, and his sister Mary, and later thought of himself during those years as "a lonely little boy."

He remembered the unusual wallpaper in the front room at the left, and he recalled the hair cloth sofa with sharp broken hairs that hurt to sit on. He also recollected that his grandmother's punishment of him was ever the same - to bed without supper. But black Caroline or one of the other women would always bring him a tray of food and tell him stories.

The summer of 1876 was a time to remember. For a while he lived with Mr. Schofield at Gaspereau Mountain, and he got there by going through White Rock. During that summer the boy's father drowned at sea, and he visited an elderly woman named Pick who had a green parrot. He liked staying with the Schofields.

When back at Wolfville he was alone again, being chastized by his grandmother who called him wicked. In that summer of 1876 he met some other young boys by the long board fence parallel to the railroad back of the large garden. The little boys sailed crude boats in the wide ditch along the tracks, and he learned from them how to make animals from potatoes and sticks. Then they asked him why he wore long hair, and he began to hate his sandy red curly hair.

Grandmother DeWolf learned that he fraternized with wicked, dirty, low boys, punished him and denied him permission to visit the garden. The high stable fence penned him in but Jim Blackaddar lifted him down and escorted Captain Crane's little boy to the wharf to play with his young friends. George Webster was sent to bring him home, lovely dirt and all, and this time the boy was threatened with Reform School at Halifax. However, he still journeyed to the wharf, and George Webster left the gate open for him.

During the final summer, when Pierson DeWolf Crane was nearly six, George made a stick for opening the gate. Back at the wharf with the other boys, he got pitch in his long hair. One lad suggested: "Why not get old man Patriquin to cut them curls off - for fifteen cents?" The boy had the money, found Mr. Patriquin, the harness maker and barber, and he went home a real boy.

Grandmother was furious, again decreed his fate as Reform School "as soon as your mother returns!" Meanwhile, to bed without supper. His mother returned a few days later and was angry, too. But Grandfather laughed: "The boy has more sense than you, Carrie." The boy loved his eighty-year-old grandfather for that.

But Pierson's amusing recollections have brought us a long way from his greatgrandfather, Elisha DeWolf. In 1780, the year after his marriage to Margaret Ratchford, Elisha bought a house from his brother Edward for five hundred pounds. According to research on the house by Norman Morgan, working under Dr. Barry Moody of the Acadia History Department, Edward had purchased the nucleus of the house and fifty-three acres of land in 1777 from Joseph Jackson and James Birmingham, two Yorkshiremen, for one hundred and thirty pounds. They had bought the land three years previously from James Atwell for eighty pounds. The DeWolf house, situated on Main Street, at the intersection with the road to the Cornwallis ferry, became a centre of social activity in the town. H.R.H. Prince Edward, later known as the Duke of Kent, the father of Queen Victoria, is said to have stayed there on his way to Annapolis to board a vessel for St. John. His mounted cavalcade must have been an impressive sight, long rememberd by Wolfville residents.

After the death of Elisha's widow, Margaret, in 1852, the house was owned by her grandson, William H., and his wife Sarah E. Lusby. The next owners of the house were Joseph F. Hea, Doctor of Civil Law, an insurance agent and Notary Public, later principal of the Acacia Villa School of Grand Pre, and his wife, Miriam. W. O. Haliburton bought the house from Dr. Hea, and in 1878 sold to William Haliburton, who in turn sold the house to Mrs. Laura Haliburton Moore, W. H. O. Haliburton's daughter, in 1896. Two years later, she began to operate the house as a summer hotel, and she christened it Kent Lodge. In 1919 Acadia students used the house as a dormitory. After fire destroyed the east wing, Stanley and Carrie Rand bought the place in 1922, and in 1947 passed it on to their daughter, Alice, who lived there until her death in 1978. Professor and Mrs. Reginald Moore then purchased the property and have endeavoured to restore it to the original layout and dignity of Elisha DeWolf's residence.

Various items concerning Elisha DeWolf have come to light. An official report of October 1828 acknowledged that he had received a certificate that the pound built by Jonathan Davison was "sufficiently good and lawful." He appears in the story of the five women of Northwest, Lunenburg County, who walked from Chester to Horton in 1828 to attend the Baptist Association Meeting:

> As they were descending Horton mountain, Elisha DeWolf, Esq., generally called Judge DeWolf, met them and in his usual bluff, kindly way enquired where they had come from and where they were going. They told him their names and their errand.
>
> "Well," he said, "this is wonderful. You five women have walked all the way from Chester. When you get to Horton Road, go to my house, Judge DeWolf's - and anyone will tell you where it is - and tell Mrs. DeWolf to lodge and feed you, and entertain you comfortable till your Conference is over."

Judge DeWolf was an Episcopalian, but many of his descendants were Methodists and Baptists. The 1828 Conference was significant because the initial plans were laid for the Baptists to found a Literary and Theological Seminary, which developed into Horton Academy.

Mrs. William Sommerville, whose recollections were published in the *Acadian* of July 1930, remembered Judge Elisha DeWolf as driving a one-horse shay, in which he would sit up very straight with his reins in one hand and his whip in the other. When the horse trotted over the rough roads, the Judge's head would go back and forth rhythmically. The Judge would not have been pleased with an item in the summer of 1843, when a young man of the same name was charged with burning a Burbidge barn.

A list of "Residents of Wolfville One Hundred Years Ago" was published in the Centennial Anniversary issue of the *Acadian* on August 14, 1930.

Over one hundred males and children were listed and eighty-six wives.

The list included these households, but gave no childrens' names:

Armstrong, Jas. L., 18, wife Lavinia (Coldwell); Barss, J. W., later married Lydia (Fitch); Bigelow, Ebenezer, 52, w. Nancy (Rand); Bishop, Ebenezer, 46, w. Anna (Lewis); Brown, Dr. E. L., 35; Caldwell, Tho., 20; Calkin, Elijah, 39, w. Rebecca; Cleveland, Deacon Benjamin, 76, w. Mary (Elderkin). Elderkin, Elijah, 27, w. Elizabeth (Johnson); Eye, Frederick, 38, w. Mary (Durant); Fitch, Simon, 40, w. Sophia (DeWolf); Forsyth, Elijah, 52, w. Nancy (Borden); Fowler, Elijah, 40; Harding, Father, 57, w. Zeruiah (Fitch); Hea, John, 30; Jackson, Joseph, 54, w. Mary Ann (Cleveland); Leonard, Mrs. Samuel, 63; Murphy, Arthur, 25, w. Mary Eliza (Pick); Payzant, Elias, m. in 1799, Ann (Martin); Pick, Wm., 28, w. Lydia (Duncanson); Rand, Thomas, m. in 1828, Eliza (Barnby); Reid, Samuel, 35, w. Elizabeth; Rogers, Rowland, 35; Wickwire, Thomas, 49, w. Jurusha (Reid); Wright, Reverend Joseph, B.A., Anglican clergyman.

Without mention of children, except for two or three of the DeWolf families, or of servants, or of slaves, the list does not give a complete account of the population in 1830. One can only conclude that the population was about two hundred.

VII.

TRANSPORTATION

1. Travel By Water

It was by sea that the founders of Wolfville came, and it was to the sea that for many years they looked for links with the outside world. From the very early days of the settlement, vessels were running to and from Parrsborough; the links between Horton and Cornwallis and Parrsborough were so strong that Parrsborough was a part of Kings County until 1840. Windsor, as the largest port in the Minas Bay area and the starting point for the overland route to Halifax, kept in touch with the smaller ports. St. John was for long the principal supplier of goods for the local merchants in all the Bay of Fundy and Minas Basin ports. Until Parrsborough and Windsor were made ports for ship registration, about 1850, St. John was the most convenient port for registration, and several hundred of the vessels built in the Nova Scotian ports were registered there. The Halifax merchants did not like this, but could do little about it.

Probably most settlers at Mud Creek and elsewhere around the Basin built themselves a small schooner for fishing and for taking lumber and produce to a merchant and bringing back flour, tea, sugar, and other necessities. These schooners would be too small for registration, and anyway there was considerable laxity in such remote areas about registering vessels. Also, in the early days ships were built at Mud Creek, at Gaspereau, at Avonport, and at the busy shipyard of J. B. North at the Kings County end of Hantsport, were registered as being built in Horton. All these factors make it difficult to determine how many vessels were actually built at Mud Creek. Recollections of old timers take it for granted that vessels they recall trading at the port were built there; the *Wolfville,* for instance, was owned by the Harrises, but was registered as built at Cornwallis.

Jehiel DeWolf, Jr., and Amasa Bigelow, sons of pioneers, are supposed to have been the pioneer builders at Mud Creek. DeWolf built a barque of 200 tons and a brig of 100 tons, but he moved on to New York and became a merchant there. After Amasa Bigelow was killed at work on a vessel in 1799, his son Daniel carried on the yard. In 1815 he built the *Emily,* a schooner of 96 tons, later rerigged as a brig, and took her to the Grand Banks for cod. The cod, dried on flakes of wood stretched out on the field behind his house, was then taken to the West Indies and exchanged for rum, molasses, oranges and coconuts. In 1821 Daniel Bigelow, owner and master of the *Emily,* was registered as of Pictou, and Mud Creek had lost another shipbuilder.

Although several of the descendants of the three DeWolf cousins founded shipping firms, at Halifax, at Windsor, at Liverpool, Nova Scotia, and at Liverpool, England, none of them seems to have had vessels built at Mud

Creek. Only Andrew Dwight DeWolf appears as owner of three schooners built at Horton: the *Shepherd,* 116 tons, built by William McKay in 1853, and registered in Wick the next year; the *Arno,* 59 tons, built in 1854; and the *Emma,* 32 tons, built in 1856, the year before Andrew Dwight DeWolf's death.

In the meantime, Wolfville, said to be the smallest registered port in the world, had developed a considerable business in shipping local products, chiefly potatoes. Ox carts would be lined up awaiting their turn to have their loads weighed and dumped on the wharf, whence they were transferred to the holds of the vessels. Sometimes as many as sixteen vessels would be outside and inside the port, the bowsprits of those within Mud Creek reaching across the early road which wandered past Mud Bridge and down again to the waterfront, would interfere with traffic and force loads of hay to use the old French road along the ridge, or be lowered in height.

In October 1814 John Ellis, blacksmith of Mud Bridge, complained that vessels tore down the bridge railings as they came into the Creek and unloaded cargoes on the bridge, blocking the road to traffic - "a perfect nuisance and annoyance to travellers."

The petitioners asked the authorities to build a wharf on the north side of the bridge where they wished to erect a blacksmith shop; this would prevent the vessels landing as they do. Signers were: Dr. T. Johnson, James Armstrong, Edwin DeWolf, Lewis Godfrey, John Graham, Charles Randall, Elijah Fowler, Edward Paisser(?), Charles Hancock, E.A. Crawley, John Woodworth, Thomas Barss, and Edwin Davison.   J. E. and D. J. Harris were the principals in this part of the port's business, and may have shipped apples before W. H. Chase, who became known as the apple king. Among the vessels owned by the Harris firm were the *Alpha,* a brigantine of 129 tons, built in Horton in 1855 and lost in the Bay of Fundy; the *Laura,* a brigantine of 236 tons, built in Horton in 1866; and the *Stella,* a barque of

About 1886. Port of Wolfville.

474 tons, later sold to Germany and renamed *Rostock.* They also owned vessels built in Cornwallis, notably the *Wolfville,* 244 tons, built in 1867, later sold at Liverpool, England.

The coming of the railroad in 1869 cut off the upper part of Wolfville's Mud Creek, where the early vessels had been built, from any use either for shipbuilding or for shipping of goods. The railroad took over the telegraph business, and the double convenience of the railroad and telegraph attracted two heads of shipping firms to Wolfville: for a time Charles Berteaux, who later transferred to New York; and, more permanently, C. R. Burgess, whose large barques and ships were built at Kingsport.   After the coming of the railroad, three vessels were built at Wolfville: the *Stella,* by J. E. Harris, already mentioned; and by W. A. Cox, in 1875, the *Sophia Cook,* a brig of 303 tons; and in 1876 the schooner *Terra Nova,* 211 tons, which was owned by William J. Stairs in 1887. An enthusiastic writer in the Halifax *Morning Chronicle,* of January 23, 1875, doubled the tonnage of the vessel then in the stocks and forecast an 800-ton vessel later. A steam mill had been built on a railroad siding to prepare the wood; did the steam mill catch fire and prevent the building of the third vessel? The writer expressed surprise that Wolfville had not had a shipbuilding industry earlier, but neither earlier nor later did any attempt to start one succeed.

In February 1764 two Acadians, Francis Arsenau and John Bourg, were given permission by the Lieutenant-Governor of Nova Scotia to continue the charges for the ferry boat which they had been running "from Partridge Island to Cape Blowme Down, Horton, Fort Edward and different Settlements on each side of the Basin of Minas." The Horton they mentioned was undoubtedly Lower Horton, but they might have included Upper Horton or Mud Creek in their rounds, if traffic warranted. How long their service continued is not known, but in 1776 a grant of 1000 acres near Partridge Island was given to John Avery, John Bacon, Jr., and Jacob Lockhart on condition that they would operate the ferry across Minas Basin. Before they could get started, Jonathan Eddy, who was about to attack Fort Cumberland, sent one of his vessels up the Minas Basin to cut communications with Fort Edward, and captured the ferry. A warship was dispatched from Halifax and forced a hasty retreat of the rebels. John Avery and John Bacon sold their lots, in April, 1777, to Abijah and Asa Scott, and Jacob Hurd of Fort Sackville. Abijah Scott then undertook to provide the ferry service, but was harrassed by rebel privateers, driven from his house, which was burned, and the Ferry Boat that cost one hundred and fifty pounds was rendered useless. When he petitioned for funds to purchase sails, in March, 1782, the council refused to give any assistance because it might set a precedent. James Shannon and Silas Crane apparently took over the ferry service, and Shannon brought James Ratchford in as partner. In 1788 Scott sold his lands to James Ratchford and Jonathan Crane. The Assembly granted a subsidy of fifty pounds to the ferry service, and in 1803 increased it to seventy-five pounds.

As James Ratchford's sister Margaret married Elisha DeWolf there were personal reasons for including Mud Creek in the ferry's schedule. In the course of the 19th century the Partridge Island — Cornwallis — Horton — Windsor ferry became Parrsboro — Kingsport — Wolfville service and continued until the outbreak of World War II. The sailing ships were superseded by vessels with auxiliary engines and then by steamers. There were occasional interruptions in the service. In 1883 the Wolfville *Acadian* reported that for the first time in years there was no packet to Parrsboro, although the steamer *Hiawatha* was running a weekly service from Horton to Parrsboro. A Kentville firm organized an all-day excursion to Parrsboro in 1887 on the *Hiawatha,* but the affair was not altogether successful, for the steamer failed to stop at Kingsport, to the great annoyance of those who had bought tickets, and was so late in returning to the wharf at Wolfville that a special train had to be sent from Kentville to pick up the passengers from there. For June of 1888 R. Prat organized another such excursion, for which it was promised that the *Hiawatha* would stop at Port Williams, and the *Acadia* would leave Wolfville wharf at 7.30 a.m. The fare was sixty cents, and the best of order was promised. The *Acadia* was withdrawn from Minas Basin in 1893 and replaced by the *Evangeline,* from which the *Messenger,* later renamed the *Prince Albert,* took over in 1904.

The Kipawo began service in 1926.

The widespread use of the automobile after the first World War, led to a demand for a ferry which would carry automobiles and save the motorist the long trip around the end of Minas Basin on the uncertain roads of the time. In 1926 the *Kipawo,* capable of carrying 127 passengers and eight to ten cars, began her service. The M.V. *Kipawo* served three ports of call: Kingsport, Parrsboro, and Wolfville, which provided the name. She had comfortable quarters. Her captain, Edward Trefry, invented a system of steel slings under each wheel for putting cars on the deck and removing them at the end of the voyage. It was a breathtaking operation to watch, but it generally worked well. When the subsidy was withdrawn, after the outbreak of World War II, the ferry was considered too costly to operate, and the *Kipawo* was withdrawn for ferry services in Newfoundland. After the war a half-hearted attempt to purchase her was thwarted by Newfoundland communities whose need was greater. Recently a movement was started to get the *Kipawo* back, not as a ferry but as a playhouse and attraction at a marina at Wolfville. She is now being put into condition at Parrsboro and will be sent across Minas Basin when she and her berth are ready.

The impact of the *Kipawo* on Wolfville has been told by Graham Patriquin who recalled his boyhood experiences of watching the Kip (*Kipawo*) land at the Gov (Government Wharf), unload, load, and leave. The wharf lay east of Mud Creek's outflow into the Cornwallis River, resting on long piles. A sturdy lighthouse stood at the western end of the wharf, a sentinel beside the road leading to the town. Youngsters swam off the wharf when not watching the Kip and her fascinating presence. The Kip's "predecessor, *S.S. Prince Albert*, was an ancient coal-burning slowpoke whose cargo-handling operations were scarcely more titillating than those of the two-masted schooners that fairly cluttered the wharves of Mud Creek's tidal road-bed." The Kip and her load of tourist automobiles proved much more

Loading Cars on the Kipawo at Wolfville. N.S.

Always an exciting time at the wharf.

exciting, as passengers and spectators got the jitters, gasped at the suspended automobile rising and floating in the air to and fro from the vessel and the wharf.

Early in the 1930's, rains, high tides, and strong winds destroyed the Wickwire dykes, and the wharf disintegrated. The Kip's new berth was a wharf beside the D.A.R. tracks at Mud Creek "where restrictions of time and tide made docking a chancy business in the confines of the shallow harbour." A new chapter was added to the legend of the *Kipawo*.

Attempts were made to provide a substitute for the *Kipawo* but with no success. Allison T. Smith of Parrsboro purchased an old R.C.M.P. Patrol Boat to run between Parrsboro and Wolfville. This boat could not carry cars, so Smith planned to provide a larger craft if traffic required it. However, no replacement was made of the *Kipawo*.

2. Travel by Land.

a. Roads

When the first English settlers came to Nova Scotia, they found no roads. The paths through the woods, which the Indians had used, were often rough and treacherous. The Acadians had begun to make paths or roads through the woods to Port Royal and La Have as early as 1701, but had not made any great progress in their road building.   In 1760 a warrant was issued to make a "carriage road from Halifax to Windsor." Governor Lawrence had visited Horton Township about this time and realized the strategic value of a good road linking Halifax to the Minas Basin communities. Members of the Nova Scotia Council had decided to reserve the Windsor area, the nearest good farming land to Halifax, for their own use, and were anxious to have a good road available, although this was not cited as one of the reasons for making the road. The road was needed for military purposes; it would enable people to attend sessions of the Legislature; it would make it possible for farmers to bring cattle and produce to the city.

In response to this warrant two Windsor men, Henry Denny Denson and Isaac Deschamp, were hired to make a "carriage road" out of the trail. In that same year six transports with settlers landed at Windsor, and some of them, and their cattle, went overland to Horton.

Overland mail delivery was slow. By 1766 it came fortnightly, on foot or by horse, from Halifax to Annapolis. Cornwallis settlers, who were off the main line of communication, could get across the Cornwallis River only at low tide and on horseback, until Thomas Lawdon received permission to run a ferry. The inhabitants complained of the high rates - two shillings per passenger — and were successful in having them reduced to sixpence for a man and a horse. Moses Gore petitioned in 1774 for the position of ferryman, and later applied for a tavern licence to provide "spiritous liquids and victuals" to travellers. James Graves, James Byrne, and John Lowden (son of the Thomas Lawdon who began the ferry?) were also ferrymen. The ferry crossed from Ferry Lane to Cornwallis Town Plot, Cornwallis, and the ferryman lived and kept his roadhouse or tavern on the north side. In 1780, a bridge, wide enough for walking or riding a horse, was built at Port Williams, and the ferry was dispensed with. However, high tides and winds washed out the bridge in the early 1800s, and the ferry service resumed. In 1835 a new bridge was completed, with tolls set at threepence for twelve years and older; under twelve, except infants in arms, one and a half pence; cattle, twopence each; swine, a halfpenny each; horses or vehicles, twopence.

By 1782 inland transportation still remained difficult. Only by being unloaded, taken apart and portaged through could wheeled vehicles cross between Fort Sackville and Windsor, or between Horton and Annapolis. The terrain was rough and rocky and the actual engineering difficulties of road building in Nova Scotia were not understood in Britain from whom funds were expected. The township had not shown a profit in the eyes of Britain, although it had been twenty years in existence, and Britain was preoccupied with the American Revolution: therefore funds were not forthcoming.

Farms were producing more crops and were anxious to have access to the Halifax markets, military and civilian. The road from Annapolis to Halifax was widened and improved, in the hope that it could handle the passage of wheeled vehicles. Farmers from different areas banded together to take cattle or other goods to the city for sale or trade. The trips were long and arduous, and both farmers and produce suffered. On their return journey they would bring necessities for the household, including leather for the journeyman shoemaker to make up into footwear for the family. The farmers began to realize their importance to the Port and to agitate for road improvements.

About 1795 the waggons were improved by big leather circular springs at the back. Benjamin Belcher imported a waggon from Boston in 1796, but few waggons and carriages were to be seen before 1800. For farm work two-wheeled carts were used. Draught horses and oxen were a rarity, and horses and cattle were small. In 1816 a Yankee peddler brought a waggon load of tinware to Horton Corner and sold the outfit to Mrs. James D. Harris.

In the autumn of 1795 Sir John and Lady Wentworth made a tour of the western townships. "The road to Annapolis was now passable for carriages," Brian Cuthbertson noted, "and Wentworth drove in state, visiting and staying with friends along the way." The Governor was pleased to find that the harvest exceeded that of any previous year, and that there were sheep and cattle on many farms.

In his *Journals* of August 1817, Lord Dalhousie, Lieutenant-Governor of Nova Scotia, wrote that he drove to the township of Horton over a very hilly road. He passed Minas and Blomidon. Horton township "was a scattered settlement of neat common houses, small farms, but rich in their way of life. A considerable extent of salt meadows dyked in, produces a great stack of hay, in which their chief wealth seems to exist."

b. Stagecoaches

In 1811 only two coach roads existed in the colony of Nova Scotia, one from Halifax to Pictou, and the other from Halifax to Windsor. The first regular stagecoach service between Halifax and Windsor began shortly before 1816, with twice-weekly trips at a fare of six shillings. Possibly the recent founding of Kings College at Windsor would have been an inducement for increased and improved travel. Then the citizens set up a transportation system for depositing passengers on the stagecoaches and picking up incoming passengers. The coaches were provided by the Western Stage Company, and Isaiah Smith was the first coachman for the six-passenger Halifax to Windsor run.

Stagecoach travel in those early years was uncomfortable and hazardous. Parts of the roads were impassable in spring, and sometimes the coach broke down and passengers had to walk. In the 1820s and 1830s, the bridges were decrepit and treacherous.

The coaches were usuaslly of the "four-in-hand" type, with four horses. A coach carried seven or eight inside passengers, on two seats facing each other. The coachman drove from the top, with another seat behind him. Joseph Howe rode in 1828 on the coach top from Halifax to Horton, "with his foot firmly on the 'dickey'," the back of the coachman's seat. A coach had window awnings or curtains, and sometimes a lighted lamp. Occasionally nine passengers were carried, three facing forward, three facing backward, and three on moveable seats stretched between the doors. In spite of braces of belts of leather which absorbed some of the shocks and bumps, coach travel created an oscillation which often induced stomach sickness.

When roads were good, Harry Kilcup and Walsh drove like Jehu. "Not faster down the steep did the devils send the swine," Joseph Howe wrote, "than our incarnate coachman drives his cattle." In wet weather, passengers were required to help pry out the wheels with fence posts. Sometimes six horses might be harnessed to get the coach through the difficult roads. Joseph Howe, on one occasion, "had some feelings of compassion for the poor devils of horses."

In 1828 a grant of 300 pounds a year was given for the thrice-weekly line of coaches from Halifax to Annapolis. The line began in 1829, and served for forty years. The coach stopped every ten or fifteen miles, and made an overnight stay at Kentville's Royal Oak Inn. In winter the Halifax to Annapolis coach ran only twice weekly. The fare was ten dollars, a considerable sum for those days — "frightfully expensive" patrons said. The journey took the best part of two days. The schedules were made up to connect to St. John by packet schooners. Steam vessels were put on the service in 1839.

A journey from Annapolis to Halifax was described in 1833:

> The day was stormy, with heavy rains, and the coach only a secondhand American one. . . . Neither was it waterproof, the canvas curtains hanging down in long shreds, and flapping to and fro with the wind. The horses, too, were poor specimens of the Nova Scotia steeds, three out of four being lame; the coachman, however, was perhaps one shade more professional in his appearance than those of the States.
>
> We continued eastward through Kentville. . . . Near Wolfville, the view of Blomidon, or Blow-me-down (as it is now significantly called, from the heavy gusts of wind which prevail off its bluff point), with the Basin of Minas and the opposite shore, is a fine and extensive one when taken from the high part of the Horton Mountains, over which the road passes. For the first time in America (a journey of 2,500 miles), I saw a drag chain used in their descent, but the road was excellent; and though closely packed with people inside, and only two seats, we travelled the ten miles in an hour and two minutes.

The Wolfville of 1851 was recalled by Dr. G. E. Day, who travelled from Sheffield, N.B., to St. John, and then to Windsor, where he went to the King's Hotel. Late in the afternoon, he left for Wolfville, with a second stagecoach behind. On his arrival in Wolfville, about seven o'clock, he learned that political conditions in Nova Scotia were "very sharp." He was asked by what coach he had come from Windsor, and was told by the questioner that he should have come in Belcher's for that belonged to the Liberals, but King's was run by the Conservatives. "When I asked what was the difference between the parties, I was told that Howe was leader of one party and Johnstone of the other." Dr. Day did not think the answer very satisfactory, but supposed "it was the best that could be given."

c. Taverns, Hotels

These stopping places were usually farm houses, sometimes altered to meet the desires of the travelling public. The coach's arrival was the great event of the day or week and frequently involved a change of horses. Of the string of taverns established along the road to Annapolis, one of the most important was Eglinton, the halfway house between Halifax and Windsor. It was surrounded by several buildings, store houses, barns and stables. It was one of the inns of the time that kept a small army of cooks, stable boys, helpers and farm workers. It was a great place for drinking parties.

Owing to the scarcity of travel on the main roads, taverns were not a profitable business, and inducements had to be offered to those willing to accommodate the travelling public. The Session gave a free Licence to the Ferry House at Cornwallis, and to Jonathan Graham in Upper Horton. The Graham house was the headquarters of the militia, the coach office, express office, and the general place of call for those who came to the community on business. In 1789 three houses of entertainment at Upper Horton, Jonathan Graham's, Elijah Fowler's, and DeWolf's were listed. DeWolf's stopping place had been mentioned in 1785, but seems to have yielded to Graham's and Fowler's.

Elijah Fowler and family had come from Georgia to Parrsborough, and then crossed over to Horton. He had married Dorothy, the daughter of John Fowler, a well-to-do Loyalist from Westchester County, New York, who had come to Nova Scotia at the time of the evacuation of Boston in 1776, and in 1778 had bought property on the north side of the main street for Fowler's Tavern, near the present Atlantic Trust building. He also bought most of the land between the present Highland and Gaspereau Avenues. Elijah bought the property on the south side of the main street, as far as the top of the ridge, in 1809. The property on the north side, which he had inherited from John Fowler, his wife's father, he sold to Andrew DeWolf. In 1814 or 1818 Elijah began to erect the American House as a hotel, and it became the stopping place between Bishop's Farm at Wallbrook and Cyrus Peck's Tavern at Horton Corner. The American House stood where the Post Office now stands, and by 1838 it was advertised as "Temperance Inn." When the building was repaired, an old document, dated December 13, 1792, indicated that Elijah Fowler had bought goods from Ratchford and Company at Parrsborough. Elijah Fowler, senior, died in 1839, and his property was left to his son, Elijah, who had married Sarah Harris of Horton.

At a later date, T. B. Messenger operated the American House, with Lew Duncanson as livery man, and Edward Chase as pioneer driver and guide. The Harrises operated the hotel for fourteen years, and in 1886 John Harris added eight rooms to the hotel, reportedly with the assistance of H. B. Witter as remodeller. In 1895 an American visitor mentioned Duncanson as in charge of the American House. The proprietor had a collection of ancient French relics, to which he had just added a coffin from Grand Pre which contaned nothing but a full set of teeth and dust. The American visitor stated that Wolfville was 'one of the most pleasant places that can be found.'' Duncanson sold the building to Joseph Starr of Kentville, but it was destroyed by fire in October of 1898. A fire in October of 1904 levelled the "worthless old building," apparently still the American House.

Lord Dalhousie's Journals mentioned that they had intended to push on to Peck's and Dennison's at the turn into Cornwallis, but learned that the County Magistrates were assembled there in Court for two days, so they could not be accommodated. "We therefore stopt at Fowler's & Graham's & did very well. This morning we ate breakfast at Peck's, a pretty spot called the Oaks." He and his party gathered acorns, and left instructions for a barrel of them to be sent to Halifax, and then he would send them to England. Mrs. Peck he described as a civil little old woman. The road was deeply sandy and uninteresting.

By 1818, travel on the Post Road was heavy enough to support two hotels. George Graham opened a second hotel at Horton. Mary Ann Norris of Cornwallis stopped at the DeWolf house of entertainment on November 24, 1825. She mentions walking to church at Cornwallis. "We had a terrible walk. I lost my Golwshoe off twice in the mud." She also mentioned riding twenty-eight miles on horseback one day.

In 1827 the Western Coach Company began carrying mail, and one of the stops for passengers was Borden's Hotel at Grand Pre. The later advent of railway depots there and at Horton Landing displaced mails by coach brought on the old coach road. Borden's Hotel was abandoned for Lyons Hotel in Kentville.

In 1830 a Temperance Hotel was built, said to be the first from Halifax to Yarmouth, but that claim was disputed by Mrs. William Sommerville, who contended that her father, Arthur Murphy, started a Temperance Hotel in 1854, during the days when the other hotels were referred to as "Rum Holes," and that it was the first Temperance Hotel between Windsor and Annapolis. Mrs. Arthur Murphy later became the proprietor of Central House, formerly the Graham House, in 1885. This hotel stood where the parking lot of the Acadia University rink now exists. In 1869 the Central House had been operated by J. N. Selfridge and W. F. Balcom. Balcom later improved the place for a livery stable. He received by train a four-horse express with side seats, to serve as a picnic waggon. He purchased a sleigh to hold twenty people, and a very comfortable barouche, a carriage with collapsible half-head, to carry a driver and four persons. After Mrs. Murphy took over Central House, the name was changed, in 1887, to Village House by W. J. Griffin who was running the place for the summer. When Griffin became ill, Mrs. H. D. Newcombe of Pereau took charge, and the place was reported as the only hotel of any note in Horton. Mrs. Murphy seems to have resumed as proprietor, but died in March 1891. John W. Beckwith, who had removed from Port Williams in 1889, took charge of Village House and improved its appearance in 1893 by adding a verandah. At some time after February 1894, the hotel's name changed back to Central House. In his "*Souvenir of Wolfville and Grand Pre*," Reverend D. O. Parker in 1891 listed the Central House Livery Stables, and the Highland Lodge on Highland Avenue, four doors south of Acadia Street, with D. O. Parker as proprietor in 1892. In all, the town had five hotels in 1890, as well as several boarding houses.

In 1879 the Acadia Hotel, E. D. Bishop proprietor, was listed. The large house had been built in 1858 by Reverend John Chase as a residence and school, before becoming Grand Pre Seminary from 1861 to 1870. It was located opposite the present Baptist church on Main Street and had been operated by J. Ells in the early 1870s. It was reported in 1887 that the hotel would be conducted as a temperance house, with Fletcher Bishop in charge.

1880s. Centre: Baptist church, with Acadia Hotel across the street. Foreground: Sawyer House, and the Drill Shed is behind it, on School Street.

By 1893 the Acadia Hotel had become the Royal Hotel. A company, led by Dr. DeWitt, purchased J. E. Jenkins' hotel and planned to move it to the rear to make room for a handsome new tourist hotel. In 1894 J. W. Beckwith moved from the Village House, and leased the Royal Hotel, which had been thoroughly renovated and had a verandah added. In the following year Beckwith built a large extension on the north side, which added thirteen rooms. In 1896, when the building suffered a bad fire, which destroyed the two upper stories, it appeared that Jodrey was the owner. The Beckwiths for a time kept the Quinn House, but moved back to the Royal in July 1897, after Currie and Bent had finished rebuilding the hotel. In 1898 a meeting was held to discuss erection of a large hotel, for which $50,000 capital, half of it American, would be required. Apparently nothing came of the proposal, and the Royal Hotel, which then had thirty rooms, continued to be busy and added two more sample rooms. The Royal was sold in 1912 to Mr. Goudey of Dartmouth, then in 1912 to Truman S. Sanford. The name was changed to Evangeline Inn in 1927 and it continued a precarious existence. From World War II on the building was used as a student residence and was finally torn down in 1969.

The Wolfville Hotel, built in 1869 by a Mr. Starr of Halifax, was located where the Imperial Oil service station now stands. It became the property of Robert DeWolf, and was later known as Hancock's, Thompson's, and Farrel's. In June 1889, when the *Acadian* agitated to have the bend in Main Street east of Wolfville Hotel straightened, the place was still in existence. The proprietor in 1895 was Charles Eastwood: the building burned in 1904.

There was also Union House, a large three-storey building located where the movie theatre now stands. It was operated by a Mr. Clark, then by Grandison Eagles, who placed a handsome fence in front of the house in 1896. T. E. Hutchinson bought the hotel in 1908 and remodelled it.

45

During the summers, when students were not using the building, the Acadia Seminary Hotel was operated for tourists by Frank P. Rockwell. In 1897 it was advertised that the building had telephone, electric lights, hot and cold baths. A bark "Wigwam Camp" in front entertained the tourists, many of whom would stay for the summer. On one occasion, Rockwell lodged Mr. Vanderbilt of New York and a party of twenty-four. The place was still busy in 1908 when a high school student, Frank L. Godfrey, worked as a bellboy during the summer holidays. Local teamsters, livery stable proprietors, and launch owners were in much demand to transport tourists to points of interest near Wolfville.

In 1901 Rockwell erected Acadia Villa at the corner of Linden Avenue and Acadia Street. By 1925 the Acadia Villa had running water in each room, but the thawing of frozen pipes by a blow torch resulted in the burning down of the hotel in 1940.

Several large houses were used as hotels. Elisha DeWolf's home, as was noted, became for a time a summer tourist hotel under the name of Kent Lodge. R. A. Jodrey's residence on Main Street was sold in 1936 to become the Paramount Hotel, administered by E. W. Balcom. It was the first place in Wolfville to fly the new Canadian flag. The building was enlarged in 1972, but was sold the following year to the owners of Old Orchard Inn, D. W. Wallace and John Patterson, who had financial difficulties operating a discotheque in the building. In 1979 it was sold to become a non-profit remedial school for high-potential dyslexias, of ages six to sixteen. Landmark East, named for the original Landmark school in New England, was instituted by headmaster Robert Kahn. The C. R. Burgess home became the residence of W. C. B. Harris, and later Blomidon Inn. It has recently been restored to its original splendour under the management of Peter and Gail Hastings. The William H. Chase house on Main Street became the Revaron, a rooming house, until its purchase in November 1973 by Arthur Speed, who renamed it Historic Inn, where rooms and meals were provided.

d. Railroads

By 1846, interest in support of a railroad for the Valley had increased. Joseph Howe and Judge T. C. Haliburton encouraged the view that a good rail service would benefit people all along the route from Halifax to Annapolis. However, because of politics, financial problems, and opposition from pressure groups, it was not until 1872 that the railroad actually ran all the way.

The line from Halifax to Windsor, a three-hour run, opened in 1858. There was still a break in the line from Windsor to Grand Pre, when a line to Kentville was begun in 1866, and the first engine bought by the Nova Scotia government had to be landed at Elderkin's Creek, one mile east of Kentville. The Windsor and Annapolis Railway (W.& A.R.), was organized in 1867, and after construction of a bridge at Mud Creek in 1868, the line ran from Annapolis to Horton Landing in June 1869. By January 1872 the line ran from Annapolis to Halifax. Before that, passengers to St. John travelled by steamer from Windsor.

The trestle bridge over Mud Creek, Johnson Bishop wrote, was built with John Clark in charge of the pile driver. In 1869 Wolfville was the headquarters of the W.& A.R. The car shops were located here, and two engines built

One of the early type locomotives built by the Fox-Walker Company of Bristol, England, for the Windsor and Annapolis Railway. Brought to this country in November, 1868

in Bristol, England, No. 1 "Evangeline," and No. 2 "Gabriel" were landed in Wolfville. Owing to lack of co-operation from owners of land, the headquarters were removed to Kentville. Chief Engineer Vernon Smith became General Manager, and lived in Kentville. In 1869 he had bought the stagecoach line in order to ensure that the railway had the duty of carrying the mail. When trains started going through Wolfville, B. O. Davidson recalled walking over the trestle bridge and expecting any moment to meet an oncoming train. For a considerable time there were only two mixed trains a day, so it is not surprising that he never did meet an oncoming train. The train conductors were Johnny Clarke and Joe Edwards, who had many a spirited tilt when either happened to arrive late.

A. W. H. Eaton recorded that "the shrill scream of the engine as it tore across the silent Grand Pre, sounded the death knell of Jehuism . . . slow travelling, good fellowship, discomfort, picturesqueness and all." Others appreciated the fact that it carried fruit without damaging it. Fruit and vegetables could be sent by rail to Halifax for shipment to European markets, and docking and unloading of ocean vessels for the British market became less important. As shipping began to decline, Wolfville shipowner C. R. Burgess involved himself in developing the Cornwallis Valley Railway. Warehouses began to appear as if by magic along the line when the railroad was completed, and the apple industry improved. In 1897 the W.& A.R. removed their tracks from the Wolfville wharf as an incentive to get the C.V.R. into operation.

About 1889. Train time, at the old station.

The first station agent in Wolfville was Samuel Prat. By 1888, Mumford was agent. The Halifax *Morning Herald* of August 1891 said a new railway station had been built in May, one of the best, second only to that in Middleton. Graves was stationmaster at the time. "The Press Association of Boston" came to visit in large numbers, and were entertained in the new station before touring the countryside in a cavalcade of carriages. In 1892 a semaphore was installed for signalling trains, green for danger and red when all was well, the newspaper said, obviously mixing its signals. The Dominion Atlantic Railway, which had been formed in 1893 to absorb the various lines, improved the grounds around the Wolfville station and levelled a barn. In 1904 electric lights were installed, and in 1910 water and sewer pipes. In 1911 the station burned, perhaps ignited by sparks from a passing locomotive, and two brick and stone buildings were erected by Rhodes and Curry of Amherst the next year. New lights were installed in 1916.

Graves had been succeeded as stationmaster by W. S. Newcomb, and in 1892 Joseph MacDonald took over. After the new building was erected, the stationmaster and his family lived over the station: Chester Coombs, Horace Jackson, and, finally, Murray Van Blarcom who lived there from 1959 and then commuted from Kentville until 1974. Edgar DeWolf, long-time resident of Wolfville, and lover of steam trains, for many years kept in close touch with Wolfville station and trains. He reported that in 1907 the trip to Halifax required three and a half hours, and that the diesel motor replaced the steam engine in 1956. Dr. Allen Gibson, in his charming little brochure, *Train Time*, recalled placing his ear to the rail to learn in advance of the train's approach, and of flattening horseshoe nails by the train wheels so that rings could be shaped from the metal. He recounted the names of the engines: DeRazilly, Blomidon, Poutrincourt, Lescarbot, Pontgrave, Kent, Champlain, Hebert, Bluenose, New Yorker, and Haliburton. To these can be added the name Howe.

In 1957, the last D.A.R. steam engine to run through Wolfville

e. Automobiles

The introduction of the motor car about 1892 made great changes in transportation, in the type of services requred, and in the quality of roads needed. Wolfville prided itself on having some of the best roads in the country, but they were still of dirt, covered by a top layer of gravel, and prone to "washout" and "washboard" effects. Many streets in town were not really roadways at all, but expanded foot and bridle paths. Sidewalks were of dirt, and hitching posts and watering troughs were scattered along the main street.

It was a long time before the automobile displaced the horse in Wolfville. In March 1904 Hutchinson's Wolfville Express began a business of livery stable, cartage and tourist excursions with horse-drawn vehicles. Two years later Hutchinson expanded his business by buying W. J. Balcom's livery stable and delivery. Inhabitants of the town remembered with affection "Tommy" Hutchinson and Mrs. Hutchinson, and also Charlie Delahunt who faithfully provided horse-drawn service until about 1960. Not once was Charlie Delahunt out in his cash receipts for the day's work.

About 1911. Well, that's quite a thing. Should I buy one?

The first motor car in town was said to have been owned by D. R. Munro. By 1904, automobiles had become common enough to warrant traffic bylaws and the first auto inspection. A. F. Rand purchased a "Queen" automobile in the spring of 1907, and W. S. Wallace bought a Ford runabout that summer. During the following year, Kings County motor vehicles were prohibited from using the roads on Thursdays, Saturdays, and Sundays. Mayor Black became owner of a car resembling a buggy, and the paper carried an advertisement for a used car. By 1911, the town had seven Fords, and F. J. Porter was the county agent. N. W. Sinclair had begun selling automobile insurance in 1909, and Hutchinson's express added an automobile in 1910. At some time, Hutchinson's smithy on Willow Avenue became a livery stable and garage. In 1912 the Wolfville Garage, which had erected a new building, advertised that cars could be stored and overhauled. The next year they were selling Harley Davidson motorcycles, and the year after they erected a Bowser gasoline tank opposite the Royal Hotel. A. V. Rand also installed one in front of his store.

Soldiers returning from the war in 1918 did not find the town greatly changed. Because the fast driving automobiles "was beginning to be a problem," signs had been placed at each end of town warning motor traffic to keep to twelve miles an hour. The town was still using "one team (a horse and truck) and men to assist in the work of removing the earth" for construction of a cement sidewalk opposite the Post Office; in 1922 the town was still buying a horse, waggon, sled and harness; in 1928 it was authorizing a grant of $50 to Superintendent Aubrey Dakin "for the cost of keeping a team at work."

Meanwhile, the Wolfville Garage had re-opened in 1919, under management of J. E. Black. A year later the Acadia Automobile Agency began business, with Phillip Illsley as president, J. Elmer Westcott as manager, and H. E. Woodman as sales manager. By 1920, motorists in Nova Scotia joined the rest of the country in the practice of driving on the right side of the highway, a change made necessary by the increasing number of American cars whose drivers were used to that practice. The bus service to Kentville was begun in the Fall of 1922 by Carleton Kinnie, who drove a seven-passenger Studebaker. T. Hutchinson had a new yellow bus on the same run. In 1923 Howard Whidden, whose father had delivered oil in wooden barrels at Halifax in 1895, opened the first gasoline pumps in Wolfville, opposite the Starr Block where Lee Johnston's insurance business now exists. Howard Whidden's son, Graham, took over the Esso Service Station in 1970 when his father retired.

The tourist trade potential and its benefits were becoming recognized, and in 1924 tastefully worded signs were placed at the eastern and western boundaries of the town to call attention to the many attractions the community had to offer. Roy A. Jodrey entered the gas station business in 1925, and young Dick Harris, who had previously set up a filling station at Aylesford, borrowed money from Fred C. Manning of Falmouth to open the Wolfville Park Filling Station. Frank Brennan was in charge of the station, which was situated on what had been the town dump. In 1930 the Irving Oil Company bought the Godfrey property next to the Baptist church on Main Street, and J. E. Westcott constructed a gas and service station. The Super Service Station installed gas tanks on the old Central House property west of the Old Cemetery, and the Imperial Oil Company's station, managed by H. J. Whidden, opened on a site opposite Seaview Avenue. In 1939 C. W. Fairn operated the Canadian Oils Ltd. garage at the corner of Main and Gaspereau.

The increasing traffic called for erection of stop signs, ten of which were installed in 1931, and for additional road improvements. The road between Kentville and Wolfville was paved. Traffic blinker lights were placed at each end of the town in 1954. A bus service to Canning was discontinued in 1955.

T. E. Hutchinson sold his taxi business to William Gue and Merritt

Coldwell, but the name continued as Hutchinsons Taxi and Transport Company. In 1946 six taxi firms, with ten cars, provided service; James MacLean took over Imperial Oil Service Station in August; the unpaved streets received their annual coating of oil. In 1947 the town sold its two horses. In March 1950 Pulsifer's Garage, corner of Main and Gaspereau, assumed management of the White Rose station on the opposite corner. In 1956 taxi drivers were Boyd F. Addington, Varley Bishop, Gordon Reid, J. W. John, and Claude Rogers.

In 1960 the Irving Service Station, managed by S. Merritt Coldwell, opened. In 1962 James Irving and Earl Curtis took over the garage previously owned by F. W. Robertson, and operated by John McKinnon until it burned. They began business in November, in association with Texaco Limited, and sold in December 1974 to C. A. McKinnon and Donald Marshall of Home Hardware. Wile's Body Shop was opened in 1964. Myron Johnson, who had been in the taxi business for thirty years, was honoured during his birthday celebration.

Main Street, about 1920.

VIII.

ECONOMY OF THE
18th AND 19th CENTURIES

1. Late 18th Century

The Basin of Minas provided the farming settlements along its shores with ready transport, and neither the Acadians nor the Planters used the Bay of Fundy as other than a supplementary source of food and employment. By land, the Minas Basin area was almost completely isolated from the rest of Nova Scotia and of North America, and all transport had to be by water in the early days. The farming communities achieved a degree of self-sufficiency above mere subsistence, but import trade was a necessity for many articles.

Economic expansion in the Valley, the most important agricultural area of the province, was slow. The land speculation which resulted in creation of new townships throughout Nova Scotia, in 1765, and some addition to the population, did not affect the Valley. However, the increasing restlessness in the 13 Colonies to the south, which led to the American Revolutionary War, stifled any further emigration to Nova Scotia, interfered with trade, and eventually shut down emigration from Britain.

The outbreak of hostilities in 1775 led to attempts on the part of the rebels to attach the Nova Scotia settlers to their side and a determination by the authorities to keep Nova Scotia loyal to Great Britain. The Americans had some success, which led to the stationing of the *Vulture* and other vessels between St. John and Annapolis to keep out rebel intruders. The failure of the attack on Fort Beausejour and the raids of Yankee privateers also ensured the loyalty of Nova Scotians. Until the beginning of the American Revolutionary War, masters of vessels had considered the voyage to Boston less dangerous than that around the coasts of Nova Scotia, and this had made Nova Scotia increasingly dependent on the New England trade. With the cutting off of trade to New England, trade within the province benefited. Halifax, the major urban centre, was faced with shortages and began to look to supplies from Nova Scotia vessels and the agricultural settlements within the province. In December 1781 a record flour shortage occurred, and a request came to Horton, Cornwallis and Windsor for sixty tons.

In 1776 the only carriage road in the province was from Halifax to Windsor. The war showed the necessity of more roads in order to move troops to threatened areas. Troops were employed in building military roads, notably the one which went straight through the woods of South Mountain so as to connect with Annapolis and Digby without the necessity of crossing the tidal streams or the marshes. The increase in military and naval establishments meant increased demand for the produce of the farms. Cattle were needed also, and could be driven along the Windsor to Halifax road, or taken by trails through the woods to the new military road. The shift toward production of cattle and sheep and hogs continued after the war, and the dyked lands were used almost exclusively for hay and pasturage. These changes had their effect on the small community growing up around the mouth of Mud Creek.

The end of the war brought 30,000 or more refugees and disbanded troops to Nova Scotia. The older communities were invaluable in supplying food, shelter, and boards for houses. Unused grants were escheated, and vast tracts of unbroken forest land were granted to the newcomers. The population of the province was more than doubled, and Halifax became a large urban market. The end of the war brought another change which was of great benefit to both rural and urban inhabitants. The trade with the West Indies had hitherto been monopolized by the Colonies which had seceded and lost their rights to free entry into the British West Indies. St. Andrews, St. John, Yarmouth, Liverpool, and Halifax took up the challenge, and there was a demand for fish, lumber, and farm produce to take down to the West Indies to exchange for sugar, molasses, spices, tropical fruits, and rum.

The Bay of Fundy became an important commercial waterway, and improvements in overland communications continued. There was so much travel that inns and taverns located along the roads were able to do a profitable business. Local agricultural societies were formed, that for King's County at Horton in 1789. More attention was paid to horticulture, and the grafting of new stock on the old Acadian apple trees was the beginning of the extensive orchards of the Valley.

2. From 1800 to 1870

A census taken in 1827 gave a population of 3,014 for Horton Township. Probably less than one-tenth of these lived in the little cluster of houses around Mud Creek and on the farms which lined the road in what is now the business section of Wolfville. Pole and brush fences lined the main road. There had been little change during the early years of the 19th century. The second or third generation of the Planters began to realize, as Loyalists and other newcomers had, that the best lands in Horton and other townships had been occupied, and to seek new areas. By 1830, as was noted previously, the population of the newly-named Wolfville was only somewhere in the two hundreds.

In 1838, from students in the newly-founded Horton Academy, there are pictures of the community. One wrote to his parents that he was boarding himself in the Academy with the other young men, and found his expenses moderate. The purchase of the cooking stove for over three pounds, twelve shillings, would swell his expenses. He wrote about the people:

> The inhabitants are frugal and industrious and are rabidly encreasing in wealth, there houses are well furnished with every kind of furniture and every other thing that tends to make them happy in this life. Every farmer has either a chaise or a wagon to carry them to meetings or any other part of the country. There are two classes of Laity among the inhabitance. The welthiest seldom keep company with the poor, or the unlarned. Some of the people are well informed and more espicial, their femals. Schools are in every direction to be found. Everything is in a cultivated state, showing the prase of him that created it, but *Man*.

A Halifax paper of 1888 provided the recollections of Peter S. Hamilton of Stewiacke, who also attended Horton Academy in 1838. He listed Wolfville houses on the north side of the road, beginning at "Willow Valley" on John Johnson's brook: "Scotch Stevens," George Johnson, William Johnson, Percy M. Benjamin, "Mrs. Judge" DeWolf, Elisha DeWolf's shop and post office, Trainholm's farm house, "Mrs. Joe" DeWolf (opposite the Academy gate), Luke Franklin, Jonathan Graham, a man named Wallace and James Graham, Lewis P. Godfrey, Thomas Andrew Strange DeWolf's shop, his house, Robert DeWolf's (which became an inn), Rev. Theodore Harding, Daniel DeWolfe (later Dr. Lewis Johnstone's house), carpenter shop, Anglican church, Woodman's, Wickwire's, grog shop, John Scott.

The houses on the south side, beginning at Johnson's brook, were: F. Elderkin, Forsyth, mother of John W. Barss, Elisha DeWolf, the Academy, "old yaller house" (the first Academy), Baptist church, a house later occupied by L. P. Godfrey, E. Fowler's "Temperance Inn," Stephen B. DeWolf's house and shop, McIntosh, Woodworth's house and carpenter shop (west of Mud Bridge), Israel DeWolf's house and blacksmith shop (east of Mud Bridge), Charles Randall (Mrs. Best's ladies seminary), Charles Randall's cottage, Dr. Edward S. Brown's drug shop and surgery, Armstrong brothers, "Aunt Abby" DeWolf, Andrew Dwight DeWolf, Rev. W. Clarke, Scott's shop (corner of the main road and Maple Avenue).

The "hungry forties" were a time of stagnation and of limited activity in many countries. Johnson Bishop wrote of Wolfville that in 1846 there were no stores except a small one of Owen Evans at Scott's corner, a small one at Mud Creek, and a third one at Kent Lodge. Evidently the store he and Johnstone had owned, with Isaac Anderson as manager, and had sold after Anderson's death to Lamont and Weir, had disappeared before 1846. By 1849, conditions were improving. J. D. Chambers, who credited Johnson Bishop for much of his information, wrote in the Kentville *Western Chronicle* of March 1912 that Reverend John Chase built a store in 1849. It became G. W. Wallace's grocery and later was C. H. Porter's first store. In the same year John L. Brown built on the opposite side of the street a store which was later to become the grocery of Porter Brothers. Next to John Chase's store, according to Chambers, separated by a pole fence and former farm land, was that of R. E. Harris. There was no house on the north side of the road from the old cemetery to Harris' store, and Chambers thought the next business was that of Stephen DeWolf, a millinery and dressmaking shop, later the Sleep property.

According to another account, Elijah Fowler, Jr., sold a piece of his property to the Baptist church, and the adjoining lot to L. P. Godfrey. Lewis P. Godfrey had come from Windsor in 1833 or 1835, and had become a maker of boots and shoes. His Horton account book of 1847 provided names of those with whom he did business and included the following: Roger O'Brien, Edwin DeWolf, William McKenzie, Sarah Fowler, Isaiah Fowler, Reverend E. A. Crawley, Reverend John Pryor, George Clarke, Mrs. Henry Best, Elisha DeWolf, Ezekiel Harris, James Fielding, Dr. Lewis Johnstone, William Johnstone, Esq., Grandison Eagles, Capt. Thompson Crane, Isaac Anderson, Robert Fudge, Edward DeWolf, Stephen B. DeWolf, Charles Hancock, James Hall, Henry Shaw, Charles Randall, Elias Paysant, William S. Harding, William DeMill, Charles Stewart, Andrew Parsons, John Ells,

Lewis Paysant, Morgan O'Brien, David Burton, Rev. A. S. Hunt, Jamy Kenny, Elisha B. DeMill, Henry Spurr, Philip Paysant, James Wallace, Asa Pick, Benjamin Kinsman, Reverend Mr. Allison, Henry Young, John Woodworth, John Scott, Jerusha Fowler, William Morine, Elijah Fowler, Jerusha Nowlin, Robert Nowlin, Flo(?) Barss, Capt. James Lockhart, Henry King, William Corbet, Reverend James Stephens, Arthur Crawley, Professor A. P. S. Stewart, Elijah Harris, George Graham, W. H. King, Thomas Crawley, Joshua Coffin, James Graham, Nathan Harris, George McKeen, James Wickwire, Thomas Barss, Thomas Fowler, Edward Trenholme, Thomas Foster, Margaret DeWolf, David Harris, Hannah Fowler, Thomas Wickwire, James Armstrong, William Johnson. Some of these names were of academy and college students and staff.

The lot next to Godfrey was purchased by Thomas Barss, and in 1855 became the property of George V. Rand, where he established his drug store. Watson Eaton bought the next lots and erected a furniture factory. The factory was burned, and afterwards rebuilt and occupied by W. C. Blackadar as a furniture store. Again the building burned, this time when occupied by S. S. Borden as a flour store, and by Temple Piers, who sold boots and shoes. S. S. Borden rebuilt, and later C. H. Borden, the owner in 1912, occupied the building for twenty-five years. The site is now Wade's parking lot.

The John L. Brown store, built in 1849, became the Porter Bros. store.

Three other stores made their appearance in the 1850s. A. D. DeWolf opened a general store at Mud Bridge, near Thomas Kelly's shoe store. James D. Morse began his grocery business in 1853, and later Fred Brown opened a hardware store on the east side of the creek.

A great deal of business was done by barter. The farmer would bring his produce to the store and exchange it for goods he wanted. There was little currency available, and it was of two sorts, Spanish dollars and gold sovereigns. Both kinds were used until 1858, when dollars and cents became official. Paper money was viewed with suspicion until well into the 1900s when its issuance was taken over by the federal government.

The increase in business activity in the 1850s continued into the next decade. The thriving shipyards at East Horton and Hantsport were partly responsible for the continuing prosperity. The store that John L. Brown had erected on the eastern part of Jonathan Graham's property, which Brown had purchased in 1852, was enlarged in the 1860s, and was taken over by Forsythe and Rounsefell in 1866. Later, Henry Witter ran the store, until it burned. It was rebuilt and occupied by Burpee Witter for nineteen years, by John Calder for two, and by J. D. Chambers for fifteen years. The small tin shop started by S. R. Sleep in the 1840s had become a hardware and plumbing business by 1858, which was moved to a store nearly opposite the new post office, and then to the corner of Main Street, where it was continued by his son, L. W. Sleep.

In 1863 James G. Patriquin built two harness-making shops opposite each other on Main Street. His own business was built up in one of them and, at his death in 1882, his son, Charles Patriquin, although only a lad of eighteen, took over. The business was moved to Earl Street.

A business directory of 1864 listed eighty-nine persons in various occupations, the largest group tradesmen, and merchants and farmers were the next largest groups. The only businesses which might be called industrial were Godfrey's boot and shoe manufactory, J. W. Barss's shipping, and a tannery, built by Charles Johnson, which stood on the site of J. W. Tuft's house. Although Wolfville was not as large as Canning or Kentville, and lacked the shipbuilding and manufacturing activities of other places in the county, it was surprisingly prosperous, and was not considered a "poor relation" of either Kentville or Canning. Nor had Acadia College added greatly to its population for it remained small until the later 1880s and 1890s.

The Province of Nova Scotia had hired Ambrose Church to make maps of various communities. The Kings County map, dated 1864, but not published until 1870, contained material up to 1869. It provided names and occupations of the residents:

Reverend J. M. Cramp, Emeritus Professor; William Elder, Professor Natural Science; D. F. Higgins, Professor Mathematics; Reverend A. W. Sawyer, Professor Moral Philosophy; Reverend Robert Sommerville, Reformed Presbyterian Pastor; R. V. Jones, Professor Classics; Reverend T. A. Higgins, Academy Principal; Reverend S. W. DeBlois, Baptist Minister; E. L. Brown, Physician; Elias N. Payzant, Physician/Dentist; H. O. McLatchy, Physician; George V. Rand, Druggist; Andrew DeW. Barss, Physician; Dr. J. R. Hea, Notary and Insurance; David Strong, Dry Goods; Forsythe and Rounsefell, Merchants; H. B. Witter, Flour Merchant; G. H. Wallace, Grocer and Bookseller; J. S. Morse, Merchant of Crockery; D. J. Harris, Merchant; S. B. Bishop, Merchant; J. D. MacDonald, Merchant; A. R. DeWolfe, Merchant; T. A. S. DeWolfe, Merchant; T. Crane, Merchant; R. I. Thompson, Merchant; J. W. Bigelow, Flour Merchant; J. L. Brown & Co., Merchants; J. W. Barss, J.P., Ship Owner, Agent of People's Bank; J. L. Murphy, Car Maker; Brown, Blacksmith; L. T. Bishop, Manager Village House; J. L. Brown, Farmer; Annie Coldwell, Teacher; W. R. DeWolfe, Farmer; Alfred Rounsefell,

Assistant Postmaster; Joseph Weston, Tailor; John Ward, Car Builder; Mason Pinio, Saloon Keeper; L. J. Godfrey, Boot & Shoe Manuf.; S. R. Sleep, Tinsmith; George C. ------------, Hotel; James S. MacDonald, Drygoods/Grocer; J. B. Davison, Photographer; James Woodman, Carpenter; George Clark, Union House; Major Theakston, Printer; E. C. Pelton, House Joiner; Robert Cahill, Painter; William Pickler, Mariner; G. A. Bishop, Farmer; James Wilson, Harness Maker; Phillip Hamilton, Cooper; James Graham, Carpenter; Nelson Strong, Farmer; J. W. Burns, Blacksmith; J. L. Franklin, Ship & Country Smith; W. J. Johnson, Farmer; William Fitch, Farmer; George C. Johnson, Farmer; James Elder, House Joiner; Elijah Elderkin, Farmer; Enock Neary, Farmer; John Rounsefell, Tailor; G. J. Wickwire, Farmer; Robert MacAloney, Farmer; J. G. Patriquin, Harness Maker; C.D. Randall, J.P.; S.L. Armstrong, J.P., Farmer; Thomas Bergin, J.P., Farmer; Angus Pick, Boot & Shoe Maker; J. E. Woodworth, Carpenter; Augustus Eagles, Master Mariner; Charles Woodworth, Carpenter; S. P. Harris, Farmer; W. A. Cleveland, Farmer; L. M. Bishop, Teacher; J. W. Elderkin, Teacher; J. J. Borden, Blacksmith; D. A. Munro, Carriage & Sleigh Maker; E. L. Brown, Jun.; John Gormley, Master Mariner; J. L. Armstrong.

The expense accounts of Professor George Kennedy, a McGill graduate, who came to Acadia in 1873 as Natural Science instructor, give a picture of prices and style of living in the 1870s and 1880s. From May 1874 until April 1875, he and his sister boarded with Miss E. A. Chipman at her residence opposite St. John's Episcopal Church, and paid eleven dollars a week for the two of them. At the Acadia Hotel (formerly Grand Pre Seminary), operated by Thomas Marshall, five weeks' board amounted to thirty dollars, and the rental of a carriage for half a day cost one dollar. The Sewing Circle Entertainment cost Kennedy ten dollars. From F. H. Brown, Importer of British and Foreign Hardware, he bought fishing gear, picture cords, and small hooks, and his bill was nine dollars.

Pew rental for the quarter at First Horton Baptist Church was nine dollars, and the financial secretary, G. H. Wallace gave him a receipt for the use of pew twenty-six. His annual dues for the Fruit Growers Association and International Show Society were two dollars, according to a receipt from R. W. Starr.

By 1877 he bought materials for housekeeping. From Theophilus A. Bishop, mason and plasterer, he purchased a bushel of calcinated plaster for $1.50. From F. H. Brown he bought an axe handle, two sets of fire irons, a can opener, a stove cover lift, saws and file, glue pot, coffee pot stand, white shellac, a pocket level, and a block plane. For four and a quarter yards of "Huckabuck" towelling, he paid seventy-five cents, and for four yards of Brussia(?) crash towelling forty cents. For clothing he paid $4.50 for a coat, and an additional $1.25 for the vest. A pair of suspenders cost seventy-five cents. C. Fritze, the tailor, made him an overcoat for four dollars.

In 1878 Professor Kennedy married Emma Langard in Wolfville. He had previously bought a set of knives and forks, and in 1879 he purchased three and a half yards of Marseilles for $2.25, and three and a half yards of fancy silesia, three yards of black silesia, and three and a half yards of "fey eclesia" for seventy-five cents. Baby Maud joined the family at the end of November 1879, and Kennedy was buying substantial quantities of milk and vegetables from John L. Brown. The milk was four cents a quart. From Caldwell and Murray he purchased ten pounds of butter for two dollars. At the same store he bought a woolen shirt and drawers for himself at two dollars, and a black straw hat for one dollar.

In 1880 Kennedy made many purchases from Alfred K. Barss, "Foot of Chapel Street," oil, salt by the bushel, a feather brush, sand soap, cedar posts, buckwheat, codfish, blue soap, box herring, hominy, and many barrels of apples at $1.25 per barrel. A chaldron of Springhill coal, delivered, cost $26.25. From F. H. Brown he bought a rat trap, six lamp chimneys for forty-eight cents, a pint measure, three window rollers, and three gallons of alcohol for $9.60. Some of his purchases were for the science department of the College.

In 1880 a one-cent postcard from J. W. Hamilton billed him for two dollars, his contribution for fencing and improving the old cemetery, and he paid the amount to J. W. Caldwell. The previous year he had subscribed for *Scribner's Monthly Magazine* through A. Coldwell, possibly the Albert Coldwell who succeeded him in the department. In the fall of 1882 he left for Windsor, where he was to teach at Kings College for twenty-three years, before retiring to Wolfville, where he died in March 1907, at the age of sixty-two.

Acadia's first *Athenaeum*, November 1874, advertised D. A. Munro's Steam-powered Carriage Factory. In January 1879 their advertisements included: Henry Rounsefell, General Store; W. Temple Piers, Boots and Shoes; William Rounsefell, Furniture (opposite Wolfville Hotel); J. G. Patriquin, Harness Maker, Barber; Daniel F. Boyd, Watchmaker; Caldwell and Murray, Gents Furnishings; J. W. Wallace, Barrister; Joseph Weston, Tailor; S. R. Sleep, Stoves, General Hardware. The previous year the same paper had mentioned the wrecking of a schooner, loaded with potatoes, off Mud Creek. The potatoes were rescued and sold at ten cents a bushel. Two Seminary girls went dashing down College Avenue to buy five bushels, and alarmed a young man who thought they were purposely going to a watery grave.

About 1880. Acadia College, Welton House, Chipman House.

In 1879 George V. Rand's drug store was considerably enlarged. Dr. Welton planned to build north of the Academy building the house that later became the DeWitt house. The Halifax *Herald* reported that W. C. Archibald's exhibition of ladies' and gentlemen's hose by the Wolfville Knitting Factory was rated equal to that made in the Upper Provinces. Also, in 1879 the *New Star* began publishing, but its brief career was terminated in June 1881 by a disastrous fire, perhaps deliberately set, which destroyed not only the *Star* office, but also a Life Insurance Office on the ground floor, the Temperance Hall above, and the nearby Knowles Bookstore.

3. Prosperity in the 1880s

There were many signs of an improved economy in Wolfville during the 1880s. Most businesses were expanding their sales and hiring assistants from the area. The *Athenaeum* added more advertising space in February 1880 to include P. S. Knowles, Bookseller, Stationer; Alfred K. Barss, Groceries; D. B. Shaw, Boot and Shoe Maker; J. B. Davison, Photographer; John Hayes, Boots and Shoes; William Wallace, Tailoring; Miss A. M. Hamilton, Millinery and Fancy Dry Goods. Advertisements in the *Acadian* became more individual, and the opening of new businesses and removal of others to more advantageous locations was noted. C. H. Borden, who had come to Wolfville in 1881, advertised American straw hats. John E. Palmeter opened a grocery business, and C. E. Bishop retired and sold his grocery business to F. T. and G. A. Porter. A. B. Rood opened a new carriage shop. J. B. Davison, Esq., sold his photography business to H. B. Saunders and in 1883 became agent for the Accident Insurance Company of North America, advertised as the first and only accident insurance company. In April 1883 the *Acadian* noted that A. C. Redden had moved his organ, piano, and sewing machine warehouse from the knitting factory to the new store lately finished by Bishop Palmeter.

In April 1884 Thomas Bird informed the public of his watchmaking business, with part of the store occupied by Rockwell and Company. Also in that year, Burpee Witter, for the satisfaction of the female population, hired Bessie Godfrey as a dressmaker for the new line in his store. In June of that year an iron foundry was opened by S. R. Sleep and Mr. MacAdam, and it was hoped that this would serve as a shining example and encourage others to start new industries.

In April 1885 the *Acadian* reported that E. S. Crawley, barrister and property agent, was learning photography. An album of his work can be seen at Wolfville's Randall House Museum.

During the summer a boom in shipping occurred, and five or six vessels were tied up at one time. Nevertheless, the town complained against paying for enlargement of the harbour channel for packets serving Minas Basin. The American tourist trade was good that summer, too, and the paper thought there was need for more "artificial attractions."

Also in 1885 J. W. Shaw installed an ice cream fountain in his shop, the third in the village. Frank L. Brown signed his business over to John W. DeWolfe in September. Arthur W. Hoare, who ran the Western Book and News Company, nearly opposite the post office, invited a young man to begin a different kind of merchandising in his store. The invitation was accepted by a former resident of Windsor, J.F. Herbin, and thus began the well-known jewellery business. Hoare later moved to Halifax.

An editorial in November 1885 brought to the fore a problem that had long been facing Wolfville and would continue for many years. The community had put off the name of Mud Creek, but the creek and its muddiness remained.

In the 1870s the *Athenaeum* had more than once complained about "the pig-sty at Mud Bridge."

> Now it is well known that Mud Bridge is a notoriously muddy place, and furthermore, that there is only one side-walk. The pig-sty is situated right alongside of this side-walk; in fact the railing of the bridge forms a part of the fence around the sty, which extends almost halfway of the bridge. In order to cross this well-named bridge, the pedestrian, whether man, woman, or child, must pass along the side next to the pig-sty, where the nostrils, if they have not been seared with a red hot iron, will be so offended with the noxious effluvia that the traveller will hesitate about travelling that road again. Now if the Road Commissioners will only provide a side-walk on the other side of the road, we will gladly take that side. Moreover, it will be helping the man who owns the pig-sty, what a dirty, disreputable sty it is! what an insult to any woman - what an insult to the public.

The Halifax *Herald*, in January 1883, had carried an item about a woman who kept a common house with a questionable individual in the Mud Bridge area. She had put out her six-year-old son one cold winter night, and he had to find refuge in a lumber shed. He was found the next day in an almost insensible condition. Dr. Bowles had treated his frozen feet, and the boy was taken to the poor house.

The *Acadian* editorial in November 1885 favoured the straightening of the street near Mud Bridge, but it took many years and much agitation by the editor and correspondents to get this accomplished.

In 1886 the oldest inhabitant of Wolfville was reported by the *Athenaeum* as saying that there were in Wolfville during Anniversary Week, "more whitewash, fruit blossoms, good clothes and brains than ever before. This is the age of progress." Signs of progress reported were the "commodious and splendid wharf now in place" at Wolfville, where the Windsor packet unloaded flour for J. H. Bishop and James Morse; a blacksmith business begun by J. I. Brown in the old DeWolfe property next to the railroad station; the painting of Fred Brown's cottage; the ornamentation of A. B. Rood's grounds; Simon Vaughan's purchase of a small-scale pickling operation (which later expanded); the platform in front of B. G. Bishop's store; the erection of a new sign by C. R. Patriquin and the arrival of F. J. Larkin to work with him; Charles H. Borden's move into a new carriage factory on the north side of Main Street; Otis D. Harris's arrival and purchase of the Glasgow House from Dodd and Corbett. (Harris later built a larger store and after doing business for thirteen years sold to his nephew, J. E. Hales).

Two people lost their houses by fire: Mrs. James Harris on the back road, and John W. Barss, who rebuilt the next year and named the new dwelling "Thornleigh." The paper also reported the arrival of a lady physician, Merle E. Bill, daughter of W. C. Bill, M.P.P., although there was no indication that she practised in Wolfville.

Conventions were bringing numerous wealthy visitors to Wolfville, some of whom decided to stay. The community was happy to receive tourists and have all the hotels filled. Too often young men tended to go to the United States and take their ideas and talents with them.

The editor of the Kentville paper visited Wolfville and reported that D. A. Munro had installed a new boiler, and an engine with an automatic cut off obtained from London, Ontario, at a cost of $1,000. L. M. Shaw imported from the United States a new barber chair with all the latest improvements. In the fall of 1889 he opened a new barber shop next to the Glasgow House, in a place fitted up for him by J. D. Chambers.

New streets were being laid out. C. R. H. Starr, who had moved to Wolfville in 1888 to be closer to the railroad and the telegraph, was the first person to buy land for the purpose of dividing it into lots. He bought property from W. J. Johnson to the west of the village, on the south side of Main Street. Mrs. Edwina Johnson, with B. O. Davison as agent, sold lots near the Presbyterian Church, on what is now Prospect Street. L. E. Duncanson, an enterprising dealer in property, owned land south of Main Street on Keen Street, now Prospect Street, and built and sold cottages on some of the lots. O. D. Harris, proprietor of Glasgow House, thought of opening a new street between Main and Keen Streets. The *Acadian* noted the need for a new street between College Avenue (University) and Chapel Street, which later was extended to connect with the old road to Gaspereau by way of Willow Avenue and became Gaspereau Avenue. Sidewalks were improved and well built up with gravel.

To advertise Wolfville's advantages, C. H. R. Starr and the local photographer, Lewis Rice, took pictures of orchards to place in journals in North America and "over the water." Rice had photographic studios in Wolfville, where he used the second floor of the building one door east of the *Acadian*, and at Windsor and New Glasgow. He also used a railway car as a studio and stopped at sidings.

1880s. Left: Sawyer House; centre: Methodist Church; right: school house; distant right: Anglican Church.

In 1889 O. D. Harris was the first merchant in Wolfville, and the second in the county, to have plate glass in his new store. In the same year the machinery of the Ideal Manufacturing Company was moved to Wolfville to make washing machines, churns, and pickling tubs, and was located next to the Munro Door and Sash Factory. For the summer of that year Wolfville, following Kentville's lead, established early closing hours for stores on Thursday evenings at six o'clock.

4. The 1890s Growing Period

In spite of one or two serious economic crises which affected most of the western world, Wolfville continued to grow steadily during the 1890s. Many communities around the Basin of Minas and the Bay of Fundy suffered from the decline in fish stocks and from the cessation of the demand for wooden sailing vessels. Wolfville's growth was dependent, a writer in 1892 stated, on agriculture and the Baptist educational institutions. There may have been some decline in the apple industry, but the College, Seminary, and Academy were growing in numbers, and the graduates of the College were achieving distinction. The incorporation of the town in 1893 was also considered to be a factor in promoting the growth of the community.

About 1890. Two friends meet on Main Street.

In 1890 Wolfville had twenty streets, five churches, sixteen stores and hotels and several boarding houses. Three of the stores had plate glass windows. Bread and meat waggons travelled the streets daily, and in season there was an ice cart. Several new enterprises were welcomed in 1891: G. F. Hamilton, with a shop in J. G. Eagle's place, was the newest young grocer; E. B. Shaw came to the town and sold boots and shoes; W. S. Wallace was a tailor on Gaspereau Avenue near Main Street; Franklyn and Fuller bought the business of Walter Brown. The most significant arrival was the patent medicine factory, a branch of the Skoda Discovery Company of Belfast, Maine. Rhodes Curry and Company built the four-storey factory, east of the station, where the preparation of sarsaparilla was concocted. In their first year they put up and shipped 6,000 bottles, and during 1892 they made and sold patent medicines. George Borden and Professor Tufts of Wolfville, Churchill of Hantsport, Mark Curry of Windsor, and Rhodes of Amherst, were among the stockholders. R. E. Harris gave the name *Skoda* to the barquentine he had bought from C. R. Burgess, and in 1894 used the vessel to carry a load of apples overseas. All very exciting, but the business soon disappeared and the empty building was moved across the tracks in 1898 to be used as a cornmill.

In January 1894 the *Acadian* reported a new business in town: J. S. Hales was engaged in the sale of men's and ladies' furnishings in the store occupied by W. S. Wallace. In November D. A. Munro was reported to have obtained the contract to erect a steam laundry, near Mud Creek, with Mr. Rafuse as its manager, but that, too, was unsuccessful, and the plant was sold by auction in 1897 and moved to Halifax. Whether Mary Kinsman, who advertised her plan to open a dressmaking establishment over the James Morse store, corner of Main and Station Street, was more successful is not known.

In 1895 a grist mill for flour and feed was located near the Harris wharf, across from Mud Creek. There was a saw mill nearby, but as business in the harbour slackened, those businesses moved to more profitable locations. In that same year a meeting was held to consider starting a creamery, either at Wolfville or at Port Williams Station. Wolfville was chosen as the site and construction was begun the following spring, with Harding Forsythe of Billtown as the contractor. The enterprise, called the Acadia Dairy, was managed by F. M. Logan of Amherst Point, and the machinery for it came from Boston. The directors of the Acadia Dairy Company (Limited) were C. R. H. Starr, President; Dr. J. N. Fuller, Vice-President; E. L. Gould, A. G. Goodacre, James Simpson, R. F. Reid, F. C. Johnson, Oscar Chase, and J. Rufus Starr, Directors. The new dairy, located on the railway grounds, fronting on Water Street, made cheese and butter of fine quality. Logan had received a thirty-four dollar butter prize at the St. John Exhibition in 1895. Although the new enterprise had been warmly welcomed, it was not long before residents were complaining about the smell. The coal and lumber business, owned by F. W. Woodman, also was criticised for the smokestacks belching out superphosphates.

Other new businesses were reported: Dr. H. Lawrence opened a dentistry office; A. J. Woodman purchased the furniture business of J. W. Coldwell; W. H. Evans went into the cranberry business; J. L. Franklyn built a store on a lot purchased from Robert Storrs, but sold his hardware business, in 1896 to C. E. Starr, who also ran a flour and feed store. Starr's wife and family moved to Wolfville from their former residence in Malden, Massachusetts. Other newcomers to the town were William Henry Chase of Port Williams, who built a fine home on Main Street, and Dr. George E. DeWitt who presided over the Wolfville Fruit Land Improvement Company and proposed to develop the land occupied by the College woods. Dr. DeWitt had a curbing placed in front of his house on Main Street, an improvement which has since been copied and widely extended. The *Western Chronicle's* G. W. Woodworth spoke of the attractive greens and stone copings which were replacing the high and unsightly road fences which earlier had straggled along the Wolfville roads.

The *Western Chronicle* also mentioned that Dr. Mallon had built a new house for his dental parlours; that Herbin's had an attractive jewelry display, and gold wire that they would work up in a customer's name for a ring or pin, for thirty-five cents, while the customer waited; and they apologized to C. H. Borden for advertising men's suits for $7.50 instead of $4.50. The *Acadian* reported that the Wolfville Clothing Company, managed by Noble Crandall, had a staff of twelve to fifteen, and paid out over $100 a week in wages; Balcom's "Beach Express" made daily trips to Evangeline Beach and the large waggon was usually filled; C. A. Patriquin was busy setting up at Evangeline Beach the merry-go-round he had bought and used the previous summer.

J. A. Woodman, Undertaker, had had an attractive hearse made for him by the Nova Scotia Carriage Company of Kentville, which was noted for its fine work; F. J. Porter had a very "nobby covered delivery waggon" in use; Wah Hup, an Oriental, had leased the Borden laundry building, and soon engaged Wah Skip as assistant; Miss Baird had opened a millinery store where Miss Welton had previously had her business; W. W. Robson had increased his photography work in Wolfville from two days to four, in consequence of having received so much assistance from Wolfville merchants after the disastrous Windsor fire; and J. D. Chambers had started a dry-goods business.

1900. Skoda building as a grain mill.

In the spring of 1898, the Skoda building was purchased by Arthur L. Calhoun and removed across the tracks in a few hours to the water front to be used as a flour mill. It was going well in November, but was later reported idle, for lack of "corn", and the sound of the whistle was missed. Dr. McKenna erected a building with two stores and dental parlour where the old post office had stood, and N. M. Sinclair, proprietor of the People's boot and shoe store, purchased part of the J. S. Morse property opposite in order to erect a two-storey building. The town's population had grown and was not distressed by noise and dust of mills and furnaces. "There can be no better place to live on this fair earth than the university town," Margaret Graham wrote in a Halifax paper.

WOLFVILLE WHARVES, N.S.

About 1900. Methodist Church at left; Skoda building at right.   19?

Although there had been some setbacks during the decade, it was considered that Wolfville had done well. Town Council had initiated many improvements, and the government had allocated $4,000 for wharf renovations at the mouth of Mud Creek. A new one was built, and R. E. Harris purchased W. H. Chase's large wharf. The Winfield S. Wallace store opened, with Captain Barberie as proprietor, for the sale of fruit and confectionery, where Flo Harris later carried on business; Mr. Haley of Hantsport opened a grocery store; Hugh Watson of Grand Pre opened a confectionery store in the premises formerly occupied by Mr. Burrell; Caldwell and Borden used the Harris store, which had been repainted; Mr. Blenkhorn bought out the blacksmith business run for several years by George V. Tupper; the Wah Hop laundry moved to the R. E. Harris building, west of the store; Stevens and Newcombe of Port Williams bought the meat and provision store of W. H. Duncanson. W. M. Black was raising White Wyandottes and making a profit of $1.50 a hen. The old century was ending on a brave note.

5. Incorporation

In August 1883 the *Acadian*, in comparing Wolfville's taxation with that of the Township of Horton, suggested that the village be incorporated. The first real push for incorporation came in July of 1887, when there was a strong desire by the community for street lights, fire protection, and a fire hall, but it took several years to achieve the goal. In the meantime, a serious problem became more agitating. The community, as part of the county, had been under the administration of the Municipal Council, to which representatives were elected from all over the county. This Council allotted funds for roads, fire protection, water supply, policing, and the care of the poor. Provincial and regional directives might have served well enough when there were fewer than two hundred families in what was thought of as a hinterland, but conditions had changed. As an incorporated town, Wolfville would be able not only to provide the best for its citizens, but to attract visitors from all over the country. It needed its own council to formulate programs, write and enforce laws, and levy taxes. The County Council had difficulty providing improvements requested by Wolfville citizens. As a result, some individuals had erected their own street lights, and some businesses had built platforms in front of their stores, but not all could afford these luxuries. The water system set in operation in 1889 was part of the push for improvement. Roads and sidewalks were a perennial problem. Hitching rails and posts studded the sidewalks, where horses preferred to stand rather than in the muddier street. In October 1891 a committee, Rev. Dr. Sawyer, Fred Brown, J. W. Bigelow, G. V. Rand, Dr. Barss, J. W. Coldwell, and B. O. Davison, was appointed to consider street names.

In December 1892 a petition of seventy-eight electors asked for a poll on the question of incorporation. Sheriff Belcher presented the petition and planned the election. Boundaries were set and published and ratepayers within those limits were entitled to vote. Some citizens expressed disapproval of the boundaries, and changes were made later. Plans for the election were set for January 23, 1893, at the store of James S. Morse, but the vote actually took place on February 18, and the turnout was light. In spite of strong editorial support from the *Acadian*, a good deal of opposition had been raised.

Incorporation took place formally on March 20, 1893, with new boundaries defined. The first Mayor, Dr. E. Perry Bowles, came into office unopposed. On Saturday evening, March 25, he assembled at the Fire Company's rooms his new council: George Thompson, George Borden, E. W. Sawyer, C. A. Starr, Clarence Borden, and A. DeWolfe Barss. They were sworn in by Judge J. B. Davidson and J. W. Caldwell, and the mayor administered the oath of allegiance to the councillors.

The first item of business was the organizing of the internal working of the council, designating the standing committees, outlining the duties of the town clerk, writing regulations concerning the procedures to be followed in council meetings, and designing the town seal (appropriately with a large apple tree as its main feature). Assessors, constables, electoral revisers, and fire wardens were chosen, as well as school commissioners and a health inspector. Residents petitioned for a temperance (Scott Act) inspector, and a recorder and stipendary magistrate were also appointed. With a telephone installed in the clerk's office, and an account opened at the People's Bank,

Town Hall was ready for business. (The council actually met in the school house until a new hall was built.)

Before and after incorporation, there was disagreement over the official name of the town. In the summer of 1888 an American, Edgar L. Wakeman, wrote to the *Acadian* to suggest the name Acadia, since such an historic name would attract a large flow of tourists. "Do they hunt wolves in Wolfville; is that the reason for such a name?" When he proposed the same name to the St. John *Evening Gazette*, they approved. A writer in the Halifax *Herald* in 1893 claimed Wolfville had no historical association, and suggested several names, the most suitable of which he thought was Grand Pre Town. However, a meeting was held in Wolfville, and although there were suggestions that "ville" was not really appropriate for so important a town, James S. Morse's motion to retain the present name was passed unanimously. At a Rotary Club luncheon in 1941 Major V. W. S. Heron suggested the town change its name to Wolfe's Town to commemorate General Wolfe.

The first year as an incorporated town was a busy one for council. By July the Committee on Bylaws had received approval for nearly twenty-five new regulations governing a variety of matters. Rules were set down regarding the disposition of rubbish, the keeping of pigs within town limits, the owning of dogs, and general conduct on the streets. Penalties for discharging firearms and exploding fireworks were established. The Clerk let it be known that licences were required for travelling peddlers, auctioneers, theatrical exhibitions, and concerts which charge a fee at the door. There were also bylaws regulating coasting on public streets, operating slaughter houses, and driving horses, oxen and cows through the town.

Almost immediately the appearance of the town began to improve. One of the council's first actions was to plant ornamental trees, some of which still remain, along Main Street. The streets themselves were in dire need

About 1900. Main Street.

of improvement, and residents, concerned with the tourist trade as well as their own safety and convenience, petitioned to have sidewalks graded and gravelled. Even the best roads needed constant care and maintenance, done laboriously with manual labour and ox teams, and one of council's first requests from ratepayers was for $700 towards street improvements. An "American road-making machine" was purchased in 1894. Plans were made in June of that year to survey and map the town for streets, hydrants, and service-pipe accommodations. A writer that summer pointed out that Kentville had a watering cart to keep down the dust, while Wolfville houses were stained a dirty grey, but it was not until 1898 that a watering cart was put in use in Wolfville.

The condition of the streets, and particularly of Main Street, continued to be bad. G. W. Woodworth wrote in the *Western Chronicle* about nearby communities and expressed himself rapturously about "historic and far famed Wolfville, except for the deep muddy streets of December." One merchant planted a bed of onions in the middle of the street, and the unfeeling street committee dumped an additional foot of soil on the onions. To remind authorities of the "humid" condition of the road, Saturday evening fun-lovers placed boats from an ancient merry-go-round along Main Street and advertised rides at five cents. The street committee was reported to be "in a state of mind." In 1898 the Superintendent of Streets removed the plank crossings and graded down the sidewalks so as to dispense with gutter bridges which did not vent the water properly.

It was reported that the town's debt of $1,636 was reduced to $500. Not a single person had been prosecuted under the Scott Act, and only one person, a stranger, was arrested for drunkenness. The slaughterhouse, operated by Duncanson Brothers, was reprimanded by council several times, and told to contain the smell of the plant, to keep their animals from escaping into

Duck Pond. Left: the 1½-story cottage lived in by the Frank Porter family, and then the George Zwicker family before it was demolished in 1964; right: approximate location of the original Mud Bridge

the streets, and finally ordered to put a fence around the works so that the public would be spared from witnessing the seamier sides of their operations.

Mud Creek continued to be a concern to the community. In 1897 the Street Committee reported to the Town Council that one new bridge had been placed on Main Street, the two bridges had been retopped, and a new gate had been installed in the sluice at Mud Bridge. In 1900 the town was trying to ascertain the exact boundaries of the Mud Bridge region, and in 1911 the whole area north of Mud Bridge was expropriated at a cost of $250, and the improvement of Mud Bridge Park was placed under the Streets Committee. Mud Bridge, at the southwest corner of the Creek, was replaced by a culvert, and a pond was made between it and the culverts which made possible the straightening of Main Street. It was found necessary to keep ducks on the pond to reduce the plant growth, and the ducks were a great attraction, especially to children. Although the name of Willow Park had been given to the improved area, the name was forgotten and it was generally known as Duck Pond. The name of Willow Park was restored in 1967 when the town's centennial project was the beautification of the area. A wading pool replaced the pond. Grass and flower beds, benches and picnic tables were installed. The Tourist Bureau asked for permission to use a building on the site, and a parking area was made. The unsightly, noisome Mud Creek has become a delightful place and an asset to the town.

Not only did the conditions of the street concern the Town Council, but naming of the streets also called for consideration. A scheme for numerical designations, Front Street to First, Main Street to Second, and so on, was mooted but was not carried out. A great many changes were made, but were not always recorded, as Dr. Kirkconnell lamented in *The Streets of Wolfville*. As far as can be ascertained, these names were established: Baseline A to Pleasant Street; Shipyard Lane to French Road to Baseline B to Ridge Road; Franklin Street to Cedar Avenue; Barss's Lane to Oak Avenue; Wickwire Lane extended to the railway tracks; Ferry Lane to Cherry Lane; Graham's Lane, west of University Rink; Elderkin's Lane; Brook Street and Lover's Lane to Willow Avenue; Acadia Road or "a road to Gaspereau" to School Street and then to Highland Avenue; Professor or College Street to Acadia Street; Keen or McKeen to Prospect Street; Water Street to Front Street; Post Road to Main Street; Railway Street to Elm Avenue; Earl Street to Central Avenue; Harding Street to Central Avenue to Hillside Avenue (Vinegar Hill); Pick Lane to Orchard Avenue; Church or Chapel Street to Gaspereau Avenue; Chipman Avenue extended south and renamed Westwood Avenue(?); Welton Street to Park Street; College Avenue to University Avenue; Wharf Street ; Blomidon Avenue ;Rand Street to Linden Avenue; Melanson Road to Maple Avenue; Starr Street not renamed.

In 1898 Acadia Street was improved by the removal of the College gates and the installation of a sidewalk on the south side. During the summer the Street Committee placed the first sewer from Main Street down Gaspereau Avenue to the creek, and the new street between Gaspereau Avenue and Linden Avenue, Summer Street, was completed. That was the first year that a watering cart was used.

In 1899 there was discussion of buying a stonecrusher and a steamroller for road care, and of erecting a three-storey hall east of Linden Avenue for

1911. Road paving, as crew uses the new steamroller.

Council Chamber, Fire Hall, Clerk's Office, and residence for the policeman, lot and building to cost $5,600. Late in the year $9,000 was voted to erect a brick building, as Town Hall, Firehall, and policeman's residence at the corner of Main Street and Locust Avenue, but the project remained in abeyance.

Street improvement continued during the early years of the twentieth century; some sidewalks were paved, and farmers were paid to haul stones to upgrade the streets. Again council proposed that proper roadbuilding equipment be bought, and in 1911 a new steamroller was procured for the first street paving. Marshall Black had persuaded the town to pave with a tar mixture, barrels of which were brought from the United States. Wolfville's streets were the first in the province to be paved with tar. The Town Offices had been moved from the old building west of the McKay building on Acadia Street to the new W. M. Black building on Main Street. Water pipes were extended across Summer Street, and water mains were laid along the streets at the centre of the town. Early in the century, permits had been required for the keeping of pigs within the town limits, after the town ruled against placards and other advertising on trees and posts. In 1912 the Streets Committee reported that 6,000 square yards of paving had been completed, at fifty cents per yard. By 1913 even those who had opposed incorporation admitted that the venture had been a success.

IX.

ECONOMY AND MANAGEMENT
OF THE 20th CENTURY

1. The Early Years

As the new century dawned, Wolfville had been incorporated for seven years; the population was approaching 1,400; the economy was strong, and the future held great promise. There were twenty-one retail stores; financial services were handled by two Halifax-based banks, the People's Bank and the Union Bank; blacksmith services were supplied by George Wood, Delahunt, and Ned Mahaney; Frank Angus was a highly regarded master mason; both Charles H. Borden and A. J. Woodman provided undertaking services; a planing mill was run by D. A. Munro; W. H. Chase and Company exported produce and apples; the Coal and Lumber Company, S. P. Benjamin Company Ltd., and W. D. Bentley sold lumber and building supplies; W. J. Balcom operated a livery stable.

Business continued healthy in 1901: hard coal came from New York; the corn mill was operating again; in the autumn the Beaver Mills added a cornmeal mill and a cracker mill, which turned out fifty bushels an hour. The *Western Chronicle* reported that John Shaw had taken over John Vaughan's store as a barber shop. F. W. Freeman and F. W. Woodman had hot water systems installed in their houses.

In February 1902 the *Acadian* carried a notice from the Acadia Dairy Company that A. M. Wheaton was now the manager. The tug *Susie*, the willing workhorse of N. M. Bentley's lumber operations, was sold to the Parrsboro Lumber Company for service on the Avon River. That deprived Wolfville citizens of a craft for excursions. Later in the year, the Misses Coldwell and Spidle began a millinery business at the premises formerly occupied by W. M. Ford's musical establishment. W. M. Black also had a hot water system installed in his house by Sleep. W. J. Balcom purchased two horses in Amherst to add to his stable. "Thornleigh" residence of the late J. W. Barss, was offered for sale. The merchants agreed to close Wednesdays at noon, and every other evening at six, except Tuesdays and Saturdays, when they would stay open until nine.

Although the People's Shoe Store had advertised in January 1904 that they were going out of business in October they were offering football boots. George A. Johnson set up business and erected a large sign over his barbers shop. He was known as "Barber Johnson" to distinguish him from the other Johnsons, who were also known by their occupations. Parker's Pharmacy advertised dulse at eleven cents a pound, and in September, Rand's Drug Store carried a large supply of spices for pickling. A. R. Morgan began repairing and tuning pianos. W. W. Robson announced that his photographic studio would re-open, with Edson Graham as manager. A. J. Woodman's new furniture store, completed in November 1904, was the town's first brick building, lighted by electricity. It also had a large plate glass window.

In 1906 there was mention of A. M. Blackaddar's furniture store east of the post office. In December it was announced that Merchants' Day, a sales promotion scheme of fun and frolic and discounts, would be dispensed with. The next year also showed little activity: Mitchell's new shoe store was opened; G. Ernest Elliott bought out the C. W. Strong fish business, where Simon Brothers formerly operated. I. S. Boates purchased a new gasoline launch for tourist excursions on Minas Basin.

The year 1908 was a time of increased activity. Laybolt and Schofield bought out J. L. Franklin and set up new livery stables near Willow Park. T. S. Boates established a new tailoring business but in the fall joined the staff of A. Crozier, who enlarged his store. That arrangement did not last, and Boates set up on his own in January of the next year. In January J. L. Herbin advertised eye testing, which prompted his rival to announce that he would test eyes FREE on Fridays. Dr. J. T. Roach purchased the dental practice of Dr. Lawrence, and located in the Herbin building. He continued in practice until ill health forced his retirement in the 1940s. Dr. Roach was also a keen sportsman and fisherman. It was noted that Mitchell's Shoe Store, the Acadian Pharmacy, and Bessie K. Saxton's Millinery had installed awnings on their stores. The water front was active, with steamers loading and unloading cargo. The steamer *Brunswick* collided with the railway wharf and caused considerable damage.

During the summer of 1908 R. E. Harris and Son replaced the unstable planking and mud of their section of sidewalk and paved with concrete. Eventually the ladies were able to give up the practice of lining the hems of their skirts with heavy material to protect against the mud. W. S. Piedmont opened a bookbinding business in the McKenna Block in October 1908, and A. J. Watson and Company moved into the building formerly occupied by T. S. Boates. In December H. E. Duncanson and Company moved their meat market into the premises of A. J. Watson and Company; W. Smith and A. W. Bishop opened for trade; a Santa Claus Toy Shop began business next to J. F. Herbin's Jewellery.

Clearly, the town was growing, and new businesses were added in 1909. C. W. Strong opened a carriage and farm implement business where the L.W. Sleep store had been. Later he started a grocery store on a strictly cash basis. In June the Hennigar Brothers set up a grocery business in a store leased from F. J. Porter, auctioneer. Eaton and Bill opened an ice cream parlor in the house east of J. E. Hales Dry Goods. In time for the fall trade, W. C. Dexter and Company introduced a new millinery parlor, and J. M. Shaw added three new oak chairs and furnished his rooms in oak for "The Oak Barber Shop." The grocers decided to close their stores every evening except Saturday during the winter months.

In the spring W. M. Black of Wolfville had purchased Evangeline Beach and had built several cottages and the Evangeline Beach Hotel. Wolfville citizens and outsiders began to take time for a holiday by the sea. The *Acadian* of April 1, 1910, announced that Charles E. Porter had opened a new store, east of the old cemetery, where he had bought from George H. Wallace in 1909. He had added twenty feet to the building, and a "Silent Salesman," for his well-selected stock. His long-established competitor, J. D. Chambers,

Excursion leaving for Parrsboro for the day.

About 1912. Rand's drug store.

installed an overhead cash system in his dry goods store. George Crozier sold his tailoring business to Mr. Vanbuskirk of Pugwash. The Misses Hennigar opened a dressmaking establishment in rooms over Rand's Drug Store. C. W. Strong moved his business into the store formerly occupied by F. C. Churchill and the Acadian Pharmacy. During the summer the community had responded with aid to Campbellton, New Brunswick, whose town had been destroyed by fire.

In January 1911 J. W. Williams came from Prince Edward Island and opened a one-price jewellery in a small self-contained building between the Baptist church and the residence of Frank L. Godfrey. J. M. Shaw sold his barber business to Mr. Dillon of Digby. A. V. Rand became distributor for Rexall Drugs. J. F. Herbin acquired a lens grinding and drilling machine for his optical business. William Smith announced that he planned to start a home milk delivery. The Chinese laundry was destroyed by fire, and restored in July. Dr. Roach moved his dental office to rooms over the Town Hall, in the Black Building. Miss Card began dressmaking parlors in the McKenna Block. F. W. Godfrey purchased F. C. Bishop's decorating business. Late in the year, Messrs. Moses and Peters opened a People's Market next to Harvey's Grocery.

In 1912 J. D. Chambers, reviewing Wolfville's business life in the *Western Chronicle*, pointed out that manufacturing had had little success, that the town was eduational and residential, with good potential for the tourist industry. J. F. Herbin, head of the Bureau of Information, reported the tourist trade as healthy. The population was 2,004, including College and Academy students.

The Royal Bank and the Union Bank, which had merged in 1910, erected a new building in 1912, with R.E. Harris as contractor for excavation, and C. H. Wright as contractor and master builder. F. J. Porter built on the site of the old laundry which had burned. M. Regan bought the Bowles store and moved it to his harness shop. R. E. Harris obtained the contract for supplies to Aldershot Militia Camp.

The January 1913 edition of the *Acadian* carried an advertisement for the T. Eaton Company Mail Order Catalogue, and an announcement by Rand's Drug Store that they had the agency for the "World's Best Motorcycle," the Indian. Hugh E. Calkin had taken over the Acadian Pharmacy; W. C. Bleakney purchased the grocery business of J. W. Barss; L. B. VanBuskirk, Tailor, located opposite the post office.

Completed in 1912, the Post Office was demolished in 1971.

About 1915. A busy Saturday morning.

2. First World War

Necessarily, the economy slowed down during the war. A great many young men enlisted from the town and from the college, and the attention and efforts of the country generally were directed towards the war. One of the Wolfville casualties was the fox ranch, which had opened on Pleasant Street, with R. W. Ford, the school principal, as president, and J. F. Herbin as secretary-treasurer. For a time the ranch seemed to prosper, but it was soon closed. A few businesses changed hands: C. D. Kappell rented J. E. Hales' Main Street store for a five and ten cent store; C. W. Strong sold his grocery business to Percy D. Barberie, who soon moved away. A few improvements were made: C. H. Wright installed a steam plant in his woodworking factory; Hugh Calkin installed a "Vortex Individual Sanitary Service System," which provided individual disposable paper cups. J.W. Williams had enlisted in the army, and his premises were taken over by volunteer women, headed by Mrs. Laura Haliburton Moore, who opened a tea room to raise funds for the soldiers overseas. There were shortages, which perhaps accounted for the appearance of moose meat in the stores. The high cost of feed led to an increase in the price of milk to twelve cents a quart.

Wolfville again began to prosper after the end of the war austerity. Early in 1919 C. H. Porter bought the J. D. Chambers Dry Goods business at the corner of Main Street and Central Avenue, where his son Ronald now carries on the business. T. L. Harvey sold his grocery business to W. O. Pulsifer, and E. A. Robertson opened a "cash and carry" grocery store in the Rand Block. J. F. Herbin invented an instrument to increase the accuracy of the shadow test in eye examination, and a New York firm manufactured the product.

Business continued healthy as Wolfville entered the third decade of the century. The Wolfville Fruit Company of orchardists and farmers constructed

The John L. Brown store now Porter Bros., at corner of Main and Highland.

a new building on Main Street, opposite Sleep's Hardware. Henry Peck managed the apple packing and exporting side of the business and Frank Welch the retail grocery. The Bank of Montreal planned a new building on the site of the old bank building at the east corner of Central Avenue and Main Street. William Regan sold his harness business to a Mr. Palmer of Canning. E. C. H. Young became proprietor of "The Palms," where female college students and town ladies consumed ice-cream sundaes at fifteen cents and banana splits at twenty-five cents at the twisted iron tables among potted palms. Hugh E. Watson had an ice-cream parlor, next to A. J. Woodman's store, with twisted iron tables and chairs, but no palms. The male college students bought baked beans with poached eggs and brown bread at the bakery and restaurant that Cecil's older brother, Arthur Young, ran at the corner of Main Street and Elm Avenue.

In 1923 the Valley Laundry announced that it would operate a steam laundry. Fred G. Herbin, son of F. J., took over his father's optical and jewelry business. Rand's Drug Store attached an outdoor speaker to the phonograph in the store and enlivened Main Street with music. In November 1924 D. Ross Cochrane announced that he would open a new drug store in the Bleakney building, where his son Douglas H. now carries on the business.

There was a general feeling of optimism everywhere after the First World War. The young men were back, except for those who had lost their lives in the defence of their country; there was hope and gaiety and high spending. In Wolfville the numbers at college had grown, and that meant prosperity for the merchants and the services. Empire Shopping Week was held in April 1928, with an appeal to "Buy Maritime Goods at Wolfville Stores." One new service had been added, with Dr. J. A. Hemmeon, specialist in eye, ear, nose and throat, opening a medical practice in the Royal Bank building.

The First World War brought a slowing down in Wolfville's activities both in the business sector and in the incorporated town's improvements. Early

About 1921. Porter Bros. store. Boy in front: Rex Porter; behind counter, L-R: Percy Porter, Grant Porter, Mrs. Gordon Murphy.

in 1918 Town Clerk Harding Bishop, who had replaced William Black in 1917, urged people to conserve water. A poll tax was levied on persons who did not own property. Wolfville joined the Nova Scotia Union of Municipalities.

As Wolfville entered the third decade of the century, C. S. Fitch was mayor, and Harding Y. Bishop, at a salary of $1,000, continued as town clerk. Merchants decided to close at six every day, except Saturday, the time beloved of shoppers from the town and country round about, for the first four months of the year. This was welcome news to the employees, who still worked ten hours a day, fourteen on Saturdays. In 1920 Mrs. Laura Haliburton Moore became the first woman to be elected to the town council, reportedly the first woman councillor in the province. The *Acadian* decried the unfair tactics of the women voters who "plumped" for their candidate. Mrs. Moore, a well-informed and capable woman, made an excellent councillor.

The town reservoir was dredged in 1920, and the residents of East Wolfville, who had earlier petitioned to be included within the town limits and had been turned down by Mayor Fitch's casting vote, won their case, and the boundary was extended to the east of Scott's Corner. The *Acadian* advocated a new town hall. The next year R. W. Ford, who had been principal of the school, replaced Harding Bishop as town clerk, and was voted a salary of $1,500. Thanks to a federal grant of $12,000, the harbour was dredged in the fall of 1922, and the waterfront became a busy place. Among the frequent arrivals at the Government Wharf was a small tramp steamer, the *Rotundus*, which carried coal and other commodities from Springhill.

In 1923 Gordon Stairs was appointed town manager, and one of his first efforts was to annouce a Clean-up Day. Installation of concrete sidewalks had continued, and by 1928 they stretched along the south side of Main Street from Highland Avenue, and on the north side from Elm Avenue to Gaspereau Avenue.

3. Depression Years

The Stock Market crash in 1929 shocked Canada and the United States, especially the latter. Optimists predicted a speedy recovery, but the depression went on for years. The prolonged drought on the prairies, which turned the centre of the continent into a "dust bowl," added to the difficulties of both countries. The urban centres, where manufacturing had been flourishing, and the prairies, suffered most. A small town like Wolfville was not seriously affected. On the other hand, hundreds of people who had gone to the States in the early years of the century, and in the prosperous days after the war, and some who had felt the lure of the west, came back to Nova Scotia, especially to the countryside and the village communities. Kings County noticeably filled up during the depression years.

The usual changes went on in Wolfville businesses. The Godfrey property, between the Baptist church and the Rand Block, was sold, and the house moved to Linden Avenue, behind Herbin's store. The small building which had housed J. W. Williams Jewellery was demolished, and Williams moved to the McKenna Block. In November 1930 five carloads of Christmas trees, each with 1,500 to 2,000 trees, were sent to the United States. A Chinese restaurant, Wong's Cafe, opened in the Orpheum Theatre building. In the spring of that year, the Wickwire Dyke was damaged by a storm and high tide, and 640 acres of dyked land were submerged. Repairs cost $30,000.

The Skoda building, which had been used as a community hall, was destroyed by fire in September 1931. E. S. Langille built several houses, and the town's first apartment building was erected on Westwood Avenue. A three-bedroom house at that time cost about $3,000. A few people had to have assistance from the town, and collection of taxes became difficult. There was little business activity. Ronald Stewart was selling Fuller brushes in 1933, and William Gue began manufacturing bristle brushes. D. H. Hirtle set up a dry cleaning business. In August 1935 Cecil Langille bought a schooner load of Springhill coal. In 1937 R. W. DeWolfe added a brick extension with a frost-proof cellar to his warehouse. T. S. Hutchinson sold his taxi service to William Gue and Merritt Coldwell, who sold it two years later to J. Myron Johnson.

At the beginning of 1938 Rand's building was completely destroyed by fire, with the tragic loss of Roy Pulsifer, electrician, one of the tenants. A brick building was constructed to house Carver's Billiard Room, MacKinnon's Drug Store, and Val Rand's Book Store. The twin "C" Foodland, managed by Charlie Cohen, was opened.

Although the depression was not as severely felt in Wolfville as in manufacturing centres, the town council was asked to supply food, clothing, and shelter for some individuals and families. Tax collecting became more difficult, and the council was forced to apply for a loan for operating purposes. In 1934 council required the officials, except the auditor and the assistant town clerk, to take a ten per cent salary cut. Householders were asked not to feed transients or give them money, but to refer them to the town office, where they could earn subsistence by cutting wood. Spurred on by disgruntled residents, the council authorized the treating of unpaved streets with crude oil to settle the dust, but the expedient annoyed mothers whose children had their clothing stained by the oil. Residents of the east end petitioned the town to stop the dumping of decayed apple skins on the dyked land, and the town complied with their request. In 1939 the harbour was dredged again, this time under the direction of J. D. Harris.

Rafuse building, possibly built in 1915, by R.E. Harris. Note high tide and spur line railway.

About 1945. Main street at corner of Gaspereau Avenue.

4. The 1940s

World War II brought about a halt in economic progress, but after the war the economy steadily improved. The Town of Wolfville made great strides.

Cecil Langille enlisted in the Air Force, and W. A. Vaughan took over his coal business. William Frank opened a bargain store. Also in 1940 a new Temperance building, with an auditorium, kitchen, two small rooms, and a basement, .was constructed on Elm Avenue. Edson Graham, who had completed thirty-five years in the photography business, changed the name of his establishment to "Acadia Studio." In July 1945 Graham retired and the studio was taken over by R. B. Macaulay.

In August 1947 the Valley Dry Cleaners Ltd., with Reg L. Boates as manager, opened on Main Street. The following year Sanisteam Laundry, owned by A. Burpee Balcom and Gerald L. Porter, began business. In 1949 C. E. Levy purchased "The Trading Centre" at the east end of Main Street; Marguerite's dress shop moved into the Wolfville Fruit Company's building; Dave's restaurant opened on Linden Avenue.

The auditor's report of 1941 showed a deficit of $9,622, much of it due to unpaid taxes in the 1930s. This was cleared by 1943, and the town operated in the black for the first time in several years. The town council began to promote Wolfville as a tourist resort, in a series of special editions of the *Chronicle Herald*, but wartime rationing, which made restaurant service difficult, tended to frustrate their efforts.

With the improvement in economic conditions after the end of World War II, plans were again made for a Civic Building. The Wolfville Fruit Company wished to occupy, in May 1946, the offices leased to the town, but consented to delay action for a year. The residents approved the expenditure of $2,500 for a site, but voted against the $60,000 asked for the building. The town purchased more property, for $16,200, and the ratepayers finally consented to approve $55,000 for the Town Hall. M. L. Wallace was the contractor. In the meantime, plans had grown, and council wanted to incorporate all buildings and facilities on one site, including the jail and fire department, which were storing their equipment in a barn. The architect's plans of December 1948 included "ultra-modern heating and wiring plans," which

1949. Fire Department, Town hall, and Truck Garage.

council modified to a simpler plan and use of their own labour. Their system broke down, and in 1950 council had to spend $2,500 to purchase a new oil furnace. Meantime, the cornerstone had been laid by George C. Nowlan, K.C., in April 1949, and the town office officially occupied in May.

In the late 1940s the Department of Municipal Affairs undertook serious consideration of town planning, and offered to help municipalities by sending a consultant to conduct preliminary studies of each town's needs. Wolfville decided to adopt this plan, especially as the Provincial Government assumed part of the cost. The possibility of a rural high school was discussed, as was the development of pension plans for town employees of long standing, and support was given to the creation of the first regional library. Wolfville did not approve the "Summer Time," and in May 1945 the council asked the Provincial Government to return the province to Standard Time, but Windsor adopted the new time, and the next year Wolfville adopted Daylight Time. In 1950 they set May 23 to September 4 as the period for Daylight Time, but extended the time, in 1956, from April 29 to September 29.

In August 1945 the taxpayers had approved extension of water facilities, at a cost of $70,000. The *Acadian* reported in June 1947 that since incorporation Wolfville had supplied its own Stipendiary Magistrates: E. Sydney Crawley, 1893 to 1922; W. D. Withrow, D. G. Whidden, and Burpee Wallace. The first Provincial Magistrate to service Wolfville was Horace B. Dickey.

5. The 1950s

Several new businesses appeared in the decade and several changes of ownership occurred. The *Acadian* noted in March 1950 that G. C. Pickford had opened a florist shop at 302 Main Street, and Murray Strum began a barber business on Linden Avenue, next to the Herbin Block. Frank's Bargain Store, in one of the town's oldest buildings, was remodelled, in March 1952. A. J. Woodman and Company ceased their furniture business in the fall of the same year. In 1953 R. S. Babcock's restaurant installed a modern kitchen and increased their seating capacity to forty. In September of that year Wade's Groceries (formerly Welch's) opened on Main Street, but was destroyed by fire the next year. Mrs. Suzanne Mitchell opened Suzanne's Fashion Centre in October of 1953.

In the fall of 1954 Grant Porter sold his grocery business to B. R. Wade. Another of the older firms, Weaver's Ltd., sold out the next year. Wolfville Fruit Company installed a modern storage plant, and Brownell Agencies, in which Austin Brownell, Walter Weaver and Ben Hiltz were partners, opened its business. In January 1956 Jayson's Ltd., a clothing store, was opened, but was destroyed by fire in February 1958; in September the I.G.A. Foodliner, owned by F. E. Wade Ltd., opened; the Acadia Food Store replaced the Dominion in March of the next year. The *Acadian* office was given a brick facing in the fall of 1957. There were two additions in the last years of the decade, Star Clothing Company Ltd., selling wholesale, and Griswold's Canteen on East Main Street, and one business closed, Marguerite's Dress Shop.

In the 1950s a group of residents, interested in building low-cost housing for themselves under a co-operative scheme, with financing available through

Stedman's Store started in November, and Coolen's Self-Service Wash began at 70 Highland Avenue.

R. C. Vanwart, who in 1961, celebrated fifty years in the hardware business, nearly half of them in Wolfville, moved to the corner of Main and Gaspereau in January 1964. In March the Sara Bliss Dress Shop, operated by Sara Watson and Bliss MacKinnon, opened, and Murray Boland began his shoe store in the Balcom block. Dykhuizen moved his business into the Dominion Store building, represented Tip Top Tailors and during the following years expanded into men's wear. Industrial Electrics opened at the corner of Main and Gaspereau. In June the Holland Bakery closed, after twenty-eight years in business, and in October Harris Bakeries opened on the same premises. Mrs. Evelyn Welch, who had begun her "Tots and Teens" store in 1952, sold to R. A. MacGillivray of Greenwood. Ronald Hobbs took over Suzanne's Fashion Centre. J. A. MacMillan opened a Home Appliance Store in December.

In 1965 the Cleveland Grocery ceased operation, and the next year Harris Supplies Limited, previously owned by William Skerry, was sold to H. R. Rafuse, who named it Rafuse Supplies. The University, for its development, removed the store at the corner of Main and Highland. The building had been erected by John F. Brown and had housed many businesses: *The Star* newspaper, Bishop's florist shop, Prat's store, R. E. Harris store, Grant Porter's grocery for fifty years, and others. At one time the building had been rented by merchants who sold shoddy goods, and residents had tarred and feathered the plate glass windows. The new Tourist Bureau opened in August 1966 at the Duck Pond site, and in September Bevan and Wilson purchased Wolfville Agencies Ltd. The *Acadian* reported that merchants desired a liquor store in the town, and a vote the next year favoured the opening by 479 to 429. The store was opened in Kings Shopping Centre. Save Easy took over a store in the same area.

In January 1967 Dalton R. MacKinnon had sold to Robert L. Bearne the druggist business he had established in 1929. The Waterbury building was demolished to make possible an expansion of Kings Shopping Centre. The Vanwart Hardware was purchased by C. A. Coll.

The addition of eight new subdivisions in the 1960s and the erection of the plant of Kent Foods Ltd. made it clear that long-range community planning was needed. The citizens demanded the creation of a Town Planning Board, in spite of Mayor Longley's assurance that the mayor, clerk and various councillors had been attending local and regional planning conferences and were satisfied that Wolfville was "proceeding in the right direction," particularly with regard to subdivisions. The Director of Community Planning for the Department of Municipal Affairs visited Wolfville Town Council in 1965 to explain the role of the Town Planning Board and council's responsibility regarding subdivisions. Approval of a subdivision by the Planning Board was final, the director stated, and no ratification by council was required. Council could, however, refuse to accept the deed for a finished street in a subdivision approved by the Board. Since Board approval did not bind council to take over a new street, it was impossible for subdividers to know if their projects, when complete, would be accepted by the town. As the minutes of council show, there was considerable confusion through the

the Nova Scotia Housing Commission, appeared before the town council in 1953 to get permission to open up a new area. They soon completed several houses in what was later called the Nowlan subdivision. In 1956 and 1958, two more subdivisions were begun, the Steele, and the Welch-Lo.

Although the Department of Municipal Affairs had for many years been urging incorporated towns and municipalities to adopt planning measures, it was not until 1951 that Wolfville appointed its first planning committee. Since the committee held no meetings between 1951 and 1954, the council set up another group. Meanwhile the housing shortage had led to much building and laying out of what came to be called subdivisions. The bylaws had been revised in 1952, but it was evident to council that building and zoning regulations should be added. A model bylaw governing the installation of TV and radio antenna was adopted in 1955, and the year following regulations regarding new streets were added.

Parking meters had been installed on town streets in the mid-fifties, but upon inspection half of them were found to be "non-functioning." The meters were intended as a source of revenue but proved to be chiefly annoyances for residents and councillors, and were later removed.

6. The 1960s

Eight new subdivisions appeared in the first eight years of the decade. The 1961 census gave the population of the town as 2,413. Additions to the public school had become necessary.

The largest addition to the town's economy was the erection of a plant valued at half a million dollars by Kent Foods Ltd. on Cherry Lane, somewhat to the dismay of residents of the western part of the town.

There were many changes along Main Street. In 1960, F. J. McEachern began a TV store at the corner of Main and Highland; Miles Thrift Superette started business at 242 Main Street; Frank's Bargain Store was closed and George N. Frank associated with his father in the main store; R. &. A. Cleaners set up shop on Main Street in place of Valley Cleaners. In 1961 Eaton's order office opened at 251 Main Street; Mrs. Mary Squarebriggs, manager of the Acadian Resturant, corner of Main and Gaspereau, changed the name to Rendezvous Restaurant; Dean's Flowers took over the G. C. Pickford Flower Shop, and H. H. Pulsifer began a second flower shop at the corner of Main and Elm; the Star Clothing store closed after three years in operation; Kelley's Restaurant, operated by Mr. and Mrs. Fred Kelley, opened; Alfred E. Milligan began Star Clothier; Ripley's Shoe Store initiated their business; Curtis Chipman purchased Brownell Agencies. In 1962 P.J. Best's Furniture Store opened; Bevan and Wilson bought the J.D. Vaughan Insurance Agency; R.S. Babcock installed new store fronts of simulated brick.

Disaster struck in February 1963, when the Balcom block was destroyed by fire, burning Ripley's Shoe Store, Northern Tire and Auto Supplies, Simpson-Sears, and F. J. McEachern Ltd. The last two reopened in the Balcom block in July. J. D. Harris sold his insurance business to Wolfville Agencies; Milligan's Restaurant opened at the corner of Main and Highland; Teunis Dykhuizen, tailor, began business above Pulsifer's flower shop.

years. The town clerk's office became overloaded with paper work, and extra staff had to be employed.

One of the startling features of the decade was the tremendous increase in both size and complexity of all town projects. Additions to the public school system cost $437,000. There was a growing involvement of "big government" in all phases of town operations, and more and more Federal and Provincial programs, involving multi-community and multi-county schemes, came to town, buried under legalistic jargon and complicated funding plans. Greater involvement by big government also meant that considerable money was available for funding new projects, and council had more time to devote to those projects as larger government agencies took over the administration of former town concerns. From 1968 to 1970, many changes were made to the Zoning Bylaws as properties were reclassified to make way for more apartment complexes, more subdivisions and more businesses. Members of council made strenuous efforts to attract new industries, but in spite of their encouragements, the industries would choose other Valley sites for their plants.

7. The 1970s

In the summer of 1970 Roscoe Construction Ltd. of Cambridge Station was awarded the contract to build the new post office. The building was put up to the rear of the old building, and the town lost one of its amenities, a pleasant garden which had been started many years before by the Garden Club. There were three other major building operations during the decade: Basin View Village, Senior Citizens Housing, and Tideways. The first to get under way was Basin View Village, a housing complex, sponsored by a private group, on a site up the hill between Highland Avenue and University Avenue. It was hoped that the location would be convenient for students who wished to rent apartments. Sponsoring the project were: Gordon C. MacDonald of Wolfville as president of the group, Earl Carey of Avonport, Frederick J. Elderkin of Wolfville, Douglas A. Seamone, and Donald E. Hiltz of Kentville. Robert A. Wrye was chosen as administrator. The first units were opened in 1972, and additional ones were built in the following years.

The Senior Citizens Housing project arose from a survey conducted in 1970 by the Inter-Church Council, which showed the need for a minimum of nine housing units for families, accommodation for thirty-two senior citizens, twenty-five mobile home units. The Town Council, realizing that the shortage of low rent housing was becoming acute, asked the Nova Scotia Housing Commission to conduct an official study so that a government housing programme could be planned. As a result of the Inter-Church Council's study, a corporation had been formed to administer a home for the aged, and designs for the project, as well as housing for low-to-moderate income families, were discussed with various bodies. By January 1972 application was made to the Nova Scotia Housing Commission to appoint a Commissioner to oversee the work. Negotiations to buy land owned by L. G. Rawding were begun but were held up by the developers of a nearby subdivision who feared that the project would lower the value of their property and refused for a time to sell a needed right-of-way. In August 1975 twenty units were opened on

Sherwood Drive. The Federal Government provided one-half the financing, the Provincial Government one-quarter, Town of Wolfville one-quarter. Each unit consisted of kitchen, bath, living room and one bedroom, and a percentage of the apartments were designed for paraplegics. There was also a common room, recreation and laundry rooms, and the possibility of a small garden plot. In accordance with the "phased" housing concept, which had been discussed with Central Mortgage and Housing, more units were planned for the future.

The housing complex, known as Tideways, at the east end of town, was built by the Habitat Co-operative Ltd., an organization sparked by the desire of Mary Black that people over fifty have subsidized group housing. The Co-operative, under Doreen Tillotson, president, Eileen Hiltz, secretary, George Fraser, treasurer, and directors Mary Black, James Crossan, Philip Gucker, James Hackett, James Potts, Fred Townsend and later additions, with the help of federal and provincial grants, purchased a ten-acre lot, and built an eighteen-unit house. A second unit was added under the presidency of W. Gordon, with James Potts as secretary, the operation headed by John Vaillancourt.

Business changes during the 1970s began with the opening of a handcraft and flower shop, Bottom Cottage Boutique, at lower Gaspereau Avenue; the sale of Macaulay's Photo Studio to Jeff Wilson; the renovation of Herbin's store; and the opening of the Dorcas Shoppe for a short time in the Harris Bakery building. In May 1972 the Royal Bank moved across the street to a new location in the Kings Centre Mall. A newly remodelled restaurant, "The Steak Out," took over the site of the former "Palms." The DeWolf house, which had been moved from its former location on the Wolfville Fruit Company premises to the corner of Gaspereau Extension and Front Street, the site of an early blacksmith shop, was demolished to make room for the Anvil Beverage Room. The Beverage Room, operated by Ken Wood, Margaret Wood, Ken Crichton, and Henry Endres, was opened in late November. Pride and Joy Fashions closed, and Hutchinson's Book Store was sold to Leo Hennessey. Clamp's Tobacco Store was relocated in the Sally Starr Craft Shop, and Keith Meerman's Beehive opened in October 1973. The Waldorf Building, which housed the Atlantic Trust Company and Eaton's mail order office, was completed in February 1974. R. L. MacDonald Insurance Services took over the Bevan and Wilson Insurance Ltd. In February 1976 Jack and Helen Maskell took over Babcock's Restaurant, and in the same month the new Sears store was opened. At the end of 1979 Wade Enterprises took over the Save Easy business in Kings Centre Mall.

In the 1970s Town Council was busy with many projects. Town workers put up crosswalk signs, checked traffic patterns, and removed the parking meters. A dog catcher and a street cleaner were hired. The taxpayers approved expenditure of $30,000 to purchase the Industrial Electric building to store trucks and public works equipment, and to house the regional library. Council borrowed $130,000 to repair and renovate the fire hall. In 1971 the town extended benefits from Maritime Medical Town Pension as well as group insurance to full-time public works personnel, and in 1972, for the first time, provided safety equipment to these workers. An integrated radio system was set up, at a cost of $9,000, to help coordinate activities between the town hall and public works, the police and fire departments.

In February 1972 the Department of Municipal Affairs ordered the council to prepare a Municipal Development Plan before March 1 on penalty of having "all existing Zoning Bylaws and official Town Plans . . . lapse and cease to have any effect" after that date. A postponement asked by council was refused. However, the department advised that the Director of Community Planning would be happy to meet with the Planning Advisory Committee, and the work began on the "Agenda for Planning," but not until May 1973 did the Planning Advisory Committee present a "preliminary statement" as its report.

Meanwhile there was continued work on sewage abatement in cooperation with Grand Pre, and tax relief was conceded to certain charitable, fraternal and recreational organizations as well as to widows and widowers, people over sixty-five, and heads of single-parent households with an income of less than $4,500 a year. The Finance Committee denied tax concessions either in tax rate or tax base to three companies: CanVin Products Ltd., R. W. DeWolfe Ltd., and Horton Development Ltd. The Planning Advisory Committee also recommended that the principle of tax concessions be opposed, although it supported concessions available to new industries under the Bonus Act. Housing was still the priority, and planning groups attempted to balance residential and commercial zoning needs, while still maintaining enough public open space for parks and recreation areas. The Planning Advisory Committee realized that one of the few remaining sites in Wolfville for industrial growth was the Front Street corridor, and negotiations to purchase those lands were begun in 1973. Council talked with Marathon Realty, whose owners, the Dominion Atlantic Railroad, leased land to Twin Cities Dairy, and to Victor Harris, the owner of lands adjacent. When the Harris Bakery had closed in the 1960s, council had twice turned down requests for rezoning the property, and had discussed taking over the property. In the early 1970s business increased and several young people opened shops there. The Kings Kable TV Broadcasting Station on Centre Street opened business and president Hugh Fairn announced in January 1974 that his company would soon be ready to provide multi-channel TV service. Council postponed its plans to assume control of the area.

In 1974 the overall Municipal Development Plan, proposed by planning consultant Dr. John Connor and the Planning Advisory Committee, headed by Jack Herbin, was accepted by the town, but the occupancy tax was rejected. In May of that year the ratepayers voted in favour of borrowing $40,000 for a new fire pumper but rejected the $540,000 for sewers. The next year the ratepayers agreed to borrow $58,000 for a street and sidewalk programme. A "Beautification Week" was declared under the chairmanship of Mrs. Elizabeth Adamson, and Gerald Porter, proprietor of Sanisteam Laundry, was awarded a plaque in recognition of assistance given the beautification programme.

There had been difficulties with the bylaw requiring removal of signs hanging out over the sidewalk. In 1972 Coastal Insurance had won a suit against the town for removal of a sign, but in 1975 most merchants complied with the bylaw.

When the Twin City Dairy failed to obtain a long-term lease from the railroad and decided to move its operations, the town took an option on the land and discussed with Marathon Realty the sale of the land. Marathon suggested renewal of the current lease for another five years, and consideration of the matter then. When council asked ratepayers to vote $115,000 to purchase the land and building of the former Harris Bakery, the proposal was turned down by a two-to-one vote, so that action on the Town Centre Development Plan was delayed. Approval had been given to spend $20,000 for renovating the Civic Building, and in July 1977, approval was given to borrow nearly $800,000 for sewage treatment facilities which began to operate in 1978.

In December 1978 a system of graduated early payment discounts for taxpayers was introduced. In July 1979 council passed a resolution asking the Nova Scotia Union of Municipalities to oppose the province's development in nuclear energy.

8. Acadia University and Taxation

In 1957 the Wolfville Town Council supported a Kingston resolution which proposed that the Federal and Provincial Governments "pay grants in lieu of taxes on tax-exempt lands and buildings of those municipalities who are providing municipal services to universities."

Under a new Assessment Act announced by the provincial government in 1966, the term "personal property" was replaced by "occupancy assessment," with properties assessed in proportion to the amount of space occupied by twenty percent of each building and the land immediately surrounding it. The most disturbing feature of the Act, from the town council's point of view, was that under it Acadia University was exempt. The university's tax-exempt property amounted to forty-four percent of the 1966 assessment roll for Wolfville. The new scheme immediately sent taxes up and the amount of Federal and Provncial grant money down. In February 1967 Wolfville communicated with Antigonish, which was caught in the same assessment squeeze because it served as a home to St. Francis Xavier University. The two towns worked together at conferences of the Union of Nova Scotia Municipalities to obtain grants in lieu of university taxes, but had little success.

In 1969 Wolfville had the highest residential taxation per dwelling in the province. The councillors, concerned with the imposition of such a tax burden, decided to explain to ratepayers the cause of the increase, and urge them to write their M.L.A.s and ministers. Council met with local M.L.A.s to discuss strategy to use when approaching the government about loss of revenue suffered because of Acadia's tax-exempt status. Meanwhile, the town did what it could. Interest on tax arrears went up ten percent on January 1, 1970, in order to discourage citizens from thinking that the town was a lending agency. During the first half of the 1960s Wolfville had enjoyed an unusually high rate of successful tax collection, and had put the money into surplus funds, but the assessment crunch of 1967 had consumed much of that reserve, and the town was back to tight financing.

The petition by Wolfville against the university's tax-exempt status had gone to the Supreme Court, and in July 1970 council learned that the court upheld the original exemption, and that Wolfville could not tax residences constructed by the university on university property. The town solicitor felt that Wolfville had won a minor victory, since university-built residences *on campus* could escape taxation, but university-constructed residences across the street could be taxed. The town's strategy was to oppose future revenue loss it might incur from Acadia's building of residences, by encouraging private developers to build off-campus rental housing, and to limit Acadia's physical plant.

The council also moved to determine from Acadia exactly what it planned for future expansion, so that the university and the town could work together on long-range planning needs. There was much discussion of zoning, and criticism was levelled against the "university" zoning classification as too vaguely drawn to be effective. Through rezoning of properties, council worked to expand the available sites for new homes and to control the university construction of more tax-exempt buildings. Meanwhile, the university continued building residences on campus, but offered to pay taxes on two commercial ventures housed in its new Students' Centre: the Bank of Commerce, and The Gift Within. This offer was accepted after council had checked to see that this arrangement would not jeopardize provincial grants for garbage and sewer services.

On February 6, 1980 the *Acadian* reported that a property tax settlement allowed $83,000 to the town from Acadia University residences and that the amount was being paid by the Provincial Government. As a result, the town council was able to lower both residential and commercial property tax rates.

9. Entering the 1980s

And then the 1980s began, with high hopes. In May the Business Development Corporation was launched, with financial assistance from the provincial coordinator, John Thorpe. In June the town took over from the Board of Trade the operation of the Tourist Bureau, with John MacFarlane and three students in charge. The Post House Restaurant, formerly owned by the Maskells, received in August the town's first restaurant liquor licence. Proprietor James Sanders employed a staff of eleven. A fire closed the restaurant in December. Council agreed on an emergency access road to E.K.M. Hospital, and property owners Donald Little and Henry Hicks agreed to deed the land to the town in exchange for the cost of development.

It is still unclear what the future will be, but Wolfville, as usual, has been cushioned from the blows other communities have received.

X.

RELIGION

The early settlers of this new land brought with them religious affiliations they had known in the New England colonies. The revivals of George Whitefield and others had resulted in a division among the Puritan (Congregationalist) churches, and many "New Light" congregations had been formed; these people claimed to have come "into the light." Illumined in their souls they were transformed from a state of perdition to one of ecstatic rejoicing in the assurance of pardon and future bliss. The mainline Congregational churches insisted on personal experience of faith (new birth) before a person could be accepted as a member. This contrasted markedly with the "Half-way Covenant" idea, whereby a person could formally agree to doctrines in order to enjoy the franchise. The new settlers were almost all Congregationalists, acquainted with, if not wholly persuaded by, this New Light movement and ripe for the revivals which were to flourish under the New Light evangelist, Henry Alline, and his successors: John Payzant, T. H. Chipman, and Harris Harding.

Among the newcomers were a few people of other persuasions who welcomed the chance to emigrate to a new land with the promise of more religious freedom. Formerly, many had settled in Rhode Island to escape persecution from the dominant Puritan establishment, and some of these would be among the "Planters." Actually, the religious freedom promised was not all that it appeared to be. The Anglican Church centred in Halifax exercised religious privileges short of outright legal establishment. It was not until 1834 that other clergymen were allowed to perform the marriage ceremony. When the Planters arrived from New England they had been accustomed to schools and churches and found the new territory devoid of the same. It was no small task to establish community life with schools and churches and other public buildings.

Therefore, when Ebenezer Moulton, a preacher and evangelist who had settled near Yarmouth, arrived in 1763, he was welcomed by the more devout people at Horton, and the result was the first church organization, in 1763, and the first meetinghouse or church building, sometime in 1765-66.

This first church was situated somewhere near the south-east corner of the old cemetery, and was used by believers of all faiths in congregational worship. This building also served for a time as a courthouse after the one at Horton Landing had been destroyed by fire. Little alteration was made to transform the church into a courthouse when occasion required, except the draping of the gallery with curtains.

The Horton Church was mostly composed of New Light Congregationalists, but at least two members, Benjamin Kinsman, Jr., and Peter Bishop, baptized by the Baptist missionary Ebenezer Moulton, later became charter members of the church organized by the Baptists in 1778. An Anglican service, attended also by other denominations, was held once a month. At first, frontier conditions necessitated a measure of toleration and cooperation in religious observances, a practice which continued on well into the next century.

The people, scattered as they were throughout Nova Scotia, and trying to sustain some kind of religious activity, were having a most difficult time, while divided by the New Light controversy. They were desperately poor and were unable to support a clergyman by themselves. Some ministers returned to New England and it was left to a few relatively uneducated men to undertake extended journeys on horseback to visit these communities and hold preaching services. The people were glad to forget doctrinal differences and to welcome these evangelists, attending the worship services of all the preachers.

1. Congregationalists

In the early years Congregationalists gradually merged with the Baptists, both bodies sharing the same form of church government. Some people of the New Light movement found a spiritual home in Methodism. One factor in the process was the preaching of Henry Alline. Though he was not opposed to the idea of adult baptism by immersion among the converts, Alline thought it a relatively unimportant issue, compared with the real question of the quality of the religious experience itself.

At the time of union in 1925 the Presbyterians, Methodists, and Congregationalists across the country formed the United Church of Canada. The Congregationalists have not really disappeared. At the present time the spirit of those people lives on in the United Church of Canada. If there is an extra measure of local church loyalty and democratic procedures in the United Churches of this area, it may well be due to the legacy from those early Congregationalists.

The Congregationalist pastors: Reverends Benijah Phelps, 1765-76; Aaron Bancroft, 1780-83; Hugh Graham, 1783-99.

2. Baptists

The Baptists and Congregationalists formed the first church group in the community, but in 1778 the Baptists established a separate group. Ten people formed this church, with Nicholas Pierson as the first pastor. He had arrived from England and was a shoemaker by trade. He was ordained with the collaboration of a church group of Congregationalists and Baptists from Falmouth-Newport. The famous New Light evangelist Henry Alline came to help with the organization of the Baptist Church.

In 1820 the congregation erected a new church, on the north side of Main Street, at the south-west corner of the old cemetery. It had an auditorium and a gallery. The growth of the community, partly through the college and academy, prompted the replacement of that building in 1860, with a new structure that had a high steeple. It was located at the south-east corner of Main Street and the present Highland Avenue. Galleries were generally for the students, and by 1880 the north gallery became the exclusive possession of students of the Ladies Seminary who were paraded to church under strict supervision. In 1908 Ernest Porter painted the spire and tower, "a daring accomplishment."

The Baptist Church, built in 1912.

Because of further need for a larger centre of worship, the local church began in 1909 to plan for a new building. In 1912 C. H. Wright was awarded the contract to build on the site of the former wooden New England structure which had been torn down to make way for a large and far grander brick edifice. The cost was estimated at $60,000.

One cannot escape the almost legendary presence of Reverend Theodore Seth Harding and his lengthy pastorate. To enter the old cemetery is to be immediately aware of his tombstone which dominates the whole scene. The Harding House at 150 Main Street is one of the oldest in Wolfville. If the university is the major industry of the town, as undoubtedly it is, and the principal reason why Wolfville is known, then Harding represents the era of expansion of Acadia College and Horton Academy.

Until very recent times the Baptist Church and Acadia University were so closely associated that either one could be regarded as an extension of the other. University people were active in all phases of church life; the relationship was mutual.

A false impression can be given of a time of flourishing and growing institutions. The truth is that periods of uncertainty arose during Harding's ministry, resulting in ennui. The Wolfville Baptist Church was actually excluded from the association for some time because they did not practise close communion.

Another problem affecting the well-being of the Congregational, Methodist, and Baptist Churches was that of church discipline. True to the perfectionist piety of New England, revivalism carried over into the culture of the newcomers and called for discipline. For example, the record stands that "a sister in Cornwallis was suspended from Church on account of levity and singing songs and had no desire to lay the least restraint on herself."

Covenant meetings on Saturdays in most churches in those early days were busy on matters of discipline. In some instances members became divided over whether the names of those excommunicated should be read from the pulpit on a Sunday. The pioneer people had growing pains for the sake of those who were to follow them.

The Wolfville Baptist Church has been the mother church of two nearby, those of New Minas and Gaspereau. In more recent years the church at the juncture of Gaspereau Avenue and the Ridge Road, named the East Wolfville United Baptist Church, can be regarded as the offspring of the parent body, though its history goes back to the old tabernacle days.

The tabernacle story is of particular interest because it tells of the turn of the century when class divisions were more apparent within the town limits than they are now. There were children in town who, because of circumstance or cultural barriers, did not attend the regular Sunday School sessions of the Baptist Church. Wolfville was also on occasion the stopping place for itinerant farm workers, salesmen and sailors. To help meet this special need, in the year 1890 Annie Fitch began a mission in the store of David J. Harris, on Victoria Avenue. Two years later a Young Peoples Union was founded in the Baptist Church which included some university students, and the enthusiasm engendered spilled over into maintaining this Sunday School and starting a preaching programme. In due time some individuals, with a view to a non-denominational programme, raised a sufficient sum of money to erect a building, constructed by Charles A. Stewart, which came to be known as the "Tabernacle." It was dedicated in 1903.

The Tabernacle became a cause for embarrassment to some extent. It was sometimes jokingly referred to as an opportunity for divinity students to get some practice in the art of preaching. Actually the people attending did not seem to mind. The Wolfville Baptist Church received the deed to the property in 1915, but the work gradually declined until the Sunday School ceased to exist. The building was sold to the town for an industrial arts centre and is at present the Canadian Legion hall.

To carry on this ministry to youth, men of the Baptist Church undertook an ambitious programme of transporting children to the Wolfville Church

The Tabernacle, opened in 1903.

Sunday School in their cars. This plan did not succeed in reaching all the children and it was finally decided to go where the people were. The "Tabernacle" money, which had been saved from the sale of the building, was in part used to purchase the Best property on Eye Road.

This work later expanded into a pastoral field which included churches at Melanson Mountain, Wallbrook Mountain, and West Brooklyn. The day came when the new highway split the Eye Road community in half, and the church programme was moved to the present site at the corner of Gaspereau Avenue and the Ridge Road, where the Salvation Army hut was made available. That building was renovated for use by the Baptists.

The church began a new kind of ministry when in January 1949 a service was broadcast over radio station CFAB, the first time a Wolfville church service was heard over the air. The church also effected a change early in 1980 when their parsonage on Linden Avenue was sold for $55,000 and the pastor bought a building in Steele subdivision. During that year electric chimes were installed in the church.

The pastors: Nicholas Pierson, 1779-1791; Reverends Theodore Seth Harding, 1795-1855; Stephen William DeBlois, 1855-1884; Thomas A. Higgins, 1884-1895; Thomas Trotter, 1895-1897; Hugh R. Hatch, 1898-1903; Lewis D. Morse, 1903-1908; Edward D. Webber, 1908-1913; George O. Gates (interim), 1913-1915; Nelson A. Harkness, 1915-1918; John H. MacDonald, 1919-1923; Albourne N. Marshall, 1924-1931; Frank H. Eaton, 1931-1947; Herman C. Olsen, 1947-1960; Austin D. MacPherson, 1961-1972; Neil G. Price, 1973-.

3. Church of England

The site of St. John's Anglican church on the north side of east Main Street can carry the observer back in imagination to the early days in Wolfville history, because this church has been in use since June 1818, when it was consecrated. Changes have taken place over the years, with doorways reconstructed, another style of steeple to replace one blown away in a storm, pews rearranged and altered, and windows reshaped. The rectory was built in 1864 and purchased in 1930.

Anglicanism developed in Nova Scotia and in the Annapolis Valley especially in a different manner than among the "dissenting" churches. The care of the Church of England communicants radiated from the bishop's headquarters in Halifax. The Society for the Propagation of the Gospel in Foreign Parts (commonly referred to as the S.P.G.) played a prominent part in this pastoral care. Gradually churches were built, and parishes established throughout Nova Scotia.

Concern for those of the Church of England tradition prevailed no matter how few the adherents might be. This care required that a missionary, such as Reverend John Wiswall, appointed by the S.P.G., besides being the first rector of Cornwallis, was responsible for the whole of King's County and as far as Middleton. He wrote to the society: "There is not one regular teacher in this part of the country. At Horton there is an Anabaptist meeting-house, and an 'illiterate shoemaker' (Nicholas Pierson) supplies the place as Pastor." In his journal he wrote, "the inhabitants are wild enthusiasts of every denomination — Independents, Presbyterians, Universalists, Allanists, etc.,

etc. — and seem to agree on only one thing, love of independence in both Church and State.'' He was not above accepting the hospitality of the Baptists, however, and welcomed the chance to use their church for a service once a month. In his journal he wrote in 1784, ''I have a very crowded audience when I preach at Horton to persons of all denominations. I am in hopes their prejudices against our church services will gradually wear off.''

Anglican missionaries had some advantages over the itinerant evangelists. They received financial support, never adequate, from headquarters, and monies were available for the establishment of schools. There was also the income from ''Glebe'' lands given by the government. Furthermore, they had the benefit of the most thorough education available, as nearly all clergymen and missionaries had been educated at the best colleges in England. Perhaps they felt a resposibility to save people from the ministrations of the itinerant preachers, comparatively uneducated, who were more indigenous to the communities.

The superiority in educational qualifications, and the church's practice of paying their clergy from the regional office, were not always the advantage one might expect. As a result of this arrangement, the Church of England followers depended too much financially on the Legislature and absentee providers, and they failed to give support to their missionaries. However, the Anglican Church of Nova Scotia would have its fair share of native-born leadership and local assistance.

Horton actually had a rector, Reverend Joseph Wright, in 1823, but there was a long period when Kentville and Wolfville shared a rector between them In the year 1841, Reverend John Storr, originally from Yorkshire, became rector of Cornwallis and Horton and filled that office for thirty-five years. In more recent times Reverend Richard F. Dixon served for over thirty years. The parish hall was built in 1960.

Around turn of century: south side of Church of England building.

Missionaries at Cornwallis and Horton: Reverends Joseph Bennett, 1762-1775; William Ellis, 1775-1779; Jacob Bailey, 1779-1782; John Wiswall, 1783-1789; William Twining, 1789-1806; Robert Norris, 1806-1823.

Rectors at Horton: Reverends Joseph Wright, 1823-1829; John Samuel Clarke, 1830-1838; John Storrs, 1841-1876; R. F. Brine, 1872-1875; Henry Sterns, 1875-1876; J. Lloyd Keating, 1876-1877; John Owen Ruggles, 1878-1888; Isaac Brock, 1889-1893; Kenneth C. Hind, 1893-1899; Richard Ferguson Dixon, 1899-1931; George A. Ernst, 1931-1936; Frank W. Fry, 1936-1954; William R. Martell, 1954-1962; J. Austin Munroe, 1963-1968; Whitley Trueman, 1968-1972; H. Douglas Hergett, 1972-.

4. Presbyterians

To do justice to the roots of Presbyterians one goes back to the earlier years preceding the building of the church on Prospect Street. This denomination is almost synonymous, of course, with Scottish history and it is no surprise that along with the presence of immigrants from Scotland and North Ireland there would be a number of missionary-minded Presbyterian ministers. Although the whole region east of Halifax became the new home for these settlers, there were clusters of Presbyterians in other parts of Nova Scotia (especially along the south shore), most of whom had come from New England to take advantage of the fishery industry. Many of the ministers were well educated, and as educators they established schools and academies.

One of the pioneer ministers was James Murdock who came from North Ireland in 1766. At first he preached in Halifax, but in 1767 he came to Horton (Grand Pre) and from that centre he carried on a ministry to Cornwallis, Newport and Windsor. He even worked as far afield as Amherst and Economy, and while living at Grand Pre he conducted a school. Many families at Horton were attracted to the church and he remained there for twenty years.

Reverend George Gilmore came to Horton in 1791 and served there until his death in 1811. Gilmore was born in Ireland, studied at Edinburgh, came to Philadelphia in 1767 and preached in that city. At the outbreak of the Revolutionary War, he fled to Quebec and was chaplain to the garrison at the settlement. He came to Hants County where he had been given a grant of land at Ardoise Hill in 1784. The land was so poor that he found it almost impossible to make a living. A story is told that Gilmore walked the thirty-five miles to Halifax and tried to trade his farm for a barrel of flour. He was buried at Grand Pre.

Inasmuch as the so-called "Old Covenanter" at Grand Pre is associated in the pastoral charge of St. Andrew's United of Wolfville, and the church on Prospect Street began with this radical form of Presbyterianism, some attention should be given to the Covenanter era.

Reverend William Sommerville was born in County Down, Ireland, in 1800. He was ordained by the Reformed Presbyterian Church in Ireland in 1831 as a missionary to New Brunswick and Nova Scotia, and eventually arrived in Horton in 1832. Because both Congregationalists and Presbyterians were worshipping together at Cornwallis and Horton, Sommerville was welcomed. Besides his church activities he began a school in Grand Pre.

William Sommerville was strict about worship, was so inflexible on the matter of singing hymns (mere man-made creations) that, when he was in charge of the Congregational Church at Cornwallis, he insisted that Psalms only should be used. Services lasted all day, generally including two sermons, with a break between, and with a fifteen-minute reprieve for lunch. The paraphrases of the Psalms were "lined" out, two verses at a time. A custom observed among the Covenanters, brought over from Scotland and Ireland, required that the men be seated on one side of the meetinghouse, and during the long pastoral prayer the congregation would stand facing the rear.

Divisions arose from the use of hymns and the form of Church government, and each Church group went its separate way. The *Acadian* reported in February, 1887, that the Reformed Presbyterian Church (Covenanters) bought the "Union Hall" on Church Street.

Possibly it was Reverend Robert Sommerville, son of the Covenanter preacher William Sommerville, who not only assisted his father at Cornwallis and at Grand Pre, but managed to have the then "Covenanter" church built in Wolfville in 1840. He later moved to New York city and became a very prominent preacher of that metropolis.

Just when and how the more regular type of Presbyterianism took over from the Covenanter is not clear. Evidently the latter began to lose ground and by the turn of the century services were no longer being held. In the meantime, however, during the early 1870s Reverend J. B. Logan supplied the Wolfville pulpit. Meetings were held in the old Temperance Hall on Main Street and eventually in the church on Keen Street. There was a great upsurge of enthusiasm during the period when the Reverend R. D. Ross was pastor.

For a period of forty-five years (1840-85) what was to become a Presbyterian church stood on the south side of the Prospect Street of today, now the site of the residence of Victor MacKay. The manse stood on the west side of the church. The church building was moved in 1885 to the location of the present United church. It must have been an undertaking of considerable

1885. Presbyterian Church being readied for removal to Main Street.

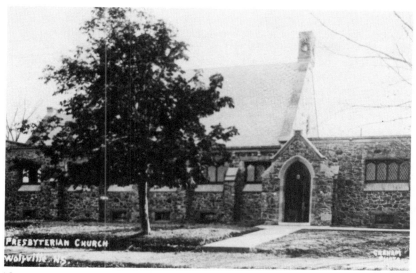

1914. Presbyterian Church, later the United Church building.

engineering skill and brought the name of the Chute and Company, into prominence. A photo taken by E. S. Crawley while the building was being moved indicated a structure with four gothic-type double windows interspersed with buttresses and a steeple large enough to accommodate a bell. After an extension had been added in 1903 to allow for a pipe organ, the Presbyterians could be justifiably proud of their achievement. Alas, in August 1913, as the St. Andrew's organ was being tuned one evening by candlelight, the church caught fire and the entire building was destroyed. This necessitated construction of the present edifice, which is of red sand-stone quarried at White Rock. Like the Phoenix, the new architecturally beautiful building arose from the ashes within the year, with C. H. Wright the contractor. It was said that when the new construction was completed in 1914 it was fully free of debt. The church was dedicated in 1914. Church union linked the Presbyterians and Methodists in 1925.

Significant dates: 1800-1830, Reverend Wm. Forsyth (Presbyterian and Congregationalist); 1827-1830, Reverend George Struthers (assistant); 1861, Reverend Robert Sommerville, co-pastor with his father over Horton and Cornwallis; 1862, Reverend R. Sommerville decided to found a Church in Wolfville, and in 1867 their building was constructed; 1883, the headquarters of Wolfville and Horton changed to Wolfville; 1885, the church moved down to Main Street, and opened January 1887.

5. Methodists

At the beginning of Methodism in Nova Scotia William Black arrived at Amherst with his Methodist parents from Northern England (1770-1775) when a number of people came from Yorkshire to Cumberland County. He went through a Henry Alline-style of religious experience and this became the initial impetus for the amazing sense of mission which motivated him with unswerving zeal on preaching missions throughout the land. He and the evangelists of the day accepted the hardships of travel which was on horseback, ship, or walking.

In 1782 Reverend William Black arrived for his first mission to Cornwallis by ship from Parrsboro. As there was no settled pastor at Cornwallis, he was welcomed by the Congregationalists. Three years later he revisited the community and at the same time preached at Horton, sowing the seeds of his faith.

One of the more significant events in the fortunes of Methodism was the arrival in Halifax of Reverend Freeborn Garretson. His coming from New England resulted from an appeal by William Black who had attended a Methodist conference at Baltimore. Garretson went far and wide on preaching missions, one of which was at Horton in 1826. Garretson possessed an almost New Light preaching style and made a number of converts in many communities. The Methodist cause languished somewhat in Horton, and followers received a preaching ministry by an Anglican clergyman, Reverend William Twining, who came from Cornwallis every third Sunday. Although an Anglican, and at the price of some disapproval from his own church, Twining was sympathetic to Methodist ideas.

The earliest formal type of Methodist Church Society must have been in the homes of the followers. In 1819 Reverend William Burt came to the circuit centered at Grand Pre and frequently held services at the home of T. A. S. DeWolf who was a "class" leader. In those early days the Methodists made much use of "class meetings" at which the supporters assembled, usually at homes, for worship, study of the scriptures and of Methodist beliefs.

A change in customs took place and a new kind of music was introduced into the Methodist Church in the fall of 1888 when C. H. Borden played the cornet and G. W. Munro the "bass-viol." Churches elsewhere had included instrumental playing in their worship services, with good results.

For some years before the time of union, the Methodist Church had grown steadily and had become one of the major religious influences in the town. The beginning of this period of growth and consolidation began when Horton and Wolfville become separate charges in 1892, with Reverend Oskar Gronlund as the first minister. But before this, a series of intense revivals had established Methodism in the town.

Whereas the present Saint Andrew's United Church building reigns supreme over the immediate vicinity from its choice location, it does not seem possible that sixty years ago another church, the Methodist, stood near the east side of the Main Street corner of Gaspereau Avenue (formerly Chapel Street). This building was of a style of architecture favoured in many Nova Scotia localities of that period. It had a lower hall with sanctuary above. The bell tower was spacious with four gothic windows, one on each side of the square tower which in turn was decorated with pleasing designs and at each corner miniature steeples. This building had served the Methodists for over sixty years when it was torn down in 1925, and the congregation merged with the Presbyterian Church. The lumber from the church building was used to build town houses on the same site and the manse was sold to the Baptists for a missionary home. A. M. Wheaton bought the land.

Other dates: 1786-87, Reverend Freeborn Garretson conducted revival services; 1789, land bought for a church building; 1794, Reverend James Boyd was in charge of Windsor circuit headquarters at Horton; 1799, Cornwallis Anglican missionary preached every three weeks in Methodist church at Lower Horton; 1812, Reverend Wm. Croscombe welcomed as minister; 1838, Croscombe returned to Horton and Cornwallis; 1923-30, Reverend D. R. Hemmeon (Methodist) the pastor as Methodists and Presbyterians combined, using the Presbyterian building; June, 1925, Church union; Reverends J. P. C. Fraser, 1931-39; Gerald Rogers, 1939-41; J. W. Bartlett, 1941-47; G. M. MacLean, 1947-54; J. Douglas Archibald, 1954-64; Robert H. Mills, 1965-67; Dewis J. Rector, 1967-69; Lloyd Archer, 1969-79; Walter Murray, 1979-.

6. Roman Catholic

St. Francis of Assisi Church had an early history that went back to the building of a church in 1853 on the south side of the Ridge Road at a site beside the Roman Catholic cemetery. At the same time a number of Irish families had arrived as the result of the potato famine in Ireland (1845-49) and had settled on both the North and South Mountains. This influx of Catholic people made feasible the building of a suitable worship centre. At this time Wolfville was part of the parish of Windsor, and Mass was held occasionally by the priest who often had to make the journey on horseback.

As often happened to wooden structures, fire destroyed this church in 1875. Mass was held for eight years at the home of James Quinn until the present edifice was erected. It was reported that a certain Charles Benjamin, a spurned suitor of a young lady supposedly worshipping within at the time, had set fire to the church in retaliation. The lady was not inside and the real victim was the building. This may have been a providential event because it did necessitate the move to a more central place in the town. Pews were salvaged from the Windsor Church and brought to replace the long pews. Earlier, benches and chairs were used.

The St. Francis of Assisi Church.

In 1883 Canon Walsh, a native of Ireland, was instrumental in building the present place of worship on Main Street. Presumably, he was a man of some independent means and able to finance the work from his own resources. Archbishop Hannan of Halifax was present for the consecration. A bell was installed in 1910.

Today, the Roman Catholic Church has a place of influence in the religious life of the community and the university and has grown steadily since the more tentative beginnings following the expulsion of the Acadians. A transition time occurred in 1959 when Very Reverend Father J. H. Durney read the official document of the Canonical Erection of the Parish of St. Francis of Assisi and installed Reverend Donald Amirault as the first priest of the new parish.

The priests affiliated with Windsor, 1883-1914: Canon William Walsh, Fr. Carmody, Fr. Daley, Fr. Kenny, Fr. Carroll, Fr. J. W. Brown, Fr. Collins, Fr. O'Sullivan.

Affiliated with Kentville, in Halifax Diocese: Fr. Donahue, 1915-1938; Fr. J. M. Brown, 1938-1943; Fr. J. H. Durney. 1943-1959.

Wolfville Parish, in Yarmouth Diocese: Fr. D. P. Amirault, 1959-1966; Fr. J. E. Leo Maillet, 1966-1970; Fr. Gerald Saulnier, 1970-1978; Fr. David Stokes, 1978-.

7. Other Church Groups and Religious Societies

This historical review has dealt only with those religious societies which have found themselves reflected in some tangible way, such as a church building. Of course, there are others, some of which have been very much a part of the religious scene. On occasion, people of the Judaic tradition have met to celebrate feast days and for other purposes. A Fundamentalist Baptist congregation has been organized since 1975. The Baha'i Faith has some supporters. The Society of Friends is active. Through the years and periodically the Salvation Army, with headquarters in Kentville, has conducted their programme and held services on occasion in the ''Tabernacle'' and in the Army hut which is now the East Wolfville United Baptist church.

8. Inter-Church Council

The first official sign of church co-operation came in 1917 when the Wolfville Ministerial Association was formed, with Reverend R. F. Dixon as president, and Reverend J. Armitage the secretary. Another evidence of common purpose showed early in 1918 when the Presbyterian and Methodist Churches united their services to conserve the supply of coal in the town. However, the Inter-Church Council expressed an enlarged scope of ''togetherness,'' to the benefit of the community. The Inter-Church Council, organized in 1970, brought together the member churches — St. John's Anglican, United Baptist, St. Francis of Assisi Roman Catholic, and St. Andrew's United — to ''provide for conference, consultation and common action in Christian witness and service in and for the community.''

A helpful service project has been the ''Wolfville Area Inter-Church Housing Society'' which assisted home owners in the repair and upgrading of their houses. Churches and individuals gave liberally to establish a capital fund for this purpose; the money was lent at a very modest interest rate. Later, this work was incorporated into the Kings County Housing Repair Society. A "Dorcas Shoppe" operated for five years until the need was met by different means. Other service projects of the Inter-Church Council were impressive and included: the Christmas-basket programme; Senior Citizen housing; Home-makers' programme; Meals-on-Wheels; and a telephone service.

9. Cemeteries

A community is made up of people and their relationships to one another, and each gravestone in a cemetery has a story. Two of the four cemeteries at Wolfville were directly church-related: the churchyard of St. John's Anglican Church which began in 1818, and that of St. Francis of Assisi Roman Catholic Church dating back to 1857. The other two, Willow Bank and the Old Cemetery, were and are public cemeteries.

Each was of great interest in its own way. The gravestones of St. John's read like the parish register, the family names of those who have supported the church. A complete list of these family names was given in the history of St. John's, prepared in 1965 by Dr. B. C. Silver. The Roman Catholic cemetery on the Ridge Road contained numerous unmarked and unknown graves. In 1969 a complete renewal of the cemetery was undertaken, the land tilled and seeded, and wooden crosses placed to mark the unknown graves.

The Willow Bank Cemetery Company was formed, with J. W. Bigelow as president and J. W. Hamilton as secretary, and trustee officers: Hon. F. S. McDonald and Albert Coldwell. J. W. Barss purchased about nine acres for $450 from Thomas L. DeWolf, and donated the land. The cemetery was incorporated in 1916 and again, with some changes in the Act, in 1923. George Nowlan carried through the legal work without charge.

Over the years many improvements have been made. Numerous citizens have taken responsibility for the cemetery. C. A. Patriquin was secretary-treasurer and manager from 1927 to 1941, and B. O. Davidson was president from 1932 to 1943.

In 1948, when Angus A. Elderkin was president, Morley Welch assumed the post as manager and as secretary-treasurer, and with the assistance of Archibald Morine, tabulated all burials and set up an efficient system of records. Morley Welch continued in this office for thirty years, and Angus Elderkin was president until 1980.

Three generations of the Morine family have been involved with the actual care of the cemetery. Archibald Morine worked a total of thirty-six years, thirty-one on them as foreman. His father Jerry Morine was caretaker, and his sons, Herbert and Gary, followed. Herbert is manager at the present time, and his wife G. Diana Morine is secretary-treasurer. Since 1932 H. H. Pulsifers has contributed at least one bed of flowers each year to enhance the beauty of the cemetery. New wrought iron gates were placed in 1973.

One of the most significant landmarks in Wolfville is the Old Cemetery. It was in use as early as 1763. There were periods in which it was sadly neglected, but in 1898 the Board of Trade appointed a committee composed of J. F. Herbin, C. R. H. Starr and A. J. Woodman to improve the cemetery; C. Y. Johnson superintended the work. New walks and old were arranged in a geometrical design, and with a suitable cairn at the centre a definite sense of order and dignity was achieved. It remained for Morley A. Welch, G. K. Prescott and Charles Patriquin to study what remained of the badly flaked stones and to the best of their ability systemize and record the names for posterity. This ambitious work was preserved in the Vaughan library.

Dr. Watson Kirkconnell composed the inscription in the "Old Cemetery." He described the place: "Beside the vanished sites of the churches of 1763 and 1820 is almost a Westminster Abbey for Acadia University in the memorial record of venerable college names." He cited and described them and then stated:

> The community itself is notably represented. Here is the beautifully preserved tombstone of the virtual founder of the town, Nathan DeWolf (1729-89), a M.A. of Yale, a lawyer and a man of property in his native Connecticut, whose home in the primordial village was just north of the 'post road' (our Main Street), opposite the present Baptist church. Here, too, lies his eldest son, Edward, the early town's chief merchant and elder brother of 'Judge Elisha'; Edward's son, Stephen, who succeeded him in the business in 1796; and Stephen's son, Charles, M.A., D.D.(Acadia), professor of Divinity at Mount Allison and president of the Maritime Wesleyan Conference. There are 39 DeWolf graves in the cemetery. Buried here is Captain John Fowler (1730-1796), a wealthy United Empire Loyalist from Westchester, New York, who bought most of the land between Highland Avenue and Gaspereau Avenue in 1780s. His grandson (1790-1860) and great-grandson (1828-1860), both named Elijah, lie beside him. Here lie William Alline, Sr. (1714-1799) and William Alline, Jr. (1742-1820), the father and elder brother of Henry Alline (1748-1784), the New Light evangelist. Here also is buried Henry's nephew, Philip Payzant (1779-1854), grandson of the French Huguenot, Louis Philippe Payzant, murdered by Micmacs at Mahone Bay in 1756, and his wife Marie, by tradition a sister of General Montcalm. Here also is Elder Moulton's first baptized convert in Horton in 1763, Peter Bishop (1736-1825), the local Baptist Church's first deacon, who at one time owned the whole university tract. A tombstone roster of Planters here includes the names of Allen, Anderson, Benjamin, Best, Bishop, Calkin, Cleveland, Cogswell, Davison, DeWolf, Elderkin, Forsyth, Fuller, Godfrey, Griffin, Harding, Harris, Higgins, Johnson, Kinsman, Martin, Miner, Newcomb, Palmeter, Pineo, Randall, Ratchford, Reid, Rogers, Turner, Wickwire, and Woodworth.
>
> This venerable spot deserves to be cherished and preserved for all for whom the history of the University and Town have foundations deeply based in the past.

XI.

EDUCATION

1. Local Schools

When the Planters arrived from New England following the expulsion of the Acadians, very few were able to do much more than basic reading, writing and calculating. Hundreds could not even sign their names. What education existed came mainly from religious instruction, discussions held within the home and from gatherings for worship at meeting houses and church assemblies.

The Planters were "a people of the Book", and consequently the children were expected to become proficient in reciting passages that were read to them from the Scriptures. To a considerable extent, they were self-taught, especially as they studied the Bible for rules of conduct.

Their education of a secular vein was not much different from that of the Acadian young people as "young men were not to marry unless the girl could weave a piece of cloth, and the young man could make a pair of wheels."

The earliest known education given in a school in Horton Township was provided through the Society for the Propagation of the Gospel (S.P.G.), and a subscription in 1763 was to add to funds provided by the society. The missionary-teacher of the Church of England served in the area for only a few years.

Most settlers preferred a non-denominational teacher and would hire itinerants on shares. Those engaged were miserably paid and seldom stayed for more than a year. A former historian of this town, Dr. Ronald S. Longley, wrote of these "travelling pedagogues", stating that "their stay in each house was too short for their comfort, but too long for their hosts who could not afford either the tax or the room." It has been reported that Cornelius Fox was schoolmaster of Horton and Cornwallis from 1772 to 1798.

The first Education Act of 1766 required that teachers be examined by a minister of the community or two justices of the peace, all of the Church of England, and no papists; this latter part was annulled in 1786.

The Act of 1811 also stipulated that the course offerings would consist of orthography, reading, writing, and arithmetic. By 1826 the government endeavoured to make schooling mandatory; but parents were expected to pay forty shillings per child, and other monies were required to be raised in a community to help offset costs, "as they see fit." A board of school commissioners was to be established in each schooling district to oversee their school. When Horton Academy began classes in 1829, Edward Fitch conducted the primary school in a separate building.

By 1830 elementary education was not only promoted and enforced in Horton Township but also throughout the province. In 1833 Joseph Dennison received a licence to teach school.

Probably 1876, from cupola of first College Hall, burned 1877. Right: Presbyterian Church; centre: school house; left: Methodist Church.

Legend has it that before the incorporation of Wolfville, schooling was first carried out in the basement of Kent Lodge, as well as in the basement of the T. A. S. DeWolf house. Prior to the Proclamation of the Free School Act by Premier Sir Charles Tupper in 1864, the first official "school" in the village stood on the north side of Main Street, where classes were held upstairs in the Temperance Hall, on the 1980 site of R. L. MacDonald and Associates. After 1864 the Wolfville School was located on Highland Avenue at the southwest corner of the present school grounds, and it was a grade school. In 1888 the building housed three departments: Primary, Intermediate, and Advanced; 161 pupils under Principal J. L. Bishop. The building also housed the town jail and had on its roof the town fire bell.

As there was growing agitation by the turn of the century for better facilities, much time was spent at "annual meetings" to discuss enlarging or building new facilities. Primary classes were held at Witter's Hall, where now stands the present C. H. Porter building, and by 1891 parents pressured for a kindergarten class. This class was held also in Witter Hall until all classes could be under "one roof".

The school board meeting of April 1892, comprised of E. W. Sawyer, G. W. Borden, C. R. Starr, B. Witter, I. W. Caldwell, and Secretary Walter Brown, voted to build and equip a new school house for children up to Grade IX. Sawyer visited Boston to view the Fuller and Warner system.

The new building, the MacKay School, was erected on what was then the extension of College Street, now Acadia Street, and named to honour Superintendent of Education A. H. MacKay. The structure was two storeys high, and had one of the most modern heating, ventilation, and sanitation systems. It was built to accommodate 300 students and was considered "second to none in the county". Contractor F. W. Woodworth erected the building.

In 1897 new principal Robie W. Ford and the School Board decided to

ACROSS THE DYKES,
FROM ACADIA SEMINARY

Second College Hall, and Seminary. Across Main Street: the Academy Rooming House, and the Manual Training building.

expand the educational offerings from Grade IX to Grade X, and possibly to Grade XI. In the *Novascotian* W. E. M. wrote that Wolfville possessed too many trees; streets were "forest tunnels". Otherwise, it was a pretty town, well-painted, fences in order. He had talked with Principal Ford and his five teachers.

The School Board used a variety of locations for teaching purposes. In 1892 the Manual Training School was located at the Edward Young Hall and gave a three-year course; Leslie R. Fairn became the new principal in 1899. Five years later the board received a report that the Tabernacle School was equipped, with Fred Woodworth as teacher.

The community expressed itself through the school. When the lady teachers petitioned for Easter Monday as a holiday, this was granted. W. H. Chase enriched the library through a gift in 1907, and the basketball team played against Acacia Villa school in 1908. In 1909 Mrs. (Dr.) Crowell formed an Anti-cigarette League among the boys, with thirty-four members who wore maple leaf badges. The *Acadian* felt in 1914 that at least one woman should be on the School Board. The graduation was held in 1915 in the Opera House. Night school began in 1920 at the school building, with twenty who desired to improve their education and could not during the day.

The town continued to grow, and according to the 1912 census there were 285 prospective students to be educated. Following World War I an extra class had to be situated in the Town Hall, where Acadia Theatre is located. The school held what was reported as its first exhibition, with sports on the college campus, followed by a prize exhibition of flowers and vegetables at the rink.

The School Board and the Town Council were under pressure either to enlarge existing facilities or to build another school bordering the MacKay School. In 1920 council initiated action to purchase land along Acadia Street to expand school facilities. However, ratepayers on purchasing the "Schofield property'' on Acadia Street, and by one vote rejected the proposal.

The suggestion was made again as the proponents became better organized, and this time they were successful. Ratepayers agreed in January 1921 to vote $20,000 to purchase the property and to construct a new school. Leslie R. Fairn, a former teacher on staff, now a contractor, was given the contract.

At a meeting in June 1921, the ratepayers agreed to borrow an additional $22,000 to complete building and equipping the classrooms. The new school, named after H. F. Munro, provincial superintendent of schools, was constructed during the principalship of B. C. Silver, (Robie Ford had retired that spring). It consisted of ten classrooms for the Advanced and Intermediate Departments, with the MacKay building housing the Primary areas. A Boys' Club organized in 1921, and a Girls' Club formed in 1922.

Difficulties at that time were the same as faced by today's teachers and administrators. The *Acadian* reported in October 1925 "the problem in local schools caused by students who either do not have the mental capacity to learn or through irregular attendance, fail to learn. It is thought that a new department with a specialized teacher be used to handle these students." It would take another forty years before a reading specialist would be hired to assist those with learning disabilities.

The local school did well in contests. The 1927 Interscholastic Track and Field Meet was held at Wolfville, and at the 1928 Maritime Junior Track Meet the town was represented by Vernon Eville, Churchill Connors, Harold Mitchell, John Eaton, L. H. Hutchinson, and B. Wade. Local students won eleven of eighteen prizes in 1935 in an English competition sponsored by Ceylon Tea of Montreal. Ernest Forbes Young obtained first prize.

In 1926, the first school on the present school grounds was demolished to provide greater playground area, with facilities for Primary students. In this same year the School Board took drastic action to enforce attendance. In October 1927, "the board agreed to enforce the Compulsory Attendance Act, whereby all children of school age must attend."

The Munro school building, opened in 1921.

1926-27. High School Basketball. Top row: Mabel Bigelow, Marion Eaton, Miss Porter (bus. manager), Miss Archibald (coach); middle row: Muriel Cox, Gertrude Duncanson; bottom row: Maie DeWitt, Ruth Ingraham, Ruth Glendinning, Ethel Ingraham.

1929. High School Football. Top row: K. Whitman, J. Eaton, W. Oliver (captain), L. Macpherson, L. Shaw, V. Duncanson, M. Hennigar, T. Baird; middle row: R. Porter, J. Roach, A. Tedford, R.W. Johnson (Vice-principal and Coach), A. Duncanson, K. Warren, H. McLeod; bottom row: W. Lockhart, R. Forbes, R. Coldwell, R. Lightfoot

School teams continued active in sports. The high school hockey team won the Valley League of 1928-1929, with players: W. Oliver, T. Baird, L. Smith, L. Hutchinson, M. Sanford, J. Roach, L. Shaw, C. Cohen. Vice-Principal R. W. Johnson was their coach. The football team of 1929 had players: K. Whitman, J. Eaton, W. Oliver (Captain), L. Macpherson, L. Shaw, V. Duncanson, T. Baird, R. Porter, J. Roach, A. Tedford, A. Duncanson, K. Warren, H. McLeod, W. Lockhart, R. Forbes, R. Coldwell, R. Lightfoot, and again R. W. Johnson was coach.

With George Nowlan as president, the Home and School Association organized in 1937; in 1938 Principal B. C. Silver went to Edinburgh University for further studies; George MacKenzie was acting principal in his absence. Silver returned as principal the next year but resigned to become Halifax County Inspector of Schools. He was replaced by O. R. Porter, teacher on staff, with Charles Eaton as vice-principal.

The students had varied interests. In 1934 they produced their first Glooscap Yearbook under editor E. Keith Forbes, and in 1941 the Glooscap was in magazine form. They won top honours in 1944 in the Kings County Drama Festival, when they received the H. F. Sipprell trophy. In 1945 the school installed a film projector, and the cadets won the Strathcona Award for proficiency in drill and marksmanship. The students won their third Sipprell trophy in 1948. The Boys' and Girls' Club united to form the Student Union under the presidency of Merritt Gibson.

By the 1950s Wolfville witnessed not only a "building boom" following World War II but also a "baby boom". The school commissioners held discussions with council, trying to determine whether the current overcrowding of schools was temporary. After many meetings, committing $4,500 to buy a vacant Temperance Hall for Industrial Arts and evening Continuing Education classes, the School Board decided that enrollment would increase 50% by 1963. Considerable controversy ensued; one councillor questioned the accuracy of these predictions.

Meanwhile, Mayor Eric Balcom stressed the need for a new high school because the present structure would provide for only the known needs of the day; additional classes would be needed. Council was urged to act quickly, to request grant money from the provincial government. Council was not as eager as Mayor Eric Balcom "to get on with the job," as major expenditures for sewer and water had been undertaken in the late 1940s. Also, the Civic Building had been completed, and town expended $100,000 for streets in 1951.

The School Board continued to exert pressure and suggested that council use money acquired from the sale of the Town Electric Commission to N.S. Power Commission. Although council was reluctant to hold a plebiscite on a new school, it did accept the recommendation to buy the Hughes property, $17,000 for the land, and to convert the property into classrooms and industrial arts facilities. The building was named the Silver Building by the Board of School Commissioners, in recognition of B. C. Silver and his years as principal.

The School Board felt that this was a temporary solution and continued to press council for a new building. The board authorized a preliminary plan for a five-room building which could quickly and easily be constructed. Local architect Ron. Peck was commissioned to draw up the plans.

The mayor met with government officials at Halifax, was discouraged about grant money for school construction, and was informed that the government disliked the idea of the town taking money from the sale of the Electric Commission funds for school expenditures. To add to the board's frustrations and dilemma, a plebiscite was held in July 1954 to approve borrowing funds to construct the five-room school, only to see the proposal defeated. The chairman of the board, Dr. Gordon Wheelock, resigned because of removal to Halifax.

High School Basketball. Bottom row: Gertrude Phinney, Teacher Ella Warren, Virginia MacLean; middle row: Marion Eaton, Waittie Stackhouse; top group: Helen Ingraham, Annie Fitch, Edna Doyle.

New chairman Nelson Grant and the board again urged council to quick action to alleviate the overcrowding. Council now decided to confer with the Minister of Education and municipal officials for permission to hold another ratepayers meeting. This was granted, and Ron. Peck was commissioned to revise his plans; a proposal for a new high school was submitted by the board. This building would have a library, science laboratory, and a potential of eight classrooms. The board proposed that, with the addition of the new building, along with the Munro Building which was to house the Intermediate section, and MacKay Building to house the Primary section, the 600 students and future needs would be completely cared for.

Construction was estimated to cost $185,000, partly covered by a $30,000 grant from the government. The ratepayers approved the project, and M. L. Wallace, local contractor, constructed the building. In 1955 council purchased for $16,000 the Longley property next to the school grounds as the new school site, and the Longley house was moved to Prospect Street. In March 1956, the official opening took place, and well-known and much-loved Dr. M. R. Elliott laid the cornerstone. George C. Nowlan, M.P. for Digby-Annapolis-Kings, presented a portrait of Queen Elizabeth.

In 1958 C. E. Eaton became acting principal, while O. R. Porter was on leave-of-absence, and on Porter's return in 1959 Eaton became principal of Horton District High School. Former teacher, and then principal of Barrington District High School, Scott Sheffield, assumed the vice-principal's duties.

By the 1960s there was a growing agitation to have better recreational facilities, as well as proper quarters for Industrial Arts and Home Economics. For many years the Home Economics Department was in the basement of the Acadia Seminary building, and the industrial arts shops, then called Manual Training, had been located in the Edward Young Hall, opened in 1892, burned in 1915. This large structure stood near where the War Memorial Gymnasium is now. The department then moved to the first floor of Rhodes Engineering Building. When Munro School was built, Industrial Arts moved to that building. From there it moved to the Temperance Building (now Legion Hall), and then to the B. C. Silver Building before finally being housed in the new high school.

For many years students used the gymnasium facilities at Acadia but after World War II, and the need by the university for the space, gymnastic activities were housed temporarily in the Curling and Badminton Building. As these facilities were considered inadequate and forced students to leave the school grounds to attend classes, many expressed the need to have all facilities under one roof, on the school grounds.

Following the provincial government announcement that it was interviewing municipal councils from Windsor to Digby about establishing such a facility, considerable interest was generated in having a multi-community vocational high school at Wolfville. If the project was completed by March 1963, all the cost would be covered by the provincial government, with three-quarters of the money reimbursed from the federal government. Teachers for the courses offered from Grades VIII to XII would be selected by the Department of Education, and maintenance costs would be divided 60/40 between the province and municipality.

Council indicated an interest in the proposal, and the School Board drew up a plan to serve 300 students from Hants, Kings, and Annapolis Counties. The Wolfville project called for a staff of twenty, with facilities for ten workshops, gymnasium and five or six classrooms, located at the intersection of Pleasant and Highland Avenues, with plenty of room for play and parking facilities.

The county had a better offer, in the opinion of the government, with county land bordering the shiretown of Kentville. There the Kings County Vocational School was built, with C. C. Cunningham as its first principal. Wolfville students were accepted in the programme.

Council hesitated to build new facilities on its own; they claimed the assessment rate too high, and some members of the council felt that education was overfunded at the expense of other town services. At this juncture a "Concerned Parents Group" organized, and a small but effective group encouraged civic-minded citizens to stand for council, pledged for the much-needed facilities. In the election of 1961 A. Burpee Balcom, Jr. defeated incumbent Mayor Ronald Longley; new councillors gave support to the project.

Chairman of the School Board, Victor MacKay, appointed a Building Committee with councillor and board member Jack F. Herbin as chairman, the mayor, O. Rex Porter, Leslie C. Crosby, Wayne C. Hatt, and Erik S. Hansen. The board requested Ron. Peck to draw up plans for the new addition.

The School Board suggested that council get money through Municipal Development and Loan Act of 1964, and Wolfville applied for $274,000, two-thirds of the estimated cost. An information meeting, chaired by Mayor Eric Balcom, explained the plans, and on July 3 1964 the ratepayers voted to borrow. V. C. Woodworth was chosen as contractor, and construction started in the spring of 1965 with the removal of the B. C. Silver building so that the addition could be joined to the existing structure.

In June 1964 the students, teachers and School Board honoured Gladys I. West on her retirement after fifty-two consecutive years as a teacher at Wolfville. Raymond Jefferson, who replaced her, organized the Junior High program.

The administration of the schools was recomposed at this time. O. R. Porter became Supervising Principal; Scott Sheffield, Principal; David Graham, Vice-Principal; and Raymond Jefferson, Head Teacher of Junior High. Mrs. Kay Mitchell led the Intermediate Department in the Munro Building, and Mrs. Joan Eaton had charge of the MacKay School. Twenty-seven teachers were on staff at the official opening on June 18, 1966. The new complex had an auditorium-gymnasium, Home Economics and Industrial Arts Departments, and four additional classrooms upstairs with an Assembly Room. The Grade XI classroom was converted into an enlarged administrative office, with two classrooms made into Staff and Library Rooms.

After Scott Sheffield's resignation in 1967, David Graham became principal, and Raymond Jefferson vice-principal. In 1969 Jefferson and Everett Pugh were appointed vice-principals, with O. Rex Porter as supervising principal.

This year was momentous, as the Minister of Education proposed that three areas in the province amalgamate their systems, including Kings County. A number of financial incentives induced school districts to agree and receive 100% capital costs for any new construction.

As the MacKay building needed replacing, the School Board and council were encouraged to consider action, but council hesitated. By 1970 council agreed to the plan for the county. Donald M. MacPherson became principal, and Raymond Jefferson vice-principal, as O. R. Porter joined the Amalgamated School Board staff.

Now the town prompted the board to build a new elementary school. Convinced that the present building was inadequate, the board agreed to a new school. Principal MacPherson and others proposed an "open classroom concept", an idea relatively new to Nova Scotia.

In 1972 Leslie R. Fairn and Associates drew up plans, and V. C. Woodworth Ltd. got the contract. The Munro School and MacKay School were demolished, and in the late fall the new premises were in use. At the January 1973 official opening Minister of Education, the Honourable Allan E. Sullivan, unveiled the plaque.

The school was unique in design, as large open classrooms or "pods" could be separated by dividers into classrooms, all under one roof. A spacious Resource-Library Centre, which included provision for a reading specialist, for music, and for art, was part of the complex.

One of the fears of amalgamation was that the high school would be closed out, the Grade X and XI students compelled to bus to Horton District High School for Grade XII. By 1974 a number of public meetings discussed the issue, one of the largest being chaired by Dr. James Perkin, chairman of the Wolfville Advisory Council to the School Board. The board revealed their decision in March 1976 that "Horton District High School could offer a wider variety of courses, and furthermore that it was more economical . . . than to try and maintain and enlarge staff and facilities at Wolfville." Students of Gaspereau School could complete their Junior High in Wolfville, by being bussed to the town.

The school staff took time out in 1976 to pay tribute to Leslie Crosby for his long service, and the Amalgamated School Board honoured Charles (Chuck) E. Eaton upon his retirement. In 1977 Raymond Jefferson received a two-year appointment to the provincial executive of the Teachers Union.

By 1980, Wolfville School offered programs from Primary to Grade IX with a staff of thirty-one teachers and a student body of 500. It has become a modern educational system, one that has developed a sense of pride and satisfaction in students and parents.

Principals of Wolfville schools: J. L. Bishop, 1864?-1891; M. S. Read, 1891-92; C. E. Seaman, 1892-94; John Fowler Godfrey, 1894-97; R. W. Ford, 1897-1921; B. C. Silver, 1921-40; Acting Principal George MacKenzie, 1938,39; Supervising Principal O. R. Porter, 1940-70; Acting Principal Charles E. Eaton, 1958,59; Scott Sheffield, 1965-67; David Graham, 1967-69; Donald M. MacPherson, 1970-.

2. Acadia Institutions

a. Horton Academy

The function of Wolfville as a social and religious centre and as a nexus of transportation routes was well established. The final influence on its growth was its development into an educational centre. This came about as an effect of the religious situation in the early 1800s.

The comparatively few Baptists of Nova Scotia, New Brunswick, and Prince Edward Island agreed to begin a school for boys, which was a daring decision but one out of necessity. The common school system was not adequate for older boys; there was need of an institution on a seminary level. The Episcopal church maintained a classical school at Halifax and later a similar school at Windsor. From these schools came graduates who were the professional leaders of society and with power and influence. Others saw this happen and desired to experience such rewards. However, the primary motive was to provide schooling towards the Christian ministry and the professions.

The founding of an academy in 1828 was not easy. The religious entry tests at Windsor discouraged Baptist families from sending their boys to that institution. This situation helped plant the idea that Baptists might have a school of their own. The Presbyterian institution at Pictou had opened in 1811, was too far away and uncertain of continuity in the 1820s.

One factor to consider at this time was the widespread opposition among Baptists to trained clergy who were suspected as less holy and sincere because of their much learning. But several clergy sensed their need of improved education for a more adequate ministry. A small group of leading Baptist clergymen decided the matter as the highly respected pastors revealed publicly their feelings about the lack of education.

Partly because Kings College graduates conferred with concerned Baptists, at Upper Horton in June 1828 the Baptist Association members were convinced of the need of a trained clergy. Strong men openly confessed their lack and of the necessity of mental culture. The clergymen's voices choked with emotion, and tears flowed. The gathering was overwhelmed with surprise, and a movement began among the people — a new era in Baptist history, as they contributed to buy property for the academy.

Just previous to the Baptist Association meeting at Upper Horton a few men convened at the Fowler Hotel to consider conceiving a Literary and Theological Seminary. They agreed to form or recommend a Baptist Education Society, which at the association resulted in Horton Academy being organized, with an expanded program to train men and boys for their vocations.

A building was needed. The structure first used was an old, low, one-storey dwelling, situated exactly next to where the Main Street now runs and nearly in front of the first college building, on the sixty-five acres bought by a society of subscribers for 550 pounds from Jonathan Graham. Another account stated that the first academy was in a yellow house on the mound where the Henry Witter hardware store stood later, on the south side and opposite the present playing field, and the farm house was on the James Graham property. The house was remembered by the first principal, Ashael Chapin, as brown in colour, while Reverend John Pryor, who succeeded Chapin, recalled it as yellow. A later writer described it as the one-storey old yellow school house.

It stood where the Main Street now runs, and a more recent chart showed it as nearly opposite the present site of the university president's house and described it as the location of the old red house.

Ashael Chapin stayed only one year before he returned to the United States. After the first three years the Provincial Treasury provided 300 pounds annually to help the school to finance.

When Dr. Pryor took charge of the academy he lived in the Randall House, according to Mrs. William Sommerville's elderly aunt. In 1835 he had three children and two servants.

The aforesaid aunt said the boys came to the school with nothing but a red cotton hankie with a few little knickknacks in it and only the clothes on their backs. In 1907 the *Acadia Athenaeum* published an account of Wolfville in the 1840s; "There was no school in those days beside the academy. The class books were elementary. The three "Rs" received most attention. Matriculation requirements for entry into the college were not very severe."

The first academy building had opened its doors on March 29, 1829, without denominational restrictions. Wolfville and surrounding areas were well represented in the list of 1830 to 1833. That earliest list named Wolfville pupils: Charles DeWolf, Elisha DeWolf, Harris? DeWolf, Stephen DeWolf, Edwin DeWolf, Patrick Cortan, Charles Randall, Thomas Neary?, Thomas Johnson, William Graham, William Johnson, Thomas DeWolf, Thomas Burns, Thomas Ratchford, George Eaton, Alexander Eaton, Isaac Graham, William Kirpatrick, James Woodworth, Edward Riley, James Kirkpatrick, John Spinney, James R. DeWolf, Edward Eaton.

The old farm house was followed by a structure for the principal and for classrooms. Before that, a private home, the Charles Randall house, was hired until the new building was ready. An academic hall, with recitation rooms, was erected, the design approved by a Boston architect. This larger building was needed to house the principal, the classrooms and a number of the students, all completed by the fall of 1831. The hall had a projecting portico of ten feet, supported by a colonnade of six Ionic pillars in front. Then a boarding house was erected in 1835 on the hill, 60'x40', running north and south and close to the Academy Hall.

The studies included Greek New Testament, Homer's Iliad and Odyssey, Euripides, Sophocles. In Latin they studied the Reader, Caesar, Virgil, Livy, Juvenal. In the English language their subjects were Natural and Moral Philosophy, Mathematics, Surveying, Mensuration, Navigation, Euclid's Elements and Algebra, Bookkeeping, Geography, Grammar, Arithmetic. This appears to be a formidable list but much of this was handled in an elementary fashion.

W. B. Hamilton, of Brookfield, attended the academy from 1838 to 1840. He and his father and a former student drove by sleigh, leaving the Halifax road at Elmsdale, travelling the Nine Mile River road to its junction with "Indian Road", then across the country to Windsor and Horton — a three-day journey. Young Hamilton was only twelve years old, amidst strangers, and had a miserable time coping with the poor food, the cold quarters. When he returned home he left Mud Creek in a little sloop-rigged open boat, without a compass or even a watch among those aboard. The stormy trip took a few days to reach Truro and then home.

Around 1840 about thirty-five pupils resided in the Horton Academy boarding house, and with as many day-scholars from the village. Food was meagre and "positively abominable" in quality, according to one boy's recollections. Wolfville families were fortunate to have the academy in their community. Some who attended during the years 1856 to 1858 included James Fitch, George Wallace, Charles Eben, and William Chase.

Horton Academy principals: Ashael Chapin, 1829; Reverend John Pryor, 1830-39; Edward Blanchard, 1840-43; C. D. Randall, 1843-51; J. W. Hartt, 1851-59; Reverend T. A. Higgins, 1860-74; Professor J. T. Tufts, 1874-81; A. W. Armstrong, 1881-83; J. F. Tufts, 1883-88; I. B. Oakes, 1888-99; H. L. Brittain, 1899-1904; E. W. Sawyer, 1904-06; C. J. Mersereau, 1906-08; E. W. Robinson, 1908-10; W. L. Archibald, 1911-26; E. W. Robinson, 1927-40; L. C. Trites, 1941-59.

The beginning of Horton Academy proved a needed boost for the village, which up to this point had the potential to be agricultural and rural, but with no motivating force to establish a stable economy. The educational institutions helped set up the community on a stronger base.

b. Acadia College, University

After providing ten years of commendable educational training and leadership for the boys and young men of Baptist and other denominations, some people felt that the educational scheme required a college level of schooling. Because a Baptist professor was not included in the first staff of the proposed provincial Dalhousie College at Halifax an unexpected stimulus was evidenced. Baptists decided in 1838 that they must have their own college for their young men. The result was Queen's College, the name soon changed to Acadia. The situation and the increased desire for education among Baptists prompted the erection of a college building, constructed "without money". This daring venture of faith began in the spring of 1843 as friends of the school sent by water transport the building materials, such as lumber, nails, glass and all sorts of contributions, some of which were turned into money.

Probably 1876. First College Hall, with Academy Rooming House to the left, and Sawyer House to the right.

Because quarters larger than the Academy Hall were necessary for college students, a three-storey building was constructed, 150′x35′ and incorporated with the old Academy Hall, running through the academy building transversely. Plans were prepared by Professor E. A. Crawley and Deacon Samuel Kinsman, with Edmond Davison and his brother Lewis, both of Greenwich, in charge of construction. They designed and made the four Ionic pillars. The east wing was ready for use in 1844, and the west wing was finished in 1854. The building also had a handsome cupola, with the roof of the Academy Hall directly under the dome of the new building.

The *Acadian* editor, B. O. Davidson, recalled that in 1869 Wolfville was a decidedly attractive and well-kept village with many commodious homes and pretty gardens enclosed by white-washed fences. The people took pride in their surroundings and particularly in "anniversary time" when the closing of the educational institutions on "the hill" was held. People vied with each other in an effort to make the village attractive to visitors. That was a great occasion when on the first Thursday in June from early morn the place was thronged with friends of Acadia, including many country people who drove in by horse and wagon especially groomed and polished for the event.

Acadia College and the town enjoyed each other during these years. Town outings were attended by both students and faculty, and college lectures and social events were of great interest to the townspeople. Some college instructors taught in the town also. Lessons in voice, music and oil painting seemed great favourites. "Town" and "Gown" had a pleasant relationship.

The presidents, principals, professors and teachers of college and academy played significant roles in developing the community and in attracting families to the area. Wolfville was very much the presence of its educational institutions. Today, there is property on the Acadia campus valued into the millions of dollars, and the university now enrolls over 2800 students. Obviously, the university is the town's largest industry.

A letter in the *Western Chronicle* of Kentville in April 1891 reported mostly on new buildings and property changes in Wolfville. Then the writer claimed that the manufacturing emphasis of the community was upon producing students, in which Americans sent raw material, and Wolfville returned the finished product.

Town and university continued to have friendly ties, evident when Dr. A. W. Sawyer died in August 1907, after about thirty-eight years of association with the university; business houses closed for the funeral. Of considerable interest to the community was the disastrous fire that destroyed in December 1920 the second college hall, when five pianos, the captured German airplane, and R. W. Tuft's collection of stuffed birds were lost. In December 1948 the town honoured past president Dr. F. W. Patterson and new president Dr. Watson Kirkconnell at a dinner at Hotel Paramount. An educational period terminated as Horton Academy closed its doors in June 1959.

Dr. James M. R. Beveridge became president in 1964. When a youth, he had come from Scotland and had received his schooling at Wolfville, including the academy and the university. He was the first Acadia president from this community. He married Jean Eaton, daughter of Reverend and Mrs. Frank

H. Eaton of the Wolfville Baptist church. A new era began in June 1974 when Nova Scotia senior citizens were welcomed by universities to take classes without charge, with or without credits. About 100 from the town and its surroundings attended the regular classes annually. In November 1978 the Board of Trade was addressed by new president Dr. Alan M. Sinclair, and in the fall of 1980 noted artist Alex Colville became Acadia's new chancellor, replacing Nobel prizewinning scientist Dr. Charles Huggins.

Some other significant Acadia events: first class, numbering nineteen, began the college course, January 1839; faculty were Presidents Reverend John Pryor and Reverend E. A. Crawley, jointly administering; Pryor served alone as president from 1847, with Isaac Chipman continuing as professor; third President, Dr. J. M. Cramp, 1851; fourth President, Dr. A. W. Sawyer, 1869; first college building burned, 1877, replaced in 1879; fifth President, Dr. Thomas Trotter, 1897; sixth President, Dr. W. B. Hutchinson, 1907; seventh President, Dr. George B. Cutten, 1910; Dr. F. W. Patterson, 1923.

c. Female Seminaries

To meet the needs for female education, private schools or seminaries for young ladies sprang up as early as 1830. These schools increased in number for about forty years, especially in the Annapolis Valley area of Nova Scotia. The New England descendants of the Planters sought education for their girls beyond the elementary level provided by the public school system. The boys attended church-related academies at Pictou, Windsor, and Wolfville but girls could be educated only at the boarding schools in communities throughout the province or join special day school classes in the cities.

Wolfville was provided with schools for girls. The first was that of Mrs. Margaret Best whose husband Henry had been an official in the navy at Halifax before his death. They had lived formerly in this area west of Wolfville, and Mrs. Best and her family returned to begin a boarding school. She located briefly at the Simon Fitch home in Wallbrook, then in 1835 at Randall House in Wolfville for about ten years. She and her two daughters taught afterwards at Elisha DeWolf, Jr.'s house on west Main Street, at "Elmwood", while the owners were in England. This school ceased about 1855.

William Troop and his two daughters began their school in 1850, ceased in 1855. The course of study at these schools involved much time in drawing, painting, music, and sometimes French and arithmetic. The school was located in Rose Cottages near Scott's Corner, now at Maple Avenue. The Misses Wells opened a school in 1855 at the Randall House, operating it for four or five years.

In July 1858 Reverend John Chase opened a boarding school for young ladies in a large residence used for his family also. His two daughters followed the Mount Holyoke plan of education, they having attended that Massachusetts institution. The Chase School was located opposite the present Baptist church where now stands Reid's Irving Service Station. The school lasted until the spring of 1859, and the building then became the property of the Baptist Education Society, with the school a branch of Horton Academy.

The staff of the school married later, most of the husbands being related to this community. Maria Chase became the wife of Acadia College President

A. W. Sawyer; Rebecca Chase married Professor J. E. Wells; Alice Shaw taught during the last term, began her own school here during the next year, and married Reverend Alfred Chipman whose home was Berwick; Minnie Johnson became Mrs. R. L. Weatherby; and Mary Beckwith taught music, no report of her marriage.

The female department of Horton Academy opened January 1861. Alice T. Shaw had graduated in 1857 from Mount Holyoke Female Seminary and had conducted a Select School for girls from August 1859 to the end of 1860, at Berwick. Because the Baptists needed to provide for young ladies, as they had much earlier for boys and young men (and the Methodists had started their ladies school in 1854), they prevailed upon Alice Shaw to begin a seminary at Wolfville.

She agreed, and twenty pupils accompanied the new principal from Berwick. Alice zealously followed the Mount Holyoke plan wherein the girls did their own cooking and housekeeping. The educational standards were high, with academic studies and the usual music and art work. Two of her sisters and a music teacher assisted in the school which welcomed the villagers also. After six months and at the suggestion of one of the pupils, the school adopted the name of "Grand Pre Seminary" because of the nearness to historic Grand Pre. Classes ceased in 1870 due to financial difficulties.

After joining with Pine Grove Seminary at Middleton until 1872, the school again became a department of the academy and moved to the Acadia campus on "the hill", with mixed classes. In 1879 they got their much-desired separate residence and quarters for classes — "the Sem.".

The first to graduate was Annie Shaw, Alice's sister, who in June 1862 represented "the dawn of a new day for females." Clara Marshall (Mrs. E. W. Raymond) graduated from the college in 1884, the first female to receive a degree from Acadia, exactly a century before this account was published.

3. Acacia Villa School

Nine years before female children of Wolfville were given an opportunity to receive an advanced form of education, a "vocational school" for boys and young men began at Grand Pre. In July 1852 the Acacia Villa School opened at Hortonville to meet the needs of youths, some as young as age seven, who wished training in practical business and academic subjects. The school also provided music instruction and prepared candidates for college education.

Joseph R. Hea started the school and was principal until 1860, when Arthur McNutt Patterson conducted it until 1907. His son A. H. Patterson had been the school's business manager for fifteen years and also a teacher part of that time. He now became the principal.

The boarding school had extensive facilities and attracted many pupils. In 1897 eighty young men attended, paying $166 per year and using five buildings by 1900. Some resided in the school and others found lodging with local families. The student body included Sir Robert Borden as a lad, Isaac Walton Killam, L. E. Shaw, W. H. Chase, and Henry Watson.

During World War I the school began accepting females, mostly for business courses, penmanship and music classes. Gertie Dennison recalled that a racetrack, skating rink, parade ground and armouries were available to the pupils. In 1980 only one of the buildings remained. Because the school became out moded, lacked student conveniences and staff, it closed in 1920. A monument marks the school's location.

A non-academic use of the local school grounds—preparing the ice for skating.

XII.

WAR-RELATED ACTIVITIES

Although wars seem to start in big cities where authority is centered it is not only the big cities that are affected. War drains the towns and little villages of their youth and vigor, and so it has been with Wolfville. Young men of the town have been involved in all of the major wars that in some way involved Canada, from colonial wars to patriotic wars. They were motivated in the same way that young men from other Nova Scotian communities were motivated, with the same results. Some made the supreme sacrifice; others returned to pick up life where they had left off.

As far as is known Wolfville was never itself in the centre of conflict, although nearby Grand Pre was militarily sensitive until the Expulsion of the Acadians in 1755, and Windsor, in the neighboring county of Hants, was part of the colony's fortification system, first against the French and the Indians, and then against the revolting colonies of America.

All communities of the Colony of Nova Scotia were affected by political decisions that sometimes resulted in war. During the incumbency of Charles Lawrence as governor of Nova Scotia (1756-60) the British government authorized him to establish a militia, and the first provincial assembly of 1758 accommodated him, requiring all males between sixteen and sixty to bear arms and attend musters and military exercises. Later, the threat of an American invasion resulted in a new act for greater protection. There appeared no opposition to compulsory military service in the Horton area but the Parrsboro portion of King's County was reluctant to conform to the requirements.

In 1760 palisaded forts were erected in the Minas townships. A.W. Eaton's *History of King's County* records that the fort erected at Horton probably was only the old Fort Vieux Logis restored to accommodate a small garrison. The fort at Grand Pre, called "Fort Mongague," was built on the hill south of Horton Landing, overlooking the river. Old cannon were readied for defence but the "Barracks" was replaced in 1780 when an enlarged provincial defence system was created.

The militia regiment was commissioned in 1761. When the government feared an attack by Indians and Acadians the militia took 130 Acadians into custody and transported them to Halifax. At the time of the outbreak of the American Revolutionary War in 1775 the Horton Light Infantry Company was made up of fifty men, and two companies went from King's County to protect Halifax. All inhabitants in the area, as well as all militiamen, were required to swear an oath of allegiance to the Crown, and magistrates were to report on each person. A special tax was levied to support the militia.

Regimental drill was regular up to about 1837 but it was neglected afterwards until 1860. The Cornwallis Company was disbanded in 1854, and this coincided with the Militia Act of 1855 which established a system of volunteer service, decreasing the practice of universal compulsory service.

In 1868 the Canadian parliament divided the country into nine military districts, and after 1870 conscription ceased. Only one King's County regiment remained.

The Village of Wolfville had a parade ground for training the militia. It was located on the north side of Main Street, west of the Graham House. Males from sixteen to sixty assembled once a year. This ground later became a cricket field where in August 1887 a new academy building was finished. The community's drill shed was located south of the Baptist Church on the present Tufts property, and the Graham House was the coach office, the express office, and headquarters for the militia.

The Militia Company had a church parade in September, 1896. Names associated with the group included: H.D. Gilmore, P. Bill, J.S. Heales, Arthur C. Starr, S. Jones, Geo. Franklin, S. Gilmore, Serg't D'Almaine, Lieut. O'Key (of Port Williams), L.S. Gowe, Lieut. Starr and Corp'l Stewart.

The first indication of the Boer War's affect on the town came in November 1899, when the *Western Chronicle* reported that Horace Jones, William Regan, and Arthur Lockwood had enlisted with the Canadian contingent to Africa. In the same month the Hon. Robert Borden donated two brass cannon to the University, and these were mounted on neat carriages in front of the College building. Mrs. Borden, wife of the Minister of the militia, requested the women to prepare emergency supply cases for voluoers to the African war. The King's Daughters assisted in this project, providing writing material.

Through the newspaper accounts the community followed the war closely. In March 1900, news of the Relief of Ladysmith arrived. Though this actually was a minor skirmish, it resulted in an overflow attendance at the Patriotic Concert given in College Hall, with a brass band, the College orchestra, the Seminary glee club, rifle and sword exercises, a reading and an address — all the essential components to feed a gargantuan patriotism, an emotion that was in Wolfville at least as fervent as the feeling towards religion. Over $300 was raised for the patriotic fund and $100 for the Indian Famine Fund.

As part of the celebration, a large procession of students from the College, Academy and Seminary, and the Council, with the band, marched through the town. Others made bonfires and set off sky rockets. They also burned the effigies of Paul Kruger, the African statesman, and other opponents of British sovereignty in the Transvaal.

When William Regan and Arthur Lockwood returned from the Transvaal they received a military parade in their honor, with "artistic and profuse decorations." Seventy citizens attended a dinner arranged by the band. Capt. C.H. Hensley, a former Wolfville resident, had died in Africa, and Charles Blair had offered his services but became ill at the embarkation point in Quebec and returned home.

Wolfville's part in the First World War was as dramatic as that for other Canadian towns. The newspaper accounts suggested that people knew little of the war because of censorship, but advertisements did appear with appeals for volunteers. The women of the community collected funds for the hospital ship to be given by "the women of Canada," and the local Red Cross collected magazines for sailors.

Evidence in the Town Council minutes reflected the presence of war. William Black, town clerk, was called up for active duty, although he apparently continued his work in the Town Office. In September 1914, the formation of a home guard was discussed. Citizens became involved in a variety of ways. Mrs. Rachel DeWolfe Archibald sent overseas more than 400 "bottles" of food, and was thanked by Queen Mary herself. In 1916 Council discussed using the local Boy Scout facilities to house military personnel temporarily stationed in Wolfville. They also looked for a place for the 219th Contingent to drill. In November 1917 Mayor J.E. Hales worked to find accommodations for the Military Exemption Tribunal during its stay in town. Later that year the Council voted to invest $2,500 of its "sinking fund" in Canadian Victory Bonds.

William Arthur Elderkin was the first Wolfville soldier to be killed in the First World War. However, many others survived and returned home. A committee formed in 1916 to greet returning soldiers. The men were met at the train by the Mayor, the Ladies Entertainment Committee, members of the Red Cross, the Imperial Order of the Daughters of the Empire, and the Give Service Girls. To come home after the fighting was a great thrill, and it was enjoyed by the veterans and townspeople alike.

The Give Service Girls were formed in 1917. They handled ticket sales and ushering at the Opera House, all their wages going to patriotic projects. The officers were: Mary Black (Pres.), Grace Shaw (Sec.-Treas.), Lalia Chase, Angela Herbin, and Hilda Fielding (executive). In May of 1918 sixty members of this group, and as many Boy Scouts, marched through the streets, led by the band. In the spring of 1918 the "Do Your Best Knitting Club," which had been organized two years before, was teaching women to knit for soldiers. The group donated $10 to the I.O.D.E. for the war effort.

First World War recruiting office.

Although most Wolfville men were patriotic and were sympathetic towards the reasons for the war, not all of them could go overseas to fight. For example, Ralph Benjamin Smallman, born in 1896 and who lived in West Main Street, graduated from Acadia University in 1917 and tried six times to enlist. He was rejected for "water on the knees." He wrote a friend in July that "all the boys I used to know have enlisted. A great many of my chums have been killed in France lately. It makes me wild to think that I can't go too." It was a common feeling among those who had to stay at home, for whatever reason. Smallman eventually got into the army, however, and was employed as an auditor in the divisional pay office of Military District No. 6 in Halifax. He wrote of Americans and Chinese landing, of convoys departing, of Ralph Connor speaking about the war. He wrote later, "In Wolfville there aren't five unmarried able chaps. Everyone has enlisted and a great many have been killed," as though both the act of enlisting and the final result were triumphs in themselves.

Then Smallman's letter of December 25 told of the "dull roar" after which glass flew in all directions. He held to a doorknob, then helped some girls and wounded down the seven flights of stairs. With all windows and doors smashed, he walked toward the northern end of the city where vast clouds of smoke spread over the place. "Dead were everywhere and hundreds of wounded were running back and forth." He had experienced the Halifax Explosion. He helped the Medical Relief Commission. Later he studied medicine and became a doctor. Wolfville's Private George Keeble died in the explosion while on guard duty.

Wolfville organized relief with a committee made up of former Mayor J.D. Chambers, Rev. R.F. Dixon, F.E. Wheelock. About sixty people came to Wolfville as refugees and they were cared for by the citizens.

Peace came in November 1918, and the town adjusted to the absence of war. The *Acadian* advocated the erection of a memorial for servicemen and a committee was formed at the suggestion of E. Percy Brown to ensure that all returned soldiers be given a suitable reception. Some of the soldiers brought back "Old Country" brides. The town imposed a poll tax of $4 on all men not owning property, but rebated to returned soldiers an amount related to the number of months they had served during the war.

In August 1919 the citizens honored the returned soldiers with a banquet, attended by Acadia President Dr. George B. Cutten and Lieut-Col. J.L. Ralston. Henry Ruffee proposed a toast, and Eugene Stackhouse responded. Musical selections were presented by Marie Wilson, Kathleen Prescott, Evelyn Duncanson, and the Wolfville Orchestra. In September the Wolfville branch of the Great War Veterans Association was formed and the officers were: Eugene Stackhouse (Pres.), Paul Davidson (Sec.Treas.), George Nowlan, George Dexter, B. Palmeter and James Amburg (Exec.)

Wolfville men who died for King and Country in the First World War are included: Frederick Abbott, Philip Beals, Robert C. Borden, George Buchanan, George B. Coldwell, Dallas C. Connor, Herbert C. Cornwell, Chester V. Dakin, H. Burton DeWolfe, Leonard C. Eaton, William Elderkin, Charles W. Ferris, Winfield A. Ferris, H. Clive Fielding,Charles W. Fitch, Frank O. Hutchinson, Stanley L. Jones, George F. Keeble, Rufus W. Lightfoot, Walter L. Lynch, Clyde C. Manning, George E. MacGregor, Arthur W. Pinch, Frank E. Porter, George A. Ritchie, E. Leslie Rogers, Charles W. Schofield, Frederick Sleep, Robert W. Spicer, Clifford C. Webster, Karl Woodman. Their names are inscribed in bronze on the town's war monument.

By 1920 the town was in the process of attempting to regroup and vitalize its progress in the wake of a devastating war. The Imperial Order of the Daughters of the Empire asked Council to help them bring a branch of the

The War Memorial.

Victorian Order of Nurses to Wolfville. In May the Council had started proceedings to raise money to erect "a memorial to fallen soldiers." The town had decorated its heroes, paid tribute to its lost sons, and turned its energies once again to the future. There was plenty of work to be done, a new social order to be dealt with, and the town's residents were eager to get on with the job.

The War Memorial tablet on the Post Office lawn was changed at the end of 1922 and placed at the base of the monument, the figure of a Canadian soldier standing at attention replacing it on top.

Canada was at war again in 1939, and Wolfville men and women went off to fight or to make the instruments of war in factories. Employment was high, and the financial difficulties of the depression years had disappeared. Although the people suffered the hardships of separation, rationing, and the constant concern for the enlisted, the wartime economy provided additional income.

Major W. Kenneth Fraser, then Mayor, organized in 1940 the No. 268 Cadet Corps, which began preparing youths for possible military service. After the First World War the community had received a German war gun and this was now shipped off to make bombs to return to Germany. The local office of the Wartime Prices and Trade Board provided sugar ration coupons, and the Wolfville platoon of the West Nova Scotia Regiment Reserve Force held their first rifle practice.

The *Acadian* reported in December 1944 that the Canadian Legion (Branch 74) had organized and about fifty ex-servicemen were present for the first meeting. Louis M. LeLacheur was chosen President.

The Royal Canadian Legion, originally a part of the British Empire Service League, now occupies a building on Main Street (once known as the "Tabernacle") and the organization actively pursues community activities related to recreational and cultural development of youth.

Bernard W. (Bob) Fullerton was the first Wolfville man to die in the Second World War, the report being made to his home in October of 1941. This convinced the community of the price that had to be paid for war, and plans were made to assist in any major catastrophe. School girls were taught home nursing and refugee work and how to raise money for the Queen's Fund or the Red Cross. Also early in 1942 the electric street lights were turned off and windows darkened due to new air raid precautions. Air raid wardens named were: Karl Nowlan, C.W. Small, Clarence Brown, R. VanWart, D. Ross Cochrane, W.D. Withrow, Otto Foshay, E. Wickwire and James Farris.

Nevertheless, there was optimism about the future, in spite of these preparations for the time when the war might come closer to home. Council began discussing post-war projects as early as 1943. These projects included building a permanent fence around the reservoir lands, completing permanent sidewalks, and erecting a new Town Hall and Civic Building as a memorial to fallen soldiers of the Second World War.

Members of the Citizens Casualty Committee and the Civilian Emergency Committee encouraged planning to make sure Wolfville might survive the attacks of more tangible enemies. Council, having been told in 1942 that "the whole of the Province of Nova Scotia has been declared a vulnerable area," dispensed two gallons of sand to each household in town and requested citizens to "cooperate fully in this effort of the council to assist in the protection of (your) premises against fire which may be caused by incendiary bombs."

The town also purchased ten stretchers for use of the fire company, and an air raid signal which, the Mayor reported, "had not been heard in certain sections of the town (during a trial blackout) and was therefore not satisfactory." In a discussion on air raids that same year Council had decided that "Church bells and the town fire bell (at Acadia) shall be rung in conjunction with the sounding of the fire sirens."

More rationing was introduced, with meat the scarce food in September. Ration books were distributed by C.W. Fairn from his office on Main Street. Air raid districts had been set up, with wardens assigned to each district. The anticipated disaster never occurred but the town was thoroughly prepared for it.

By 1945 plans were being made to care for returned soldiers, and a rehabilitation committee was formed, with A.R. MacPherson as chairman. The town was ready for victory in May of 1945. Flags flew, the siren sounded, church bells rang, car horns tooted, and the V-E Day parade was accompanied by fireworks and a bonfire on Raymond Field. When the Japanese surrendered in August it seemed anti-climactic, and there was less excitement.

Veterans who gave their lives in World War II were: Cyril G. Cavanagh, Kenneth W. Eagles, Bernard W. Fullerton, F.R.W.R. Gow, Samuel R. Kenny, Leo M. Regan, Donald M. Smith, J. Beverley Starr, Alfred G. Stevens, Jack Stewart.

After the war 200 veterans returned home and were met by a committee providing each man with a scroll and a wallet. As the Korean War began in 1950 there were nineteen Wolfville and vicinity men enlisted in the Canadian contingent. Weldon Barkhouse failed to come back.

The continued threat of war suggested the need for adequate civil defence and a committee was formed in 1950 to prepare for the consequence of an atomic war. Brigadier H.J.B. Keating consented to be the first Civil Defence director in Wolfville. He was succeeded in 1955 by Major L.M. Clairdale. Mayor Eric Balcom attended a federal conference on civil defence in 1952 as one of three appointed delegates from Nova Scotia. In 1953 the Council provided the Red Cross with storage space for emergency supplies in the basement of the Civic Building. Supplies worth $830 were bought in 1959, with the federal government assuming ninety per cent of the cost.

Civil Defence had also become a government-funded concern since the volunteer days of the Fifties, and the provincial director wrote Council in 1960 to announce that the salary of the Town Civil Defence Director would be cut from $800 to $600 to put it in line with other towns of similar size.

Council was granted a civil defence budget of $3,500 for 1961, with ninety per cent of that amount recoverable from federal and provincial sources. About $1,600 was used to buy a small trailer stocked with rescue equipment, some folding chairs, and a movie screen for showing emergency preparedness films. Another $100 went to purchase a "portable loudhailer."

Interest in civil defence had dropped off sharply after the first panicky days of the bomb, and when the incumbent director died in 1962 Council spent two fruitless years searching for a replacement. No one wanted the job, and the civil defence office was finally closed down.

The story of Wolfville's role in wars can only be partially told. The real story, the personal story of the men who fought, has died with the leading actors. How many heroes there were among those who went to the Africa war, who fought in First World War trenches, no one really knows. The Second World War and the Korean conflict being closer in time, a few of the recognized heroes can be identified. Among them are Max Forsythe-Smith (Military Cross), David Waterbury, Q.C. (Distinguished Flying Cross), Keith Forbes (Distinguished Service Cross), and George E.M. Ruffee, who won the Military Cross in Korea.

SIR SAM HUGHES REVIEWING THE HIGHLAND BRIGADE, CAMP ALDERSHOT, JUNE 14TH. 1916.   33

XIII.

HEALTH AND WELFARE

The health and welfare portion of the history considers the developing sagas of sanitation, water supply, garbage disposal, the control and prevention of diseases, the physical and material well-being of the indigent and handicapped, as well as numerous lesser concerns. In 1888 a health officer had been appointed — druggist George V. Rand.

With the community enjoying merely settlement status until incorporated in 1893, sanitary conditions were in a poor, indeed perilous, state. About the mid-nineteenth century the names of two medical doctors were in the early records. These were Dr. H. O. McLatchy and Dr. Edward L. Brown; the latter also ran an apothecary shop, while Dr. McLatchy was not only a physician but also a pioneer in orchard culture. First consideration of the town's public health was in the report of a "Health Society" in 1899, presided over by Dr. A. W. Sawyer, president of Acadia University.

1. Sewers

A modest sewer system had been installed some fifty years before incorporation, and although modern for the times it had deteriorated badly by 1894. A resolution in 1902 "to have our town sewered" was hailed as a memorable event. In his 1903 annual report the mayor dealt exclusively with the sewerage problem. Mayor J. F. Herbin won his point when council was empowered to borrow $35,000 to install sewers. Although this was a considerable step forward in sanitation, it was not enough for the medical health officer of the day, the doughty Dr. George Erasmus DeWitt. In 1905 he expressed regret that so many households had not availed themselves of the sanitary convenience of the sewers and urged compliance with the by-laws requiring citizens to do so.

He had reason to complain. More than 100 cesspools "of various makes, shapes and sizes" still existed in use. He also declaimed against the practice of allowing manure to accumulate about properties, citing especially the livery stables. Under stern pressure, improvement of unsavory conditions continued, and by 1923 the health officer could state that of the once-numerous "privy pitts" only a few remained. Sewage treatment, as handled at present, did not exist in those early years. Instead, all connections to the system were equipped with "gates and strainers" to break up the material before it went out to sea. Because of the extremes of the famous tides, difficulties were encountered in placing the sewer outlets.

In the 1920s sewerage was still primitive and menaced the well-being of the town. People were well aware of the peril and in 1943 voted $70,000 for additional water mains. This eased the situation somewhat but pollution created by sewage remained a problem. For the Municipal Joint Planning Advisory Committee the conclusive study on sewage abatement called for a "lagoon" system requiring some thirty acres of land, with pumping stations at various locations. Such a plan would entail great cost. In 1972 council filed a "statement of intent" to implement the development of a sewage abatement plant in the years 1974, 1975 and 1976. The location of the required "treatment ponds" caused considerable debate. Finally the matter was settled, with location in the east end of town dictated when Grand Pre, a member of the joint committee, sought co-operation with Wolfville in a system of shared treatment ponds.

2. Water Supply

Another serious concern from the beginning, and an abiding problem for the early councils, was the supply of good water. With chemical purification not yet accepted, contamination was an ever-present danger. Reservoirs, which fed from a series of dams on the Gaspereau Mountain, were the main sources. However, especially during dry summer spells, this source was neither reliable nor safe. A new well was dug in 1904; this, along with the reservoirs, was constantly tested for contamination. Bad water and an uneven supply of it continued to plague the town for years.

Medical Health Officer Dr. George DeWitt was the first to call for chlorination of the water. Others joined him to urge development of a safe, reliable supply. Much debate took place in 1919 over adopting a modified chlorination program but the plan was rejected as too experimental. In 1925, Dr. C. E. Avery DeWitt took up his father's task in the battle for treatment of the water. Dr. Avery DeWitt set up practice in 1910 and also became the town's medical health officer. The outstanding work done by father and son spanned some sixty years of service.

Not until 1950 were the townsfolk convinced and a chlorinator was installed. The fight for fluoridation was briefer, and that form of treatment was adopted in 1959.

The building boom in the late 1950s and early 1960s, with expansion at the university, put a severe strain on the water supply. Residents were urged to use water sparingly, and the mayor was forced to warn the university that further building grants would not be provided unless consideration was given towards handling the increased load. Angry ratepayers demanded to know how much longer they must boil water for household use. In 1971 the commission agreed to drilling of test wells, on condition that they be monitored by the commission for the first six months. Ratepayers had already approved in principle $210,000 for this project. Test wells were established on railway property at Cherry Lane and on the grounds of Eastern Kings Memorial Hospital. The water committee reported that summer that water was plentiful and the quality was "excellent".

3. The Poor, Housing

From the beginning the problem of maintaining health and well-being was compounded by the extreme poverty of many of the residents. In the early years no institution existed where such unfortunates could be cared for. The homeless were adopted into voluntary households, with charges paid through the village tax system. The problem of the destitute was partially solved by auctioning them to the care of families, who in many cases were in need of financial aid themselves. It was, in essence, a form of slavery, as labour was expected for their keep. Whoever charged the township the least got the care of the auctioned.

This treatment of the indigent was acknowledged to be inadequate and degrading. In 1850 a Poor House was proposed as an alternative, but not until ten years later was one established, situated in Horton District West (now Greenwich), to serve both Cornwallis and Horton areas. Vagrants, such as one Kitty King who was observed "walking the streets and making a poor appearance," were placed in the Poor House, from which they drifted from time to time. In 1891 the Poor House was managed by Fred Eye, with nineteen adults and seven children under his charge. Those able to do so worked on the farm to assist in their upkeep. This first poor house burned down in 1893 when an inmate upset a stove.

The Municipal Council took the matter in hand and rebuilt the Almshouse on the same property with a grant of $1600, plus insurance of $1400. An official visit in 1896 had praise for Mr. and Mrs. Forsyth who managed the place with its seventeen inmates. But the annual report of the Wolfville medical officer left little room for complacency: "We have expended $213.91 on this service, and you have reason for gratitude that so few are compelled to seek public aid. You are supporting two half-orphans in the poor house, in ignorance, idleness and misery, and some effort must be made to improve their condition." The structure served as the depository for the indigent until the 1920s, when its use ceased. Those in need of such maintenance were then placed in the Kings County Municipal Home at Waterville.

During the depression, calls for help for the poor and sick dominated council reports. Appeals for aid for orphans, illegitimate children and unwed teenage mothers were staggering. Council resolved in 1940 that only relief recommended by the V.O.N. would be allowed. The magnitude of the task merited a personal citation that commended Daisy West who served for thirty-five years as secretary of the executive.

The work load of the "Poor Committee" decreased markedly when the depression abated, and the new Social Assistance Act in 1960 further diminished it. The town now paid one-third of assistance costs, with the government paying the rest. By 1965 the number of welfare cases was small. By 1967 the Family and Children's Services of Kings County took charge. However, the case load of this organization became insupportable, and Wolfville was requested to seek aid from the municipal social assistance agency at Windsor. Adults were now processed by their office, which was available for consultation at Wolfville two days in the week. Child care continued to be the concern of the Family and Children's Services of Kings County.

The introduction in mid-century of universal federal government programs, such as the "Baby Bonus" and Old Age Security did much to improve general conditions, especially for shelter and food. With the Canada Health Act in 1968 providing largely free medical attention and hospitalization, the town's health showed marked improvement.

The welfare of citizens of retirement age and over became a matter of vital concern. Due to the rising inflation, the cost of maintaining shelter rapidly exceeded the means available to many of the aging. An Inter-Church Council, formed to evaluate the homes of the poor, conducted studies which showed considerable need for low-rental housing. Mostly due to these studies, a corporation was formed in 1970 to administer a plan to create group houses for senior citizens. Council met with representatives of the N.S. Housing Commission regarding designs of houses for low-to-moderate income families. By 1972 a Wolfville Housing Authority was established, chaired by John W. Murphy. A site was selected on Sherwood Drive, and although opposition came from some owners of neighboring properties, land was acquired, and building began. The N.S. Housing Commission, in co-operation with Central Mortgage and Housing Corporation, financed construction of fifteen units. The operating costs of the projects, over and above the tenants' rentals, was borne by the town on a percentage basis with the provincial and federal governments. The town also shared in the debt retirement.

The fifteen units officially opened in December 1973, were promptly filled, and Roy E. Loomer became the first administrator. The apartments consisted of a kitchen, bath, living room and one bedroom, with all amenities provided. Additional accommodations were needed, and twenty units were added on two separate occasions. Blomidon View Manor supported forty-five units, with some common room and recreational facilities for the use of all. For those disabled by age or physical handicaps and unable to maintain their own households, private nursing homes and rest homes provided shelter and total care.

4. Infectious Diseases

Along with inadequate sewerage, impure water, and the needs of the indigent, other conditions threatened health and welfare. Infectious diseases could appear with terrifying suddenness, and in the early years, only the vigilance of the medical health officer and the Board of Health was able to combat them. An outbreak of scarlet fever in 1896 prompted speedy passage of sanitation by-laws and health regulations. Dr. DeWitt, aided by police, checked all households which had open cesspools, inspected the sewer system of all residents, fined violators of the by-laws. All houses which harboured contagious diseases were disinfected and fumigated. When smallpox appeared in Kentville in 1901, all Wolfville residents were vaccinated, on penalty of $50 fine for failure to co-operate. In effect, the entire town was ''sealed off'' from outsiders until the disease was controlled and quarantine could be lifted. These emergency controls proved so successful that the Board of Health had little trouble in similarly confining other threats, such as typhoid and diphtheria.

Dr. George DeWitt served for twenty years as medical health officer and inspector. He was widely regarded as a pioneer in the field of preventive medicine and in using progressive measures of sanitation and health. In his annual report of 1902 he expressed his satisfaction: ''I do not know of a town . . . which has been so immune from infectious diseases as the town of Wolfville within the last few years.'' Dr. DeWitt kept abreast of progress in medicine, attending and contributing to the chief medical societies in the dominion.

From early years a menace of deepest concern was the growing incidence of tuberculosis or "consumption" as it was commonly called, the consistently greatest killer of the time. One victim of this dread disease was Carrie DeWitt. Dr. DeWitt accompanied his daughter to Gravenhurst, Ontario where existed the only Canadian institution for the treatment of tuberculosis. He remained long enough to observe the care given patients — rest in fresh air the year round, with graduated exercise and medication, such as Scott's Emulsion.

Upon his return home, Dr. DeWitt created a centre for similar treatment. He acquired two small neighbouring houses above the town (on what is now Skyway Drive) and joined them by a glassed-in porch. A caretaker and wife lived in one of the houses, while Carrie and others "took the cure" on the porch. "Highland View Sanatorium" seemed to have begun about 1899, operated five or more years until the provincial sanatorium opened at Kentville in 1904. The 1901 report of the Canadian Association for the Prevention of Consumption listed Wolfville's as one of three private institutions in Canada. Dr. DeWitt reported to the Maritime Medical Association in 1903 that during the previous year he had ten patients under sanatorium treatment. Patients had been admitted from Wolfville, Halifax, Windsor, and Parrsboro.

The threat of epidemic diseases continued to be dealt with alertly and forcefully. For instance, when the deadly Spanish influenza appeared in 1917 all Wolfville schools and public buildings and some businesses closed for several weeks. Again, in 1946, as a precaution against polio, high school swimming coach Fred Kelly ruled that no meet be held. When Salk vaccine became available a few years later 100 school children were given its protection.

Compounded by the increasing population of both Town and Gown was the contentious and unsavory garbage problem. The dump soon proved totally inadequate and by 1940 was declared insupportable. Residents threw their trash over the embankment behind the structure when the supervisor was off duty, thereby creating a notable rat problem. Incineration was finally agreed upon.

In 1960 council agreed to build a new incinerator and asked the university to contribute towards capital and maintenance, and in 1961 Acadia provided $3,000 for a facility costing $5,000. Charlie Delahunt collected the garbage until 1967 when council was informed it would not be eligible for certain provincial grants unless the town did the collecting. The town could not ignore this ultimatum. The town's garbage staff and equipment now collect the garbage which is then disposed of by William Tracey at Municipal Sanitary Landfill site at Meadowview, just north of Kentville.

A long stride in preventive medicine was taken in the 1920s when milk was suspected of causing bovine tuberculosis and undulant fever. Pasteurization of milk was introduced into dairies, which helped allay the danger, but pressure was exerted for fuller control. In 1936 a major step was taken with the ruling that only pasteurized milk might be sold at Wolfville, the first town in Nova Scotia to have 100% pasteurized milk.

5. Hospitals

By the end of World War I a strong desire existed to have a hospital. Payzant Memorial at Windsor was the only general hospital in western Nova Scotia between Halifax and Yarmouth. A limited amount of laboratory and x-ray work could be handled by the N.S. Sanatorium through the co-operation of Medical Superintendent Dr. A. F. Miller, a considerable assistance in the diagnostic field, but an acute surgical case faced the alternative "between an operation on the kitchen table or a long journey in a baggage car." In 1919 Dr. Avery DeWitt purchased the W. F. Parker estate on Westwood Avenue and set up a hospital of a limited capacity, which he operated privately until 1929. It was then taken over and run as a general hospital by a committee of: Doctors M. R. Elliott, P. S. Cochrane, C. E. A. DeWitt, R.N. Viva Bengston, and George Boggs, while negotiations continued towards a new hospital.

Prominent citizens of the town and university discussed plans, and at one time the Municipal Council and the towns of Kentville and Berwick took part. When Berwick proceeded to build Western Kings Memorial Hospital, Wolfville decided to take action on its own. With the promise of substantial grants from prominent families, the university and town, a hospital board was formed under chairmanship of W. H. Chase.

The cornerstone was laid on October 22, 1929 at the selected site on Earnscliffe Avenue. Leslie Fairn was architect, and Rhodes-Curry Construction Company built the hospital with such speed that it officially opened May 26, 1930; the first surgical case was operated on that night. The construction cost, including land purchase and furnishings, was reckoned at $117,800.

Through the aid of fund drives, fairs, memorial gifts, constant progress rendered the hospital efficient and creditable. In 1978 the addition of a modern out-patient department, named for Dr. M. R. Elliott who had for fifty years served as a medical doctor, greatly enhanced services. In 1980, at the fiftieth anniversary of the hospital, a plaque was unveiled to honour the memory of Dr. P. S. Cochrane, former chief of staff. With the passage of time and the acquisition of needed improvements, Eastern Kings Memorial Hospital received accreditation from the American College of Surgeons and the Canadian Council of Hospital Accreditation. Since the league's formation in 1929, the Hospital Auxiliary has greatly added to the hospital's effectiveness.

6. Victorian Order of Nurses

The need for more comprehensive welfare services was keenly felt throughout the town, especially by the doctors and teachers. A move was started to consider establishing a Victorian Order of Nurses service. Spearheaded by Dr. Malcolm Elliott in 1921, a local council of the V.O.N. was formed, and soon the first nurse took charge — Mary Harry, a memorable figure, recalled as "a weatherbeaten little English woman on a motor scooter." She was on the job for over seven years. Aided by a strong council, the V.O.N. became the chief welfare agent in the area. Under Miss Harry's direction, the health of school children became a prime concern. Her first annual report stated: "Thanks is due to Dr. Elliott and Dr. Cochrane for medical examinations; to Dr. L. Eaton and Dr. E. Eaton for dental examinations, who gave services free."

In 1949 a school dental clinic was set up, with office equipment purchased through financial drives. Town dental teams conducted surveys and did what treatment could be done with the equipment on hand. The priority of dental care continued, with needy cases sponsored by various local service clubs.

Changes in the town's health care management and inspection came with the creation of Health Units by the Provincial Department of Health, each unit under the direction of a doctor with post-graduate work in Public Health. Wolfville came under the jurisdiction of the Fundy Health Unit. Inspection of sanitation and supervised testing of water and milk were carried out in conjunction with the town medical officer. Restaurants came under scrutiny of the local Board of Health and were required to conform with Provincial Regulations. Health inspection of schools was taken over by Public Health nurses attached to the Windsor office. This change freed the V.O. nurses to provide nursing care in the homes. Control of infectious diseases became the responsibility of the Health Unit, with follow-up on such cases as tuberculosis done by the Public Health nurses.

7. Mental Health

The first community-based clinic of its kind in Nova Scotia, the Fundy Mental Health Centre, was established in June 1955 at Wolfville, with the following founding directors: Dr. M. R. Elliott, of Wolfville; Dr. J. Earle Hiltz, superintendent of the N.S. Sanatorium at Kentville; Dr. J. Clyde Marshall, the province's first director of mental health services; Dr. Marion Grant, Professor of Psychology and Dean of Women at Acadia University; Dr. Eric Cleveland, Psychiatrist with the Stirling County Project at Digby, N.S.; Dr. Douglas Denton, of Wolfville; E. D. Haliburton, of Avonport; Dr. G. Michael Smith, of Windsor; and Lewis MacMillan, high school teacher at Berwick. Dr. A. A. Giffin, of Kentville, attended subsequent meetings. Three groups founded the clinic: Acadia University Institute, Kings County Mental Health Association, and the Provincial Department of Mental Health.

The clinic began providing services in September 1955, in a university-owned house west of the president's residence, with an agreement that the province pay the major expense for the programme, the board to raise the remaining fifteen percent. Dr. Cleveland became the first director, and Mrs. Margaret Margeson was engaged as secretary and receptionist, one of the chief strengths of the clinic. Dr. Marion Grant was with the staff as part-time psychologist and later as full-time, and continued for twenty years with the association. Also, Margaret A. Godfrey, R.N., was the social worker on the staff. Many patients were cared for, and numerous referrals were made.

Acadia University treasurer, Frederick J. Elderkin, served as treasurer until 1961, when he was succeeded by John Colson. The local board selected the staff, and in 1958 Dr. Mortimer V. Marshall became the second chairman of the Fundy Centre. Dr. Ralph Townsend had joined the staff in 1956 as psychiatrist, remaining until 1967. Psychiatrist Dr. Douglas Archibald was appointed, and became medical director in 1971.

Wolfville welcomed the clinic which had close ties with the university. The centre was the first to use public health nurses to assist with home visits to patients. The programme served an area of 55,000 people in Hants, Kings, and Annapolis Counties. Annapolis County later joined with Digby County.

Responsibility for the clinic changed in the spring of 1958, as communities became represented on the newly formed advisory committee which developed into a valuable aid to the programme. In January 1962 a new building opened near Eastern Kings Memorial Hospital, the property bought at a nominal charge. Architect Ronald Peck designed the structure, and the citizens paid for it through contributions. A new wing was added in March 1974.

Staff changes took place. Dr. Cleveland retired in 1972 as executive director but continued with the centre until 1976. He was succeeded by social worker John W. Murphy who became administrator, while Dr. Douglas Archibald assumed the office of medical director.

The clinic's program has led to and encouraged the development of other services, such as child guidance, parent effectiveness training, speech therapy, and programmes for the learning disabled and mentally handicapped children. The centre worked closely with Dr. Charles Taylor's pastoral counselling training course, providing a recovery programme for patients from the N.S. Hospital at Dartmouth and from the Waterville institution. The centre also prompted the alcohol and drug-abuse program treatment centre at Miller Hospital, Kentville.

The centre has been affiliated with the Maritime School of Social Work, providing field placement for students, and is used by Acadia students in clinical psychology and counselling courses. The school system benefited through testing services and from the efforts of Dr. Grant, Barbara Archibald, and Carol Armstrong to help children with learning disabilities. Down through the years the several facets of the mental health clinic have provided an essential service.

At the close of 1980 the staff included: Mrs. Margaret Margeson, Dr. Douglas Archibald, John W. Murphy, Dr. Jacqueline Milliken, Dr. Edward Strok, Carmen Enzinas, Ernest Enzinas, Eleanor Chase, Carol Armstrong, Margaret Bayer, and Jeff Moore.

8. New Needs

Several community groups organized to meet special needs, first in the 1890s to aid George Lynch buy an artificial hand he lost in an accident. Mrs. R. G. D. Harris opened "Restholm" on Main Street in 1929. In the 1930s a few women collected clothing at Waterbury's store and outfitted needy children; barbers gave free service, and some children got baths. With E. W. Balcolm, president, and Nurse Mrs. Edgar Child as matron, the Maritime Maternity Home opened at the former W. H. Chase property. In 1965 and later, a group, led by Mary Williams, Macha MacKay, and Claudia Tugwell, operated the Women's Centre over Mitchell's store, giving instruction in family life. A youth hostel opened in 1979 at 1 Prospect Street. In 1975 the Children's Centre, administered by Pat Moore, farewelled assistant Nancy Faulds, and Claudia Tugwell presented gifts to Elaine Ferguson, Anna Hutton, Joanna Stonehouse, and Ulla Tirroner. Landmark East, in the former Parmount Hotel, began in 1979 to treat children with learning disabilities,

Robert Kahn the administrator. In that year "Communiversity" began a swim program for mentally handicapped, co-ordinated by Betty Bowers, and the Central Avenue Workshop amalgamated with the Flower Cart at New Minas.

In addition to having welfare and relief services available, Wolfville has several benevolent groups and clubs which seek to better the lot of the less fortunate. The "Meals on Wheels" program served nourishing dinners to the ill and aged; day care centres for preschoolers freed mothers for employment; aid to refugees, notably "The Boat People", was provided generously; "Crippled Children" programs gave expert medical attention. It is surely safe to state that citizens of Wolfville are attentive and caring concerning welfare needs within their town.

XIV.

CIVIC PROTECTION

The need for maintaining law and order became apparent soon after the settlers arrived at Horton Landing. As early as June 1761 men were accused of stealing fish from the fish "ware", and John Atwell was charged with breaking the Sabbath by carrying grain to the mill. John Bishop, Jr., was charged with labouring at the mill and grinding the grain on the Sabbath.

In the fall of 1773 John Bishop, Jr., and Andrew Davison were charged with introducing smallpox to the township. The case came up again in 1776 when Andrew Davison threatened to shoot anyone who attempted to remove Andrew Jr., apparently still suffering from the smallpox, from the house where they resided. Eventually, he and others were removed.

The coming of age for any community brings concerns and problems for its citizens, and Wolfville was no exception. In the early 1800s efforts to solve these problems led to the formation of police and fire departments.

1. The Police Department

The courthouse and jail for Horton Township was first located at Town Plot, and then removed to Upper Horton. When Horton Corner, Kentville, had become the commercial centre of the county, it was made the shiretown in the early 1800s, and the courthouse was moved to Kentville. Little is known of cases in the early years of the century. In April 1802 Stephen Rider, the constable, laid a charge against Elijah Fowler, the innkeeper, for allowing card playing for liquor, and accused the innkeeper and his son with assault. They charged the constable with assault. Charges of assault against a number of young men from the academy were laid by a Wolfville resident. The students were accompanied to court by a teacher, John Leard, and Reverend John Pryor, who bound the students to keep the peace, with payment of money. In the same month James Stephens and Johnson Elderkin were bound by law to keep the peace.

In 1879 there was a tragic case in Wolfville, that of thirty-one year old Albert DeWolf who had studied medicine at Edinburgh, and returned to Wolfville where he married. He then spent two years in Halifax — there seems to be some doubt as to whether he was a patient at the lunatic asylum or the doctor in charge — and returned to his parents' home. He asked his wife to resume their marriage but she refused, and he shot her. He was arrested and jailed, and the case was scheduled to come before the Supreme Court, but before that could happen he hanged himself in the jail at Kentville. According to the newspaper report, he had fastened a sheet to an axe handle and placed it across the stovepipe hole in the roof. He then kicked away the chair and "launched himself into eternity."

Otherwise, 1879 was a quiet year. The *Western Chronicle* of November reported that "Cabbage night has come and gone, and very little uproar was made." Cabbage night was the local term for Hallowe'en, and was also used in other parts of Nova Scotia.

The *Acadian* reported in 1883 that the "pound had been broken open twice and cattle feloneously liberated." In 1885 it suggested that there was real need for a lockup, particularly after a robbery occurred. When the robber fled, authorities broke in his barn door and found him, armed with a knife and gun, under a pile of potatoes. When he was taken to Amherst for trial, he escaped from the train, still wearing handcuffs.

The need for a policeman was brought to people's attention in 1887 when it was reported that there were "a number of suspicious characters in our village . . . We would advise people to keep a sharp lookout over their moveables." Further news items claimed there was need for a policeman to deal with unruly drunks. No doubt these citizens were habitues of the "two gin mills now gracing or disgracing our village. Some knowing ones said there *were* three, one of which has been temporarily suspended owing to the force of circumstances." During that summer the community moved to get police protection from street loafers gathered about shop doors. Meanwhile, a street lamp, to be paid for by public subscription, was placed at each end of Mud Bridge, to discourage rowdyism.

A questionable practice was reported later that summer when three suspicious looking individuals, two offering fifty cents and ten cents a gambling chance, the other selling a remarkable kind of soap, attracted a large crowd. Since the men lacked a licence, the magistrate closed up their games. Afterwards they were watched, and the merchants of the town kept an eye on their safes. At the end of 1888 there were references in the news to Policeman Barry, and a lockup, and it was suggested that a courthouse and jail be placed in Wolfville. The County Council resolved to establish a police department at Wolfville. James Toye, at a salary of $400 per annum, is credited with being the first policeman. He took office in 1894.

In 1891 a newspaper report stated that "Counterfeit quarters and 20 cent pieces are in circulation in Wolfville. The counterfeit is a good one but the pieces made of lead have no ring." In 1894 the chief of police had difficulty in handling a parade of seventy-five college students. Also, a reward of fifty dollars was posted for information leading to the conviction of those who burned the bridge on University Avenue, apparently on Hallowe'en or Cabbage Night. In 1897 a man was ordered fifty days in the county jail for assaulting one of the two Wolfville Chinese laundrymen.

Changes were made in the police personnel. Policeman Quipp was released from his duties in 1899, which left boys free to enjoy riding bicycles on the sidewalks. He was replaced in May by Mr. Sutton as chief. "Let the evil doers now beware." Older boys caused trouble in 1900, and in the following January the County Court heard a case of Wolfville versus eight college students who congregated before the Post Office and elsewhere. Avard Pineo appeared for Wolfville, and W. V. Roscoe for the students. Policeman Porter stated that the students blew horns and sang the following refrain: "We are the college police and we do as we d--n please, we don't give a d--n for any d--n man, who doesn't give a d--n for us." They were walking four abreast and did not pay any attention to Mr. Porter. The students were fined two dollars each and appealed the case but final outcome was not reported. Chief Sutton resigned in March 1901.

In February 1902 the Chinese laundry was robbed of fifty dollars, taken from the cash box. In 1904 boys solicited donations from house to house but the money never reached the designated person.

Town Clerk Frank A. Dixon advertised for a policeman, and in December 1903 the long career of Freeman S. Crowell of Pereaux commenced, and continued until his death in 1941. A week later the paper reported the laying of two charges in the Town Court, under the Scott Act, the first such charges for years. In January 1904 the Acadia Electric Light Company advertised in the *Acadian* their troubles with vandals: "$10 Reward! As we are under considerable expense in repairing street lights that are maliciously broken, we offer the above reward for information that will lead to the conviction of the guilty parties. Offenders will be prosecuted to the full extent of the law." In 1909 the company was still offering the reward.

As ever, the editors of the *Acadian* displayed their concern for proper behavior. In February 1902 they had suggested that since the Acadia Seminary fined girls five cents for singing or whistling "Dolly Gray", those youths who offended in this way in the local rink might be penalized by an even larger sum. In 1907 they were complaining about rowdyism in the streets, evidence that Policeman Crowell needed an assistant and also help from the citizens. During the next year Town Clerk A. E. Caldwell warned against littering the streets: a conviction meant a fine or jail term. In November clothing was stolen from Miss Davison's yard on Summer Street, and the year closed with two family men sentenced to fifty days for being drunk and using profane language.

An unusual occurrence took place near the exhibition building in 1911 when Scott Clark was attacked and robbed of sixty dollars. A new reason for police action was noted in 1913 when offenders rode bicycles on sidewalks. A $1,000 reward was offered to discover the persons who poisoned several young cats belonging to C. R. Bill. Hallowe'en passed quietly that year, but in 1915 precautions were taken and an extra constable was engaged by the town for Hallowe'en. In 1915 Temperance Inspector Patriquin arrested an inhabitant of Saxon Street for violating the Temperance Act, and nearly 500 gallons of cider and about ninety gallons of beer were destroyed. In 1916 reckless car driving became a matter of concern and the police were busy enforcing the laws against it.

There seems to have been a minor crime wave in 1918. The frequency of thefts prompted council to place an advertisement in the *Acadian*, offering ten dollars to anyone having information leading to the conviction of persons found guilty of "theft, breaking into homes or buildings, trespassing, destroying public or private property, use of profane language . . . or the selling of intoxicants." Council also felt the need to tighten the bylaws concerning disorder and impropriety, and conduct on the public streets.

With the increasing number of automobiles in 1921, the Police Department worried about speeding cars, and agreed that something should be done. Council finally authorized purchase of a stop watch and a motorcycle, "so that the police officer can determine accurately the speed of passing automobiles." By 1925 the police officer was also "inspector for the enforcement of the Temperance Act," the truant officer and janitor of the Town Office. In addition, he received in 1927 the title and responsibility of school attendance officer. Altogether he was a busy individual.

Early in 1926 the town offered a reward of $100 for information concerning those who tampered with the electric system, particularly the fire alarm. A disturbance took place when a man placed in jail for vagrancy was taken from the jail at midnight by a group of masked men who tried to run him out of town. The police succeeded in thwarting the attempt. The police charged a woman for operating a "punch board", and she was fined five dollars and costs, or thirty days in jail. A drunken driver was fined $100 or sixty days in jail by Stipendiary Magistrate Whidden, who said he would show no mercy in such cases.

By 1933 the effects of the depression were evident. The town experienced a "severe epidemic" of hen stealing, and Chief Crowell advised citizens not to feed hoboes. The Police and Licence Committee of 1935 instructed people to report beggars. In a concern about slot machines, council instructed Solicitor W. D. Withrow to take criminal action against all operators of gambling devices.

There was excitement in August when Police Chief Crowell and Special Officer Willard Stewart made an arrest and a large crowd stormed the jail and smashed down the door. However, Crowell succeeded in pacifying the group before the R.C.M.P. arrived. Judge Burpee Wallace fined the prisoner ten dollars. The paper reported that the ringleaders of the assault were not of Wolfville. In 1940 the police erected speed limit signs at entrances to the town.

Changes took place in the Police Department. Late in 1940 Henry K. Eaton became the second officer, to be on duty during night hours, an improvement long sought by the *Acadian*. After thirty-seven years as police "chief", Freeman Crowell died in July 1941. H. K. Eaton resigned in 1944, and Lawrence B. Parker of Kentville soon afterwards became the replacement, at $100 per month. He obtained an assistant in June when Harold Spencer became an extra constable, and was later on duty as a night policeman.

The Bank of Montreal installed a hold-up alarm system in 1947 to augment the police protection. A week later money was stolen from the safe of the Acadia Theatre.

The concern for speeding continued to be an issue. In 1949 the Police Committee made a recommendation to the Home and School meeting that new speed limit signs should be placed at the entrance to the town. In the summer of 1950 the town placed parking meters on Main Street to limit parking to two hours. Two years later there was a complaint that vandals were attacking the meters.

Throughout the summer of 1959 the *Acadian* reported complaints of purse snatching. The Sanisteam Laundry lost $800 to thieves. An additional constable, Carman Fraser, was hired as an assistant.

In the 1960s crime increased, and the town minutes referred to a "near riot at the recent Battle of the Bands in Kentville" where Wolfville police had been asked to assist in keeping order. Other serious concerns were "hoods" on Main Street, a rash of minor break-ins, and reports of young boys sniffing airplane glue. At least one meeting discussed other rumours of drug use but the members of council were not certain that the stories told were substantial enough to demand action.

There were reports of personnel problems in the Police Department. Police officers complained of longer hours and lack of an Arbitration Board to hear their views on long hours and underpayment, and there were resignations. At this time the constables lacked use of an official police vehicle, although they sometimes were able to make use of the chief's car. In "hotly pursuing" speeders and other lawbreakers, the police were handicapped, and the calling of a taxi for conveyance did little to ease the situation. An improvement was made at a later date. Although the Town Council increased the full-time force to a chief and two constables in 1968, a high rate of turnover continued into the 1970s. In 1972 the Police Department was expanded from a three-man to a five-man force. With an increase in the student population in town and in university residences, a growing use of drugs, and more unemployment, the department was very busy, and some members felt the salaries were too low.

Relationships between the town and Police Department became strained. In 1974, after one man was reprimanded and then dismissed for what the council considered unprofessional behaviour, the entire department, except the chief, applied to the Labour Relations Board for certification of a union. At the same time the association drew up its first collective agreement for negotiation with the town. The Labour Relations Board upheld the Town Council's action in dismissing the constable. In June, terms were agreed upon between the council and Police Association but problems continued. Three more constables resigned, and another was dismissed within the next two years. After one member of the police force was injured during the "Basin View fracas" in 1975, Councillor Robert Wrye wondered if members of the department should not be given riot training. He also asked the council to write the Attorney General to express concern for the long delays experienced by police in the trying and sentencing of lawbreakers. In May 1975 council voted to approve the use of firearms by police.

In 1975 Chief G. Alex. Kendrick was honoured by the Maritime Association of Police Chiefs for entering the thirtieth year of service at Wolfville. Early in 1979 he resigned, and was appointed the bylaws enforcement officer. At the end of 1975 the town had hired Kenneth McQueen and Eric Roy McNeil, the first Holland College graduates, professionally trained police, to be engaged by Wolfville. The paper started an illustrated series, beginning with Chief John McLeod, to introduce the local police to the public.

In 1979 the police inaugurated a system of guards for the crosswalks near the school, with five guards financed by a federal grant. Later, Gwen Phillips, representing fifty petitioners, requested that the guards be employed permanently. Another introduction was Operation Identification, intended to discourage thievery in homes. Five young people stamped valuable articles with the owner's Social Insurance number. In 1980 a further introduction was made when the Police Department purchased a breathalyzer to test drivers suspected of impairment. Thus the Wolfville Police Department continues to keep up with the times and the introduction of new techniques.

2. The Fire Department

In October 1886, the *Acadian* advocated a volunteer fire department for Wolfville. Kentville had one, and would soon have a steam engine for the use of the fire department. Possibly as a result of this suggestion, early in 1887 the County Council appointed a fire-escape committee for Wolfville, and authorized them to check every building and to ensure that an exit for every inhabitant was available in case of fire. The *Acadian* editors hoped that the committee had authority at the College as well. The Odd Fellows Hall had burned, possibly because of a defective flue, and the Lodge lost all their books and papers; and Farrell's Hotel had a narrow escape. Few people were at the fire, and it was suggested that the town needed a fire alarm.

Destructive fires continued. In February 1889 a disastrous fire levelled B.G. Bishop's store, owned by Mr. Higgins; the McDonald store, owned by Dr. Barss; the building owned and occupied by Patriquin, and Larkin's store was badly damaged. Wooden buildings were fire hazards, and the local paper continued throughout the early 1890s to agitate for a fire prevention service. When the fire department was properly organized, it was able to save buildings and property.

In January 1890 it was announced that the Fire Department would build a hall on Main Street, below the Methodist Church, and tenders were invited for the construction. In July about twenty young men met at Witter's Hall to form a fire and protection company, and elected officers: Pres. - E.W. Sawyer; Vice Pres. - Burpee Witter; Sec. - G.W. Munro; Treas. - B.O. Davison. The Hose and Ladder Company: Capt. - G.W. Munro; Vice. Pres. J.F. Herbin; Marshall - D.O. Munro; The Protection Company; Capt. - J.F. Franklin; 1st. Lieut. - F.P. Rockwell; 2nd Lieut. - J.D. Chambers; Marshall - J.W. Coldwell. The Company had forty-nine members, and some apparatus had been purchased. Early in August the Fire Company was still meeting in Witter's Hall, but the new engine house was expected to be ready soon. In April 1892 the Hose Company drill tested the water strength and was able to throw water over the top of the Skoda building. In June 1893 a telephone was placed in their building. They won the hose reel race in Kentville, and in July 1899 at Windsor when they received a silver cup. There is a picture of the group action at Randall House Museum.

At the annual meeting of the Fire Department at the Main Street Station, in February 1900, it was reported that there had been three runs during the year, but no need to turn on the water. Chief J.F. Herbin resigned and was replaced by G.D. Ellis. The membership was then twenty-nine. In 1904 the Company enjoyed a sleigh drive to Kentville, where they dined at the American Hotel, with Chief J.E. Hales presiding. The Company continued to meet regularly and to test their equipment. In the fall of 1911 the Town erected a new fire station at the corner of Front Street and Central Avenue. The building contained two cells for a police lockup, a repair shop, and a stable. Parts of the fire equipment were kept at both the east and west ends of town in case of a sudden alarm. Ernest Eagles was foreman of the construction, and it was hoped that the erection of the new building would permit lower insurance rates for community properties.

At the 1912 meeting the Fire and Protection Company elected Ernest Eagles as Chief, W.C.B. Harris, Vice Chief, and Secretary Treasurer, William

Regan; the Captains of No. 1,2,3,4, Hose Reels were Ed Mahaney, Harry Fraser, William Murphy, I.S. Boates; of the Ladder Truck, E.J. Ellis; of the Salvage Corps, W.H. Fraser. J.E. Hales, Charles Fitch and J.F. Herbin constituted the Executive Committee, and A.M. Wheaton, William Regan, and W.C.B. Harris the Finance Committee. The meeting discussed the advisability of having some firemen paid.

Mayor Thomas Harvey encouraged the use of brick rather than wood, for new construction within the business district. In 1912 the ladder wagon and hose reel that had been purchased in 1894 came clattering out of the new all-brick station. The Fire Department received continued support. Work was started in 1915 on drawing an outline for a new fire district. A new fire alarm horn, bought in Chicago in 1921, was tested on the roof of the new school building in October, but, according to reports in *The Acadian* in August 1922, the new and expensive fire alarm had yet to be installed; in the next month it was placed on a tower behind the light station. "It works great," was the verdict. On Fire Prevention Day in October, steps were taken to improve the fire-fighting force, and the Company was reorganised, with H.E. Fraser as Chief, Wm. Murphy as Assistant, and W.O. Pulsifer as Secretary. The *Acadian* also advocated paying firemen. The Town Council, late in 1922, decided that "the Wolfville Fire Prevention Company have, temporarily, the room on the ground floor of the Front Street House adjoining the Police Lockup, for meeting purposes." Early in 1924 Council approved an expenditure of $10,000 for purchase of a triple combination pumper, chemical, and hose car. In December of that year, thirty-five firemen were given a banquet by the Town Council. In 1927, the Fire Company adopted its own set of bylaws. The next year, they played the Kentville Firemen at the University Rink. In spite of the efforts of H. Sleep, goal, Rogers and Fraser, defence, Hutchinson, Caldwell, D. Rogers, forwards, with Murphy and Carey as spares, Wolfville lost.

In 1931, *The Acadian* favoured the sounding of the fire siren at noon, to ensure that it was in working order, and this became a daily ritual. In 1935 the Department sponsored an "Ice Frolic" at University Rink, with a children's carnival, a hockey game between the firemen and the merchants, and a tug-of-war between firemen and university. A new hose truck was welcomed by the Fire Department at the close of 1937.

In the 1940s the Town Council decided that the Fire Department needed to be reorganized: it was then operating with a membership at times as high as sixty, too many for a manageable group. It dissolved the Company, in 1945, set a membership limit of twenty, and took over selection of new firefighters. A yearly remuneration of fifteen dollars for each man was set, and efforts were made to obtain comprehensive insurance for them. In 1948 the Council considered the need of a new fire hall, and the old fire station at the foot of Gaspereau Ave. was torn down in May 1950.

Better fire protection meant lower assessment and insurance rates, so that the Town Council gave a sympathetic hearing to requests from the Fire Department. In June 1950, $13,000 was appropriated for purchase of a new pumper and ladder truck, and three years later $1,000 was donated from a surplus fund for a new Mercury truck. In 1956 the Department purchased a two-way radio. In 1954 and in 1959 the Department reported no fire losses, for the first time in twenty-five years. The ratepayers were happy to vote $18,000 for a Pierre Thibault pumper to replace the twenty-year old LaFrance model, and the new equipment proved convenient in protecting the considerable new construction that appeared in the next few years. In May 1971 the Department moved into a new building, and in July 1974 a new pumper was welcomed by Chief Gerald Wood. By February 1980 the rescue equipment included a pneumatic bag to lift weights and a device to pry open crushed metal pieces. The derailment of a train loaded with chemicals at Mississauga led Gerald Wood and the Department to call for a disaster organization.

The *Acadian* reported in November 1980 that volunteer firefighter Maurice Lightfoot had been presented with a long service medal by Premier John Buchanan. Lightfoot's term with the Department had begun in 1947 and had taken several forms: lately he had been the radio man. He recalled that the number of firemen had more than doubled and equipment had tripled during the past thirty years. The burning of firewood had caused more fires in earlier years than in recent years.

XV.

PUBLIC UTILITIES

1. Postal Service

The postal service to Upper Horton was in operation shortly after the settling of the area by the New England Planters. The military government had inaugurated the post office at Halifax in 1754, and mail began to get through to Horton by 1766. The postmen then were soldiers, and when on foot they carried the mail in their jackets, and a gun to shoot partridge to sell. By 1786 the highway from Halifax to Windsor was travelled fortnightly, part of the way by mail carrier on foot, partly on horseback.

With growth and activity in the Minas settlement, Halifax tried to improve connections between the capital and the rural territories. Therefore, the first regular mail service to Annapolis was inaugurated in 1786, as a carrier delivered the mail on foot once every two weeks. By 1796 the mail was delivered in saddle bags by horse, and the trip between Halifax and Horton Corner (Kentville) took forty-four hours, with stopovers along the way.

Twice-weekly mail service began in 1814 to Annapolis, and after 1816 mails from Halifax to Windsor were carried by stage, driven by Isaiah Smith. In 1817 Joseph Howe reported that the only postal service in the province was between Halifax and Digby. The accounts differed. James Ratchford DeWolf wrote in 1900 that in 1828 the mail from Halifax (carried on horseback) was due weekly at Upper Horton on Wednesdays at ten in the forenoon, after more than forty-four hours.

By 1829 the stage coach carried the mail and had a regular thrice-weekly schedule between Halifax and Annapolis Royal. Steamers from St. John connected with the mail carriers and passengers at Windsor and Annapolis. In 1830 there were only twenty-one post offices in Canada, seven of these in Nova Scotia: Halifax, Windsor, Horton, Parrsboro, Cumberland, Annapolis, and Digby. The colonial office had charge until Nova Scotia took over postal affairs in 1851.

The service improved, and in 1848 it increased to four days per week, provided by both passenger and mail coaches drawn by two horses. At this time an exciting interlude occurred. An attempt was made by some enterprising coach lines in 1849 to speed the delivery of mail and messages from Europe through to New York, via Digby, by pony express riders. The Associated Press spent $20,000 on the venture and two coach lines became rivals. These were the Davison Coach Line and the King Coach Line, and both companies had steamers at Victoria Beach ready to cross to St. John. The "pony express" riders galloped 144 miles and provided entertainment for the people where horses and riders exchanged. This magnificent effort to speed the news ended after nine months, when the telegraph office was opened at Halifax on November 15, 1849, making the carrying of messages by hand unnecessary.

Of local interest was the visit in 1899 of Thomas O'Brien after thirty-five years in the United States. He told of Mr. Hyde of Truro and Mr. Barnaby of Cornwallis competing to get mail first from Halifax to Annapolis, with $14,000 as the reward. O'Brien had charge of Hyde's horses at the Wolfville Hotel, kept by Charles Hancock. Hyde's crew won by four minutes over the 123 miles, doing it in eight hours and forty minutes.

The first official way station at Upper Horton was opened in 1784, and Elisha DeWolf, Sr. was appointed postmaster in 1790. The total receipts at his office were $16.00 per annum. Elisha DeWolf, Jr. took over from his father in 1817.

Postal practices were simple, with postage regulated by distance and no limits on weight. Envelopes were unknown and stamps were not dreamed of. The cost of carrying letters was expensive — from Halifax to Upper Horton seven pence. Drivers did not always report collections, and passengers carried letters, evading postage charges. Newspapers were usually carried free. Sometimes, mail bags would purposely be unsealed on the way, the letters read, even removed.

The largest amount of correspondence was carried by people, owing to the scarcity of post offices and mail routes and the high cost of postage, according to the number of pages. Delivery was uncertain, for a letter might lie in the post office for weeks before it was sent to the proper community.

Occasionally, letters were written across a page of a single sheet of paper, of various sizes, and then the writer would turn the sheet sideways and continue to write, at times doing the same on both sides of the sheet. This procedure would mean a saving.

In 1841 Elisha DeWolf, Jr. complained to the postmaster general about the postal system. ''Respecting my franking privilege, my father was appointed post master, I believe in 1790, and held this commission from Mr. Herriott, and also from Sir Francis Freeling. At that time the whole proceeds of a quarter amounted to only about 20s, with very little increase for several years. I have been acting as postmaster since 1817, and always accounted to the postmaster at Halifax until the year 1827, at which time a mail stage was first established; and in order to accommodate the stage in exchanging mails, I consented that the office should be removed to Kentville, and have since that period accounted with that office, and received no compensation or commission, except the privilege of franking my own letters, which to me has been an object as I am doing a mercantile business in this part of the country, and have also a large circle of friends and connections both at Halifax and St. John, N.B., and other places, with whom there has perhaps been a more extensive correspondence carried on than otherwise would have been, were it not for the privilege of franking. At the same time the franking privilege to country postmasters generally would not be worth 40s per annum.''

DeWolf claimed that the office should be restored and the one at Kentville be kept up only as a way office. He argued that the presence of the college and academy, and a bridge between Horton and Cornwallis, had made the office more important, and steamer packets had increased the number of letters. Letters went seven miles farther than necessary, remained overnight, and were then sent back to him. The Kentville postmaster got about 100 pounds per annum from him, received a commission of twenty percent for doing nothing, and he (DeWolf) worked for nothing. In 1830 DeWolf had become an M.L.A. for Horton, and in the 1830s the postage receipts increased to $400, of which the postmaster received $80. Wolfville became a post office in 1841, and in 1850 postage stamps were introduced into Nova Scotia.

By 1830 the name of Horton had been changed to Wolfville and its postage business began to increase when the Acadia institutions became larger. An indication in the fall of 1877 of increased attendance at the seminary was the shortage of one-cent stamps at the local post office. In 1889 the post office building was provided with ash letter boxes, sixty fitted with locks, and now it was the property of the federal government. Postmaster G.V. Rand announced that the office had been made into a post office savings bank. William Johnson had preceded Rand as postmaster.

In 1894 the *New Star* reported that framework for the new post office arrived, and in that year the office was burglarized, the safe blown open, and a sum of $35 stolen. A new post office building was constructed in 1912, when the postmaster was E. Sidney Crawley who took over from G.V. Rand. On December 26, 1913 a new safe, weighing two and a half tons, was installed.

During the following years the post office served as a centre where the townspeople met daily to exchange greetings and gossip before starting across the street to the coffee house or to return home. Ninety-three additional mail boxes were added in 1950 to accommodate the growing population, and two years later three street mailing boxes were placed on Main Street and on Highland Avenue.

Recent postmasters have been: Brighton L. Fielding who retired in 1953 after forty-four years service; Carl E. Angus, in office until March 1963; Charles Fry, until 1974; Donald Tanner, from then to 1979; Ian Raines, the present postmaster. In 1971 a new building, with a garden front, was built. However, many citizens preferred the architecture of the previous structure.

2. Newspapers.

The daily or weekly newspaper represents a near-essential public utility which has been appreciated by Nova Scotia pioneers and also by readers of this century. The students of Acadia college, the academy, and the newly-formed female seminary, provided Wolfville's first newspaper when they wrote by hand two copies. Reverend David Freeman was the financial agent for the college and recorded in his diary of February 20, 1861: "This evening spent with wife in the newly opened female seminary (later named Grand Pre Seminary) under Miss Alice Shaw. A paper was presented by an appropriate speech from Reverend T. A. Higgins, as the first paper of the kind in Wolfville, called *The Budget* executed with a pen. A couple of large sheets of thick blue writing paper closely filled . . ." The first issue had come out that very day, and the paper was published twice each month, one copy for the college and the other for the seminary.

In 1859 *A Small Sheet* had been published by Campbell Stevens, a deaf mute at Canning, with only a few copies printed. After their publication venture during 1865 and 1866 was disrupted by fire at Canning, Major and William Theakston put out the *Acadian* at Wolfville during 1868 and 1869. Their building was ransacked and the plant destroyed by vandals. At this time the *Novascotian*, edited by Joe Howe, and the Tory *Colonist* came out each week from Halifax but the village wished its own newspaper.

Other publications were produced. The Acadia *Athenaeum* was put out by college students, beginning in 1874 and carrying occasional local items. The Berwick *Star* originally appeared in 1866, moved to Kentville, returned to Berwick, then to Wolfville. The second issue published by James A. Halliday of the *Star* seems to have been printed October 8, 1879 at Wolfville when Halliday's *Star* removed hurriedly after fire destroyed the Berwick printing plant.

The *New Star* at Wolfville had Walter Barss as editor and proprietor for a short time. He retired from journalism at the close of 1880 when J. A. Steele bought the *Star* and continued publishing, despite the disastrous fire of June 1881. A. J. Pineo operated the *New Star* in 1884 at Wolfville. At Berwick Halliday sold later to Walter L. Barss who sold to C. W. Knowles, who transferred the publication to A. T. Stodd, and soon the paper ceased.

Then the *Acadian* story was renewed. In April 1883 Arthur S. Davison, aged seventeen, started a small paper with his limited assortment of printing material, mainly for his own amusement. Whimsically first called the *Bumble Bee*, because he lacked a sufficient number of Bs, he changed the name to the *Young Acadian*. The paper was dedicated to "help our fellow men by a strong and steady denunciation of the many frauds perpetrated on them . . . , ignoring the biased mono-maniacal style of those lesser lights," referring to other newspapers in the area.

In the paper Davison created a way of sizing up the issues, raising questions, and the paper reflected the moral and social standards of the day. Though a small village in the 1880s, Wolfville was portrayed as a cozy, comfortable place. Such interests as cricket matches, the number of boats landing or loading potatoes at the docks, and the problem of some scoundrel freeing all the cattle from the pound undoubtedly more closely linked the people who were already connected by family and geography.

In 1883 the item constantly mentioned was the need of a wharf at the mouth of the Creek. While the editor seemed to feel that "everyone" in town desired one, he also knew that paying the bill made few people elated. In May the Churchills of Hantsport were willing to pay the cost of a new dock, but for a wharf to be effective there must be a road leading to it. Wolfville balked at the expense.

In the opening issue of the paper the editor promised that integrity and honesty would determine the paper's goals and that the good of the community was the whole purpose of the *Young Acadian*. One can imagine the excitement when the paper made its weekly appearance. To the small community this was *their* paper, which urged readers to participate in various activities. The *Acadian* helped make the cricket field, the skating rink, and Witter's Hall to become gathering places where friends could enjoy entertainment and one another.

Arthur Davison's brother, Benjamin O., joined him in the fall of 1883 when the paper became the *Acadian*, a bi-monthly publication. Two years later it became weekly, distributed on Fridays. Shortly after 1885, A. J. Pineo of Wolfville, but then in Kentville, made a journalistic venture, tried to resurrect the *Star* as the *New Star* which soon removed to Kentville as a semi-weekly. This paper was sold in 1892, and Dr. F. H. Eaton changed its name to the *Advertiser* which had been founded in 1880, with the Wolfville edition

THE YOUNG ACADIAN.

Vol. I.   WOLFVILLE, N. S., APRIL, 1883.   No. 1.

POETRY.

THE CASTLE BUILDER

A gentle boy, with soft and silken locks,
  A dreamy boy, with brown and tender
    eyes,
A castle builder, with his wooden blocks,
  And towers that touch imaginary skies.

A fearless rider on his father's knee,
  An eager listener unto stories told
At the Round Table of the nursery,
Of heroes and adventures manifold.

There will be other towers for thee to build;
  There will be other steeds for thee to ride;
There will be other legends, and all filled
  With greater marvels and more glorified.

Build on and make thy castle high and fair,
  Rising and reaching upward to the skies;
List to the voices in the upper air,
  Nor lose thy simple faith in mysteries.

LONGFELLOW.

Miscellany

ARTEMUS' "EPPISODES"

DEAR SIRS: I take my pen in hand to inform yu that Ime in a state of blis and trust these lines will find yu enjoyin the same blessins. Ime reguvenited. Ive found the immorkal wafers of yooth, so to speak, & am as limber and as frisky as a 2 year old steer, & in the futur them boys which sez "go up old bawld head" to me, will do so at the Perril of their hazzard individooally. Ime powerful happy. Heaps of joy has desended to on ct & I feel like a bran new man. Sumtimes I arsk myself "is it a dream?" & suthin within myself sez "it air", but when I look at them sweet little critters, know it is a reallerty—2 reallerty's I ma sa—& I feel gay. There's considerabul human natur in a man after all.

I returned from the Summer Campane with my unparaleld show of wax works and livin' wild Beests of Pray in the early part of this munth.

The people of Baldinville met me cordully and I immejitly commensed restin myself with my famerly.

The other nite, while I wos down to the tavurn tostin my shins again the bar room fire & amuzin the krowd with sum of my adventurs, who shood come in bare heded & terrible excited but Bill Stokes, who sez, sez he, "Old Ward, there's grate doins up to your house."

Sez I, "William how so?"

Sez he "Bust my butrons, but it's grate doins," & then helarfed as if heed kill hisself.

Sez I, risin and puttin on a austeer look, "William, I woodent be a fool."

But he kept on larfin till he war black in the face until he fell over on the bunk whare the hostler sleeps and in a still, small voice sed, "Twins!" I assure you, gents, that the grass didn't grow under my feet on my way home, & I was follered by an enthoosaastic throng of my feller sitterzuns, who hurrard for Old Ward at the top of their voises. I found the house chock full of people. There was Mis Squire Baxter and her three grown up darters, lasyer Perkunses wife, Taberty Riyley, yung Eben Parsuns, Deaken Simmuns fokes, the Schoolmaster, Doctor Jordin, etsettery, etsettery.

Mis Ward was in the west room, which jines the kitchen. Mis Squire Baxter was mixin sumthin in a dipper before the kitchen fire, and a small army of female wimin was rushin wildly round the house with bottles of campfire, peases of flannil, &c. I never seed sich a hubbub in my born dase. I cood stay in the west room only a minit, so strung up was my feelings, so I rusht out and ceased my dubble barrild gun.

"What upon airth ails the man?" says Taberthy Ripley. "Sakes alive, what air you doing!" and she grabed me by my cote tales. "What's the matter with ye?" she continnered.

"Twins, marm," sez I, "twins!"

"I know it," sez she, coverin her face with her apun.

"Wall," sez I, that's what's the matter with me."

"Wall, put down that air gun, yu pesky old fool!" sed she.

"No, marm," sez I, "this is a nashunal day. The glory of this here day isn't confined to Baldinsville by a darn site. On yonder woodshed," sez I, drawen myself up to my full hite, & spekin in a show action voise, "I will fire a Nashunal saloot!" saying which I tared myself from her grasp and rusht to the top of the shed, where I blazed away until Squire Baxter's hired man and my son, Artemus Juneyer, cum and tuk me down by mane forse.

On returnin to the Kitchen, I found quite a lot of people seated be4 the fire, a talkin the event over. They made room for me & I sot down. "Quite a eppisode," sed Doctor Jordin, litin his pipe with a red hot coal.

"Yes," sed I, "2 eppisodes, waiing about 18 pounds jintly."

"A crack coop de tat," said the skulemaster.

"E pluribus unum iu proprietor yersony," sed I, thinkin Ide let him no how as I understood ferrin langwidges as well as he did, if I wasent a schulemaster.

"Its a momentous event," sed yung Eben Parsons, has been 2 quarters to the Academy.

"I never heard 2 twins called by that name afore," sed I, "but I suppose its all rite."

"We shall soon have Wards enuff," sed the editor

Continued on last page

called the *Acadian Orchardist*, first published in January 1894, but in Kentville a year hence. The Windsor *Foreword* and the *Maritime Baptist* were papers also dated at Wolfville for short periods.

The *Acadian* editors enlarged their scope of influence. In 1888 the Davisons took in the Berwick area and the paper was called the *Acadian and Kings County Times*. Reverend D. O. Parker had charge of the Berwick office in 1893. A Wolfville *Acadian* letter suggested in 1894 that there was not enough room in town for two newspapers. A change had taken place in the summer of 1885 when the *Acadian* office moved from the Higgins building to two doors west, over the Customs House. Then, in May 1899 the paper moved into the McKenna Block, located where Elmer's Restaurant is today.

The *Acadian* took a keen interest in local affairs. It chastised those who may have felt in the 1880s that good times were what life was about. The second issue pointed out the need for a lockup for people who consistently violated the Scott Act and in their intoxicated state bothered the more temperate people of the town. The paper acted as a catalyst in several cases. The editors constantly badgered the commissioners of roads and streets about wash-outs and unsafe bridges. Concerned citizens now had a public forum in which to state their demands.

One of the crusades fought in the paper in 1885 was for straightening Main Street. At this time the main road of the village took a wide swing southward opposite where Mud Creek emptied into the harbour. Some of the buildings along the road were what the editors referred to as "tenements" which could be demolished and the road be made over their remains. Later, that same year, some of those buildings were destroyed by fire, an all too-common disaster . . . The paper continued to push to renew the main street, the area from the Odd Fellows building to Munro's shop.

In 1884 the *Acadian* had questioned the road commissioners, whether a term of service longer than one year would be more effective; since the roads and sidewalks were of dirt, the job of keeping them repaired was a full-time one. The paper continued to agitate and told of Anthony Lantz, a cooper by trade, forced to move his business to New Minas because of high rents and taxes in Wolfville, and the paper criticized the school for being "extremely dirty and the uncouth appearance of the different rooms."

During that summer an editorial reprimanded the people for "the dangerous and obnoxious, as well as criminal practice, of tying horses across the sidewalks again." Evidently, the owners wanted the animals to have such little shelter as would be provided by awnings or protecting eaves, and because the sidewalks would not be as wet and muddy as the road. The *Acadian* also showed considerable concern about tenements or derelict houses rented to the poor, by owners who failed to repair the buildings. The citizens were warned of disease, bad living conditions, and danger of fires, and the paper asked for a writing shelf to be placed in the post office.

The *Western Chronicle*, founded in Kentville in 1873, and the *Acadian* entertained their readers as they found fault with one another's policies and accomplishments. The *Acadian Orchardist* also entered the fray but the Wolfville *Acadian* firmly dissociated itself from the *Orchardist* printed in Kentville.

The *Acadian* editors reveal their puritan background when the paper complained that boys were pitching pennies, a form of gambling. The paper disliked "sickly-looking lads in knickerbockers puffing away at the stub of a cigar or cigarette." These offenders were referred to as under-age boys and there should be a law against it. The *Acadian* reported in the spring of 1890 that a new business began when a public house opened, and the drinking customers caused noise and disorder in the streets of the village in the evening. The writer of the account warned, "watch." He advised his readers to beware of more trouble.

The paper recommended in 1893 that a policeman be engaged, and still complained about half-grown boys: "those brainless creatures who wear caps on the backs of their heads and bangs in front, turn up their coat collars, display a watch chain all across their stomachs, smoke cigarettes and cheap cigars." The editors themselves were capable of change, as in September 1919 they altered their surnames from Davison to Davidson in the paper, a matter of interest to the editor of this account. A change had been made earlier when in 1915 Paul Davidson enlisted.

The paper undoubtedly sensed the need for improved facilities in the community. In 1897 they called for a public library, agitated in 1898 for a board of trade, complained in 1911 that Kentville's population was larger than Wolfville's by 1,000, advocated in 1921 the reorganization of the town band, and encouraged a town planning campaign, besides complaining about bootlegging, and advocated a curfew. The paper suggested that "Randall Hill" be made into a park, influenced the town to procure a manager, proposed that a tourist booklet be distributed, and denounced use of "punch boards", also denouncing the government for passing the liquor bill in 1930.

The *Acadian* got recognition for its excellence. The paper won in 1930 a Canadian Weekly award, and, for the third time, in 1939 received an award as the best all-round newspaper of its class in Canada. The paper conscientiously continued to take a stand on contentious issues. In 1947 the editors favoured importing margarine to replace butter, and in 1954 praised the town for purchasing a snow plow that could be attached to a truck, with efficient results. The paper was decidedly displeased with rock and roll music — "a monster." Maxine Williams' sketch of Blomidon topped the front page for many years.

Changes occurred in the paper's format. The *Acadian* modernized, introduced color printing in 1960, and during the next year carried T.V. programs on C.J.C.H. (Halifax). And in 1962 the paper actually carried an ad for Oland's Export Ale.

Difficulties arose. In 1965 Waldo Davidson sold the *Acadian* and retired. The paper was bought by Lancelot Press Ltd. of Wolfville, with William Pope as president. The paper was soon reduced in size and sold in 1968 to the News Publishing Co. of Truro. Although they published again in the regular size, the last issue was put out in July 1968 before the paper was taken over by the Kentville Publishing Company, with the *Acadian* only a supplement of the *Advertiser* since July 1970.

3. The Telegraph

In 1753 a British surgeon, Charles Morrison, conceived of the idea of telegraphy, and the first instrument is usually credited to S. F. B. Morse who constructed a simple one in 1837. He devised a code and sent the first message in 1844. The practice spread rapidly, and Canada hooked up in 1846. In 1874 a line extended from Montreal to the Maritimes, though a line had run in 1848 from Calais, Maine, to St. John, N.B., and from Amherst to Halifax in 1849, making fairly complete connections.

George V. Rand arrived at Wolfville from Canard in 1853 and began his drug store. Before 1869 he had taught himself telegraphy within ten days, and used the Morse code in a part of his shop where he also served the public as postmaster. When the railroad came through Wolfville in 1869, the W. & A. R. had eight of their stations equipped for telegraphy, and Wolfville was one of them. G. V. Rand then turned over his Nova Scotia telegraph business to the station agent, although another report stated that in 1884 the local Acadia Rapid Telegraph Company system was extended to connect the W. & A. R. Station, the post office, the Custom House, the People's Bank, Rupert Prat's store, and the Western Book and News Co. Store. Shops and houses connected with the telegraph lines. These were broken by a severe storm in January 1890, and became unusable for a time, until repaired and extended to the east of the village.

George V. Rand was the second telegraph operator in the county, as L. DeV. Chipman of Kentville had preceded him.

4. The Telephone

A central telephone office began serving the public at Halifax when in December 1879 the Western Union Telegraph Company offered the "Universal Telephone" private lines. Progressive individuals installed their own units, and the telephone arrived near Wolfville by the summer of 1888 when S. P. Benjamin strung a wire between his residence and mill at White Rock. He extended the line four miles by the end of 1889, at a cost of about $300.

The Valley Telephone Company began at Middleton in 1891, and continued west to Digby and east to Hantsport. The Company divided into twelve circuits or exchanges; Wolfville had ninety-eight telephones, the second largest in the group, and one more than Kentville. The company charged each resident $15.00 per year, $20.00 for business houses. The line connected directly to the N.S. Telephone Company, making long distance calls possible. The rate from Hantsport to Halifax was twenty cents. The line reached Wolfville by about the last of August 1892.

The Valley Telephone Company invested in equipment for this new utility. They bought 200 hackmatack poles in 1892, also fifty "Unique" telephones manufactured by John Starr of Halifax, and an equal number of "Bell" sets at $22.50 each. By the end of that year, the line stretched from Annapolis to Hantsport. The customers now learned the "crank and holler" strategy of handling this new-fangled machine which could prove both a blessing and a nuisance.

In 1838 an English novelist humorously divided the people into two sorts: "Peerage folks and Post Hoffice Directory folks." Below the middle class lay the largest group of the English population. Wolfville citizens who first owned the telephone were few in number, segregated above the "Directory". Ownership of a telephone probably indicated social position in the beginning, but the merchant class were more able to finance this innovation. Their advantaged financial status enabled some heads of businesses to place telephones into both their work establishments and their homes.

The *Acadian* of April 1902 informed the public that G. V. Rand's telephone was now in his drug store, not in the post office as before. Others with telephones were: Dr. A. DeW. Barss, Capt. Baird, Dr. E. P. Bowles, E. Sydney Crawley, Dr. G. E. DeWitt, H. W. Davison, R. E. Harris, also his branch store, T. L. Harvey, J. F. Herbin, residence, Harvey & Ellis, Arthur C. Johnson, Dr. H. Lawrence, Royal Hotel, L. W. Sleep, C. W. Strong, Stabb & Co. Coal Office, Wolfville Coal Co., Wolfville Clothing Co., A. J. Woodman, F. W. Woodman.

By 1892 Wolfville was represented, through C. R. H. Starr, on the Valley Telephone Company Board of Directors. The company instructed users to talk only five minutes and to speak directly into the receiver. The president's report for 1905 told of new poles at Wolfville, "Metalicted (sic.) the old main line from Middleton to Wolfville, thus cutting out a large amount of induction and cross talk." In 1907, Starr was replaced by C. H. Borden as director.

The Wolfville exchange later included: Acadia Seminary, Acadia Dairy Co., Academy Home, Acadia Villa, N. N. Bentley, W. M. Black, S. P. Benjamin, C. H. Borden, W. J. Balcom, Mrs. Burgess, R. Earl Burgess, Bank of Montreal, Beaver Mills, W. H. Chase, Chipman Hall, R. A. Cohoon, J. D. Chambers, Reverend H. T. DeWolfe, D. A. R. Station, W. H. Davison, W. H. Evans, Dr. E. H. Freeze, Charles Finch, C. M. Gormley, J. E. Heales & Co., Hutchinson Express, Miss Jacobs, H. D. Johnson, E. H. Johnson, Kent Lodge, Reverend M. P. King, Henry Laupould, J. E. Morse, Dr. A. J. McKenna, F. J. Porter, Porter Bros., W. F. Parker, Robson's Studio, E. W. Sawyer, J. Elliott Smith, C. R. H. Starr, W. J. Stephens, Mrs. J. D. Sherwood, J. W. Selfridge, Town Clerk's Office, C. J. Townsend, J. H. Tabor, Dr. T. Trotter, Union Bank, Young's Bakery.

With the demand for new technology, and the burden of increasing costs, the Valley Telephone Company turned over its assets to the Nova Scotia Telephone Company in 1906 for stock shares. By offering in 1908 an all-night service, the company attempted to get new subscribers. Adverse circumstances necessitated sale in December 1911 to the Maritime Telegraph and Telephone Company, which made improvements. In 1914 the service became continuous, and on October 8, 1920 the first direct call was made to New York, when J. D. Sherwood spoke to Maurice Low. In October 1922 a single battery system was installed, which ended cranking to get "Central".

At Wolfville a new structure housed the telephone office. A brick and stone building, Rhodes Curry Co., contractors, was erected in 1932 on the same site as the old one which had been destroyed by fire. Ninety-two year old Elmer Kinnie had recalled that John Shaw's barber shop had stood on that corner before the first telephone office. He also understood that Ida Wagner has been the first operator.

The office provided employment, and six or eight operators worked in the office in the 1930s. By 1944 the number of subscribers totalled 900 names, and Board of Trade asked the town to number the houses for the telephone book. The *Acadian* reported in August 1949 the death of the town's first telephone "Central", Charlotte L. Hutchinson. For a number of years she also operated a tearoom. She had been born in 1858, had married Reverend John Hutchinson, and they served as missionaries in India. When her husband died she came to Wolfville, where she was a member of the Baptist church and had a special interest in the Telugu mission field in India.

More recent changes have been made: The first telephone booth was placed on Main Street in September 1951, set up between Weavers' and Pickford's establishments. The new dial system was installed in 1952, all telephone numbers having seven digits by 1962. The Maritime Telegraph and Telephone Company introduced long-distance dialing in 1976.

5. Light and Power

The first reference to the use of artificial lighting appeared in the August 1884 issue of the *Acadian*, with the announcement that the college grounds were to be lit with new oil lamps of great power. A year later J. M. Shaw placed a light outside his store, and then the American House placed a lamp in front. This was a good example for others to follow, and now the town wanted them everywhere. The electric light began when in 1881 D. A. Munro installed an arc light "of wonderful brilliance" in his rink, with power from his wood-working factory. Signs of real progress came when a street light, paid for by the citizens, was placed in November 1888 on the corner of College Avenue and School Street.

By 1890 the local light companies that served the Valley communities had installed incandescent lamps of twenty-five candle power each, to burn until 1:30 a.m., for twenty days of a twenty-eight day month. Meanwhile, a number of citizens had placed street lamps in front of their houses.

The *Acadian* announced in December 1891 that Wolfville was to have electric lights, through the enterprise led by D. A. Munro and J. A. Woodman. Lights were turned on in February, but they were not up to full candle power, as the existing engine was not sufficient for the dynamo, with 200 lights in operation. By December the post office had the lights. Lines and poles gradually climbed the hill towards Gaspereau.

In 1895, with good streets on which to travel, residents now wanted the benefits of electricity. This new and exciting predecessor of a thousand other inventions was the most tangible proof that Wolfville was a modern town. The Acadia Electric Light Company erected a new station in 1893, and council agreed in 1894 to have power supplied to the town. Coping with the disturbing paradox of an electric company with a mind of its own and a citizenry which demanded more and more services and then complained about their cost, council tried to get electric power into the homes of the residents. Late in the 1890s an episode produced irate editorials in the *Acadian* concerning fifty-five recently-purchased street lamps. The paper castigated council for apparent extravagance, then charged it with placing too many (forty-five) of the new lights in the business district, "leaving the rest of the town in total darkness." In turn, council was annoyed about the uncooperative attitude of the electric company which had a thoughtless habit of cutting down trees, then informing council that it had been done.

The electricity was produced by a plant at the east end of town, approximately on the present site of Nova Scotia Power Commission building, and operated by D. R. Munro. Power was turned off at ten in the evening, requiring citizens to use kerosene lamps for further lighting requirements. In most homes electric light was installed in the downstairs living quarters; electricity in the sleeping quarters was considered an unnecessary affectation.

After enduring many inconveniences, the town became convinced that it needed its own power plant. Actual negotiations did not begin until 1906, and when ratepayers finally authorized an expenditure of $20,000 to buy its holdings, the company had increased its selling price to $35,000. Not until twelve years later was the deal completed.

Several people enthused about electric energy prospects as power developments on the Gaspereau River promised energy for Wolfville and other localities. A report to the *Western Chronicle* in April 1913 contemplated a good future. Changes took place, as the light company installed a gas engine for all night service, and new globe lights were installed in front of the post office.

By 1914 Nova Scotia had electric light companies in twenty cities and towns, powered mostly by steam generated by coal. In Wolfville, the Acadia Light Company burned both coal and fuel oil, and after operating for twenty-six years the plant worked only seven hours out of twenty-four, and provided only a faint light. The Wolfville Board of Trade, with L. E. Shaw as president and George C. Nowlan as secretary, asked Charles H. Wright and Roy A. Jodrey to investigate the Gaspereau River as a possible source of power. Shaw wrote several years later that the two men "never came back to report." They found a waterfall and set up a hydroelectric plant on their own.

Back in 1901 the Nova Scotia Electric Light Company bought land, but by 1914 only rusty machinery remained from efforts to establish a plant. Roy Jodrey located his own efforts at another part of the river in 1917, and got Kempton Bezanson of Wolfville to build the power plant. Jodrey and Wright completed their project in 1920 at Stivers Falls, White Rock. Poles and lights came to the communities in that year, as did the first telephones. Charlie Wright had already built the Kentville Sanatorium and was erecting the university gymnasium and rink.

In 1917 Roy Jodrey and his family moved to Wolfville and lived from 1918 to 1936 on west Main Street in a large house which would become Paramount Hotel. On the site earlier was a house occupied by James Elder, later bought by Arthur C. Johnson who tore it down and erected a more modern house, owned and lived in by Marshall Black, and then by R. A. Jodrey.

By 1925 Jodrey had investments in Canadian corporations and was still the manager of Wolfville Apple Storage Company. About that time William H. Chase of Wolfville got control of Windsor Electric Company and secured Jodrey as manager. This required regular trips from Wolfville for Jodrey. He had much on his mind and often was indifferent to his driving. However, he was not the victim of this attitude; rather, his good friend Charles Wright died at the wheel.

Tragedy silenced Wolfville on July 16, 1929 as news reached the town that Charles Wright, president of Minas Basin Pulp and Power, his son Graham (10) and his daughter Jean (15), his sister-in-law Mrs. Ruby Huston, and his father-in-law Nason W. Eaton had died at a train crossing near Falmouth. The loss devastated the family and the Valley community. Mrs. Charles Wright, the former Annie Louise Eaton, was a leader in church and other community activities, is now aged ninety-one and lives with her daughter Rhoda, wife of artist Alex Colville.

In 1919 Wolfville finally purchased the Acadia Electric Company for $20,000. After taking charge of the complex equipment involved in establishing new power lines, checking meters and sending out bills, officials might have wondered if the long fight for ownership had been worth the effort. The town had spent over fifteen years negotiationg this deal and was determined to run the company well and at a profit. It did so for the next thirty years until it sold the operation to the Avon River Power Company in 1949.

Residents wanted an attractive, modern-looking town, and they were willing to pay the price while they could afford it. The Streets Committee was busy in the 1920s, installing new lights and recommending others. During the depression, the Wolfville Electric Commission provided a boost to the town budget, with an annual profit of between $3,000 and $4,000, given to the town as a ''grant''.

The electric commission operated at a high profit for many years but in 1947 the Public Utilities Board forced the commission to reduce its rates, which lowered profits. The N.S. Light and Power Company had approached council previously with an offer to buy the plant for $28,000, and was turned down. In 1949 its subsidiary, Avon River Power Company, again approached the council, offering $50,000. Council agreed in December to sell for $56,000, and the electric company once again changed hands.

In 1968 new street light poles of concrete were installed with lights on curved ''davits''. During the following year illuminated overhead signs were placed over crosswalks.

XVI.

RECREATION AND SPORTS

1. Cricket.

Cricket was played as early as 1860 by the college and academy students, whose playing field was adjacent to the present football field. The Evangeline Cricket Club organized in 1883, reorganized in 1884, and held several matches that summer. The club officers were: President, F. L. Brown; Secretary, A. M. Hoare; Treasurer, G. W. Munro; other members included: E. G. Woodworth, D. R. Munro, Winfield Wallace, C. A. Patriquin, J. E. Farrell, Walter S. Evans, B. O. Davison. One of their sorties was a scratch match on the college grounds between elevens captained by D. R. Munro and F. L. Brown.

During the 1890s efforts were made to revive interest in the game, but it was 1899 before a match was reported, this time a business men's contest between married and unmarried men. Also in that year Wolfville lost three games — to Hantsport, to Kentville, and to Canning. On the Wolfville team were H. Brown, C. Patriquin, J. Herbin, G. Munro, E. Brown, Thompson, Michener, Caldwell, Harberie.

Interest lagged again until 1908 when the club was reorganized, with new officers: President, W. H. Chase; Secretary Treasurer, J. F. Herbin; Captain, Mr. Robinson. It was agreed to use the campus field for games, and the equipment was stored at J. F. Herbin's store. Wolfville played Halifax in July 1915, though the Great War generally disrupted the games.

The Cricket Club reorganized in May 1920, with a slate of officers: Patron, W. H. Chase; President, Reverend R. F. Dixon; 1st Vice-President, R. W. Ford; 2nd Vice-President, G. S. Bauld; Treasurer, J. Elliott Smith; Secretary, G. H. Ruffee. The town held a "Big Day" of sports that summer, that included cricket, baseball, tennis, tug-of-war, and a Boy Scout tournament. By 1921 and 1922 there existed a Valley Cricket League which included Windsor, Kentville, Annapolis and Bridgetown, and was presided over by Reverend R. F. Dixon.

Changes took place, as by 1924 many adult cricketers had moved away, and the death of J. F. Herbin removed an outstanding enthusiast of the sport. New officers were chosen, with Reverend R. F. Dixon still as President, A. C. Cox the Manager, and Nelson Grant as Captain. In 1926 Wolfville had teams in cricket, baseball and tennis. This appears to be the final reference to cricket.

2. Skating and Hockey

The January 1877 issue of the *Acadia Athenaeum* reported a community interest in establishing a skating rink in the east end of the village, but this did not happen until four years later. D. A. Munro operated a carriage factory and woodworking plant just east of the harbour, and his son D. R. Munro was a leader in sports activities. He played cricket and baseball, built sailboats and motorboats, and with his father constructed in 1881 the town's first rink, circular in shape, on the street leading to the government pier, north of the Munro residence.

The *Acadian* advertised weekly carnivals and skating parties, and in 1885 races were held involving a One-Mile Forward, and the Half-Mile Backward competition. At the beginning of 1887 Munro announced the rink open on Friday nights under electric lights, the skating fee ten cents, and five cents for the promenade. A successful carnival was held in 1892, with 150 skaters on the ice, and the Kentville band providing music. The rink was torn down in June 1894, and S. P. Heales built a new rink on Front Street opposite the Skoda building.

Hockey was a popular sport, and Aberdeen Rink was often in use. Top scorers for Wolfville early in 1899 were Harry Johnson and B. W. Lockwood. The rink was used also for the special ice carnival features of the year, with fancy dress and band music. The band played also for summer concerts. In 1898, Rink Manager Heales procured a mechanical piano for the rink, and the Wolfville Victorias, the town's top team, defeated Windsor, but later lost to Canning. For Wolfville were: Shaw, Sherwood, A. Johnson (Captain), Shaw, Gilmore, Jones, Cox. The reporter explained that "the ball was kept, most of the time, in Wolfville's territory." In 1899, the team reorganized, with Stanley Gillmore as Captain, G. L. Starr as Secretary.

1906. Girls' Hockey. Top row: Hettie Crandall, Nell DeWitt; centre: Emma Murray, Gladys Harris, May Woodman; bottom row: Enid Tufts, Lou Crandall.

1906-08. Junior Shamrocks. Top row: Leonard Eaton, Fred Sleep, John Gould, Judson Harris; middle row: Willie Murphy, Lloyd Woodman (manager), Harry Fraser; bottom row: Frank Godfrey, Harry Sleep.

The hockey team of 1904, pictured at Randall House Museum, shows the following players: W. Godfrey, Spare; A. Lockwood, Centre; H. Pineo, Rover; J. Kennedy, Right Wing; F. Fraser, Point; S. Gilmour, Business Manager; W. Harris (Captain), Centre Point; G. Loomer, Left Wing; G. Regan, Goal. At the end of 1904 the club reorganized, with Ernest Easterman as Captain, and Dr. Fred Beckwith the Secretary Treasurer.

The record-breaking snows of 1905 levelled the rink but by February 1906 a new rink opened, with Mr. Stevens the proprietor. The rink was regulation in size, and included a curling alley and waiting rooms. Music played weekly, and occasionally by the Wolfville Brass Band.

In January 1907 the club sent a team to Lunenburg to play in the N.S. Western Hockey League. The team included: J. S. MacLeod, Right Wing; H. Pineo, Centre; R. Spicer, Left Wing; F. L. Faulkner, Rover; R. W. Churchill, Cover; W. C. B. Harris, Point; R. H. Ells (Goal); and W. S. Wallace, Business Manager. Lunenburg won, 8 to 1. A couple of months later a ladies hockey game was played in the Evangeline Rink between Wolfville and Windsor. Playing for Wolfville were Lue Crandall, Goal; Nellie DeWitt, Point; Nettie Crandall, Cover; J. McLeod, Left Wing; G. Crandall, Right Wing; Enid Tufts, Cover; Gladys Harris, Cover. May Woodman, Left Wing; and Emma Murray were also listed elsewhere. The game ended 1-1.

The years 1906, 1907, 1908 were busy ones for the hockey enthusiasts.

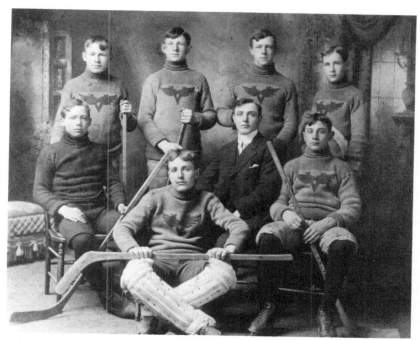

1907-08. Wolfville Victorias. Top row: H. Baird, B. Eagles, E. Barss, H. Corey; bottom row: C. Webster, C. Robinson, F. Godfrey (manager), B. Shaw

1914. Top left: Violet Sleep. Who are the others? Advise the editor.

The Shamrocks were champions of Kings County Junior Hockey League for those three years. The players were: Leonard Eaton, Fred Sleep, John Gould, Judson Harris, William Murphy, Harry Fraser, Frank Godfrey, Harry Sleep. Other members included: Lloyd Woodman, Business Manager; Aubrey Dakin, President; and R. MacGibbons, Secretary. The second Shamrock Team, 1909, was made of: J. H. Gould, J. W. Eagles, F. Murphy, A. B. Young, B. D. Eagles, P. F. Cook, G. H. Ruffee, C. A. Manning, J. F. Eastwood (Business Manager).

Evangeline Rink was built in 1906 by S. D. Stevens. It was purchased in 1908 by H. D. Johnson and H. D'Almaine, and on December 18 of that year it was officially opened, with music by the Wolfville band.

Skating and fancy dress carnivals were also popular at the rink, and the Hockey Club was a member of the Western Hockey League. In 1910 the club looked for support from the town merchants, and borrowed the Nicklet Moving Picture Theatre from Mr. Bustin to raise money for the club.

In February 1911 the Wolfville club covered themselves with glory by becoming the undefeated champions of the N.S. Western Hockey League. Players were: Winfield Spicer, Cliff Webster, Harry Fraser, Robert Spicer, Brent Eagles, G. Christie, Leonard Eaton, Blake Shaw, Herman Baird, Leon Archibald, and Harry Sleep. The team won the Halifax *Herald* Trophy, and two years later they repeated their triumph. If Harry Fraser and Herman Baird were playing today they probably would be in the pro league.

The community responded well to winter sports, enjoying their carnivals also at Evangeline Rink. That of February 1912 called for D. A. R. special trains from Aylesford and Hantsport, with the Berwick and Kentville bands providing the music. The Masquerade Carnival during the next month was

May an abundance of the Christmas Spirit
be with you this Season.

Very Sincerely,

Wolfville. N. S.   C. A. Patriquin

The 1930s. Skating on the Duck Pond. Centre: Patriquin house, now Randall House Museum.

even better attended, with about 1,200 persons. D'Almaine and Johnson, the proprietors, had arranged for special trains and for the band of the Royal Canadian Regiment — a great success.

Girls got into the act again in 1916. Those playing were: Marguerite Coldwell, Minnie Godfrey, Marie Wilson, Grace Shaw, Frances Stackhouse, Gladys Elderkin, and Clara Chisholm. There was a lady's team also in 1923.

Around 1919, league play resumed in Evangeline Rink with new players: Allan Parker, Ted Stackhouse, Waldon and Gordon Kennedy, Stub Hirtle, Molly Morrison, Karl Mason, Paul Tingley, Murray Beardsley, and Fred Eagles.

In 1920 Wolfville became a member of the Valley Amateur Hockey League, and in 1921 were top winners. In the early 1920s the town team included Barney Bishop, Miff Kennedy, Lloyd Vaughan, and Graham Harvey. In 1925 new players were: Wally Barteaux, Gil Rand, and Jack Williams. Shortly before World War II new players were: Gerald Harrington, Maurice Lockhart, Murray Lockhart, Gordon Shaw, Neil Sanford, Don Williams, Erne West, joined later by Wilf Reading and Max Noseworthy. This team entered the Nova Scotia finals.

The rink was sold to the Athletic Association of Acadia, and taken over by the governors in 1926. Fire, strongly believed to be the result of arson destroyed Evangeline Rink. Plans were made for a new rink, Leslie R. Fairn the architect, and C. H. Wright, builder. Ice was made in the rink in January 1928.

The official Wolfville team came out on top of the Valley league twice more: February 1931, and again in 1937 when the team members were: Goal — West; Defence — Williams, Burns, Mitchell; Forwards — Harrington, Reading, Shaw, Sanford, Kennedy, Baird, Lockhart.

During 1938 Varley Bishop directed the team but no organized play occurred through World War II. However, a team was organized under Frank Regan after the university installed artificial ice in 1946, the first maritime university to do so. Players were: veterans Gerald Harrington, Maurice Lockhart, Gordon Shaw, Murray Lockhart, Don Williams; and new players: Lorne Cavanaugh and Ronald Coldwell.

Hockey was the organized sport, but casual skating was enjoyed at Willow Park where the frozen Duck Pond provided outdoor exercise. A rink was made also on the school grounds.

In 1949, Charles Patterson became hockey manager and procured Billy MacIntyre as coach. At this time the players, not listed above, were: Rhodes Hennigar, Carl O'Brien, John Regan, Roy Forsythe, Roddie and Eddie Crowe, Claude Rogers. When submitting his "Story of Hockey" to the *Acadian* of February 1949, G. E. Angus also credited Dr. P. S. Cochrane, Dr. Morton, Cecil Hansford, and Eddie Hennigar for helpful assistance to the teams. During that year the team became known as the Falcons, and during the following March became again the Valley league champions.

Other organized groups played. In 1956 Wolfville helped form a suburban league with seven teams participating. During the following year a Church Hockey League came into being, with Baptists and Anglicans taking part. In March 1960 the Falcons won the mainland Intermediate Hockey title. Four years later the Valley Hockey League reorganized.

In 1967 the Minor League was again reorganized, and by 1970 had several competitive teams. The Pee-Wee teams of 1970 and 1974 won the N.S. "B" championships, and the Midgets came a close second in the 1974 Provincial championships. The young players had wider interests. The *Advertiser* of March 1975 reported that "An exchange of Peewee and Bantam hockey teams was held for about five years as Wolfville and Cambridge, Mass. boys visited the other's rinks and homes. Mayor Paul Kinsman and the hockey association president William Parker received from Gerald Wood and Mrs. Ferne Davidson a large trophy. These had received it previously during a visit to Cambridge Youth Hockey Association." Ralph and Donald Mosher assisted in the arrangements for this first international hockey exchange.

Wolfville had also formed in 1967 a Figure Skating Club, and in 1979 and 1980 held successful carnivals at the university rink, with sixty members taking part. Terrie Logue was professional instructor, and Mrs. Sally Martins was chairperson for the event. The Minor League Club had completed in 1979 their 200 club financial program, with Ferne Davidson as chairperson.

Another noteworthy entertainment was held in the 1980 season — that of the Firemen's Ice Carnival, with prizes donated by merchants for best costumes; Mayor William Kenny and Lois Gower were judges. Harold Stewart was prime mover of the carnival which was highlighted by a tug-of-war between Wolfville and Port Williams Fire Departments.

3. Baseball

In 1878 college students talked of baseball, and in May 1888 an attempt was made to form a baseball club. Organized in July, the group included: J. F. Herbin, Catch; D. Munro, Pitch; G. Munro, 1st Baseman; W. Wallace, 2nd Baseman; E. Sawyer, 3rd Baseman; Walter Brown, Short Stop; C. Patriquin, Right Field; Blenkhorn, Centre Field; Tugwood, Left Field. The team played Kentville in August. Sport flashes from the *Acadian* showed much activity through the next two years. In June 1888 the club officers included: G. H. Wallace, J. W. Caldwell, O. D. Harris, Geo. W. Munro, E. W. Sawyer, Charles Patriquin, W. S. Wallace, Fenton Harris. The team played in July a picked nine from the Cornwallis valley when Charles Eaton captained the visitors, and E. Sawyer had charge of the local team. In August, Wolfville's second team lost to Canard. Two summers later an excursion took a large group to Parrsboro where Wolfville played against Springhill. Munro pitched a fine game, with Herbin at 1st. Other players included: Cox, Hemmeon, Patriquin, L. Brown, Murphy, Higgins, H. Brown.

Almost nine years passed before the next report of a game, in October 1899, when Wolfville defeated Windsor. In 1908 a high school team played against Acacia Villa School at Grand Pre. By 1910 the Wolfville team was named the Victorias who in the following year lost two games to a visiting team from Andover, Mass., and in 1913 defeated Parrsboro.

The war intervened, and it was not until August 1919 that baseball came back to its own. The sum of $25 was requested to outfit the players with the necessary equipment, and by 1920 and 1922 the team was a member of the Valley League. In 1923 they did not join. Instead, it was announced that a Town League had been formed with three teams: West End, East End, and The Hill, in hopes of developing a team for the Valley League. During these years Wallace Barteaux displayed his baseball skills, and Allan Parker excelled at football.

The year 1950 was a good one for baseball. The town team was now called the Monarchs and was comprised of Bordie Carey, Willie Henderson, Rae Swanson, Ron O'Brien, John Sproul, Fred Kelly, Doug Spidel, Ernie LeBlanc, Lloyd Smith, Hugh Fairn, Merritt Gibson, Burton Bowlby, and Ralph Mosher. The team's bat boy was Eric Smith.

Twenty-six boys were enrolled in the local "Little League" program in 1951. The boys playing were: B. VanZoost, E. Young, C. Giffin, F. Cole, D. Stevens, T. Cochrane, M. Beach, J. Cochrane, D. Purdy, K. Manzer, M. Burke, L. DeWolfe. The Lions Club Committee member was Reg. Boates, and Burton Bowlby served as Coach. "Donkey-Ball" was played that August on Raymond Field, the Rotary and Lions Club members risking their necks. In June 1979 the Wolfville Recreation Department organized Minor Baseball.

Between 1955 and 1979 few organized ballgames were played, but several young players joined the Kentville Minor Baseball program. The Van Blarcom brothers: Sandy, Brian, and Kirk, along with Ian and Monty Mosher, became five of the best senior baseball players in Atlantic Canada.

4. Other Group Games

The college students adopted Association (Soccer) Football in 1876, with fifteen players. In 1882 Acadia played rugby rules for football, and games were played sporadically in the community through the years. In 1897 a rugby football competition was arranged for a trophy prize, when Avonians, Kings College, Wolfville, and Kentville took part. Most of the teams were from mercantile establishments and each team played two games in the competition. In the fall of the next year Wolfville won over Windsor, and Horton Academy defeated Kentville Academy. Albert Green was captain in 1899.

Possibly the first local reference to basketball appeared in the *Acadia Athenaeum* of March 1894 when Nova Scotia played against New Brunswick in the college gymnasium. An 1897 game ended 9-6 for Nova Scotia students.

In the summer of 1931, a Softball League of Baptists, Anglicans, United Church, and Married Men was formed, and by 1947 was mentioned as being a member of the Valley Softball League. Reorganized in 1974 by the Recreation Department, several area teams participated in the game. Volleyball was mentioned in March 1962, with four teams playing for the Jack Herbin trophy.

In the early 1950s the Rotary Club developed Rotary Field on King Street, the members assisted by school children. They laid out two softball diamonds and a football (soccer) field, with bleachers and backstops. The present clubhouse was constructed in the late 1950s.

5. Swimming

In July 1883, some enterprising young men solved a problem for the swimming population of the place. A wharf was constructed during that or the next year, and the harbour became an attractive spot for a dip on a summer day. However, the cold water and a gentle breeze discouraged the wet swimmers because of the discomfort. Therefore, in the summer of 1890 the young men raised some money by subscription and built what came to be

About 1889. Swimming at the wharf.

called fondly, "The Bather's Retreat". This handy little structure, on the wharf, allowed people to change while protected from the wind off the Basin, and also kept clothes dry and clean.

In that same summer a swimming tournament was held at the wharf. Contestants were: Brenton Quinn, Stanley Gilmore, and Jack Heales. The fancy swimming contest involved Bennie Newcombe, Clarence Quinn, Samuel Prat, Jr. Another race was swum by John Farnham, Ernest Porter, and Clifford James. In the Men's race, A. C. Patriquin, Louis Brown, A. V. Rand, C. R. Higgins, and Harding Bishop competed. The high and long diving by J. F. Herbin was much admired. The barrel and tub racing were failures.

Another entertainment during the summer of 1890 was held at the wharf and was greatly publicized. That event gave the public a chance to see "Miss Maggie Burrell — the World's Greatest Skipping Rope Dancer."

First mention of the Wolfville Triton Swim Club was in February 1973 when Operation Olympics declared those qualified to compete. Heather MacKay won the 50 m. butterfly, and Patti Murphy got a third in her event. Among the boys, Jimmy Williams received a bronze in the individual medley. Other winners included Rod Murray, Pauli Williams.

In the summer of 1974 Director Terry Moore of the Town's Recreation Department formed a swimming instruction group. In 1974 Heather MacKay placed 6th in the 50 m. butterfly in Operation Jr. Olympics and made a new provincial record. For the 1975 All-Star Team Trials Chris Ryan was chosen a member and placed second in ten and under 50 m. breaststroke. At Greenwood in December Heather MacKay made the finals in all her events, and obtained two firsts. Chris and Maggie Ryan and Angela Watts did well. Ann Ryan, Stephanie MacDonald, Rickey Hansen, Cathy White, and Darryl Bent also took part.

Dr. Robert Watts helped organize the club which had David Fry as coach, and Charles Fry as president. Others in on the founding were Mr. and Mrs. Victor MacKay and Mary Anne Ryan. In 1980 the officers were: President, Shirley Marston; Vice-President, Joan Seaman; Secretary, Beverley Williams; Treasurer, John Horton.

Associated with swimming was the Wolfville and District Water Ski Club which operated between 1967 and 1974, based at Mike Smith's cottage at Lumsden Pond. Approximately thirty-five young men and women were instructed in the skills and in small craft safety, first with "dry-land" performance. Members participated in area tournaments, and several competed successfully in provincial contests and in the Canada Summer Games of 1969 and 1973. A highlight was a visit from George Athanas of Kelowna, B.C., Men's World Champion. He demonstrated his skills and gave instruction.

6. Golf

By about 1895 a golf course was laid out above the college campus on Baptist church hill. The August 1900 issue of the Halifax *Mail* reported golf at Wolfville, with about twenty members, including two from Kentville. The officers were: President, C. R. H. Starr; Vice-President, J. W. Wallace; Secretary Treasurer, Professor F.C. Sears. Other members included:

Professor R. C. Haley, George W. Munro, and W. H. Chase. The links were crowded with players.

The Ken-Wo Country Club was incorporated in April 1921 to serve both Kentville and Wolfville on a sixty-acre golf course. Only a few holes were laid out for the first few years, but by 1924 a nine-hole game was being played. The club procured a Scottish professional, Boswick, during the summer of 1920 to give instruction and to superintend the greens. George Graham was the first president. R. S. Babcock, a professional golfer who came to Wolfville in the late 1940s, was chairman of the greens committee for many years. The club procured more land and extended the course to eighteen holes.

7. Bicycling and Horseracing

In May 1879 the editor of the *Acadia Athenaeum* endorsed a manual on bicycling, which could teach riders the skills to get to Kentville and back in an hour. Later, in 1891 the Wolfville bicyclists organized a club, and in May enjoyed an outing to Kentville. They had sixteen members: George Munro, Captain G. F. Herbin, W. E. Butler, J. E. Hales, C. R. Borden, H. M. Sleep, J. W. Shaw, C. R. Higgins, M. S. Read, W. J. Spurr, A. V. Rand, J. W. Litch, J. L. Masters, E. Porter, J. Vaughan, B. Wallace. They took tea at the Lyons Hotel and returned to Wolfville. By 1895 there were twenty-five bicycles in the town, and a couple of years later two daring ladies "of about forty summers" attracted considerable attention because of the picturesque and brief costumes they sported. The Bicycle Club members received a reduced rate when they used the Speedway.

Bicycle racing was a popular sport in 1927 and 1928. Gerald Hughes and others participated in races, such as from Wolfville to Halifax.

Another form of racing was popular in the 1890s. Wolfville's Mayor Bowles operated a Trotting Park in 1893, and the Wolfville Speedway was open to bicyclists in 1894, completed and ready for horsemen and cyclists.

8. Tennis

Tennis was popular at times but often needed to be revived. In June 1891 Wolfville organized a Tennis Club, which used the college courts for playing. Officers were: President, E. W. Sawyer; Vice-President, Mrs. Ernest Brown; Captain, J. F. Herbin; Secretary, M. S. Reid, Treasurer, F. R. Higgins; Committee: Misses Sherwood, J. Brown, A. M. Fitch, E. Burgess. An annual meeting was noted in 1893, and an organizational meeting in 1894 had new members voted on by ballot. E. W. Sawyer was the secretary. The club apparently was in operation for a few years, and presented a three-act farce at Evangeline Beach two years in succession, viz. 1909 and 1910, presumably to finance tennis equipment.

During the war the Methodist Tennis Club reorganized in 1916, and after the war the Town Club reorganized in the summer of 1919. President R. W. Ford encouraged new members to sign with Secretary-Treasurer R. W. Tufts. The first mention of an actual competition came at the end of the 1924 season when Wolfville won the Valley Tennis Championship. In 1927 the Provincial Championships were held at Wolfville, and in 1934 the town players won the Valley Championship for the third year in a row. The club was reorganized in May 1947, and again in 1961, when the officers were: President, Willie Morine; Vice-President, Annie Piggott; Secretary-Treasurer, Fred Seaman.

Recreation Director Terry Moore formed a tennis instruction group in 1974, and by June 1978 the club had fifty-eight junior and senior members. Winners of contests were: Beverley Harrison, Geoff Douglas, Colin Cochrane, and Stephanie Bearne, followed by Paula McGuinness, Glen Cheney, Tommy Thompson, and Tom McGuinness.

9. Curling

In February 1895 a Curling Club was formed with a membership of sixteen who played in the Aberdeen Rink. They curled the following year also, but possibly lost interest; they contemplated a new beginning in 1908, but it was not until 1931 that the Curling Club began to prepare the rink for action. Then in the fall of 1935, a Curling Rink was erected on land east of University Rink. It was a fireproof building, costing $8,700 and housed both the Curling and the Badminton Clubs. (Badminton had been organized in 1931.) C. W. Fairn was president of the Curling Club.

The first matches played in the rink took place on New Year's Day, 1936, with the competing teams comprised of: 1. Dr. Avery DeWitt, J. D. Harris, G. C. Nowlan, B. W. Wallace; 2. O. H. Foshay, G. H. Ruffee, Robert Bauld, R. G. Callander; 3. H. B. Bowlby, F. G. Herbin, E. Scott Eaton, R. G. Callander; 4. G. A. Boggs, Dr. Avery DeWitt, I. Emerson, C. W. Fairn. In 1947 artificial ice was installed in the building, and in 1955 a new Badminton Club had Bruce Laidlaw as president. Bob Stirling's Rink won the N.S. Past President's Curling Bonspiel in January 1960.

The club renovated its premises in 1965 at a cost of $60,000, and in 1974 added a Ladies Lounge. They sought new members in 1980, and President Blake Porter reported that the forty-five year old club had more than eighty curlers playing on four sheets of ice in 1979. Secretary Johnnie Johnson named the regular fee at $110 for the male members.

10. Table Games

The community also engaged in table games as a form of recreation, enjoying one another's company during tests of intellect and manual skill. In 1889 Wolfville and Windsor competed in several correspondence games of chess, and in January 1899 the Whist Club met at the home of Robert Baird, next at Sydney Crawley's, then at Mrs. Ernest Brown's, and at Mrs. O. D. Harris's. Their first meeting of the fall was held at Mrs. Robert Rand's home. In February 1901 the club discontinued for the season.

Other kinds of games were played. At the end of 1900 the young people formed a Euchre Club of weekly meetings, and earlier, progressive crokinole had become a popular indoor recreation.

Still another kind of table game had its devotees. George Smith applied in 1900 for a license to operate a pool room but council, as at River City, regarded the game unfavourably, turned down the request. William Bauld's petition during the next year to open what he called a "Billiard Hall and Reading Room" was also quietly denied before action was taken. However, a pool room did open later and taught Wolfville youths the skills of the green table top.

The further attempt was made in 1910 when G.H. Ruffee reportedly opened a pool hall in the Wallace Block where the Box of Delights now stands. He had tables and an up-to-date ladies' and gentlemen's shoe shine stand, and sold soft drinks. This report is questionable, for young Ruffee, according to his daughter Jeannette, was not old or prosperous enough to handle such an enterprise. In the 1930s, Starr Fullerton did operate a pool hall in the MacKenna Block, later Eaton Block, near where Pulsifer's flower shop now stands. It was taken over in 1935 by Clyde D. Carver who sold to Wilbur Vaughan. Then Cyril Evans transferred the business to the rear of Waterbury's store where he had two pool tables and two snooker tables in the 1950s. In 1966 the M. & R. Billiard Club opened at 216 Main Street, with Ralph Brown as proprietor.

11. Other Outdoor Sports and Entertainment

The community was alive with organizations in the 1890s. In the summer of 1894 the Gun Club planned a trapshooting tournament, and representatives went from here to other localities to participate. Three years in a row D. A. Munro came home with prizes, won the first permanent cup for that distinctive honour.

About 1900. Wolfville Gun Club. Bottom row: F.P. Rockwell, C.A. Patriquin, O.D. Harris; back row: J.F. Herbin, D.R. Munro, G.W. Munro, Dr. Geo. DeWitt, C.H. Borden, a friend, Kate Munro.

In 1895 quoits was played on the school grounds by many people, so that during the summer a Quoit Club was organized, with President, E. S. Crawley; Vice-President, C. W. Borden; 2nd Vice-President, J. W. Caldwell; Secretary-Treasurer, C. S. Baker. The club revived two years later, with E. S. Crawley the banner player.

Another activity involved both Town and Gown. The Bulmer Race was in a class by itself. The *Western Chronicle* of October 1912 gave the origin of this event when it reported that Mr. Boomer (Bulmer) of the class of 1897 offered a cup for the class which won an eight-mile relay race from Kentville to Wolfville and around the campus. He also offered four prizes of $25 each for essays on topics chosen by the editor of the *Athenaeum*. Partly because of bad November roads, the run from Kentville was replaced by a run on the college track. Four college classes and the academy competed, with a large crowd of spectators from the town and the college. The academy won. The Bulmer race was revived from time to time.

Not all recreations and sports were so well organized or involved with team members. C. A. Patriquin bought a merry-go-round for Evangeline Beach in 1897 where some Wolfville families established summer residences through the years since then. In 1909, as at other times, a steamer took citizens for an evening sail in the Basin or for a day's excursion to Parrsboro. Sleighing parties were a popular pastime until highway traffic on snow-cleared roads made sleighing impossible. In 1938 the council arranged that King Street be available for coasting on Wednesday afternoons under police supervision.

Entertainments also took a bizarre nature. U.F.O. (Unidentified Flying Object) sighting became popular in the 1960s and 1970s, and in 1974 Frank Evans was one of three men reported making parachute jumps at the Waterville Airport. Less exciting was the occasional arrival of the small circus, with its few animals, games of chance, and sideshows, but these events were spectator occasions. Having had experiences in New Zealand with lawn bowling, Maurice and Anna Hennigar endeavored in 1977 to introduce the game to Wolfville. By 1980 some classes of instruction had been held, and some of the town and nearby residents began to show interest.

12. The Quadrille Club

Dancing in an organized way appeared in Wolfville earlier than might have been expected. A Dancing Class opened in 1867 on the second floor of Fred Brown's Hardware and General Store, now 176 Main Street. Quadrille Clubs became popular in the 1880s. Still, some people preferred the traditional as when a successful ball was held in June 1884 at Canning, with the following present from Wolfville: Mr. and Mrs. C. B. Munro, Mrs. C. R. Burgess, Misses A. Burgess, Gladys Starr, Prat, the Misses Sherwood, and Messrs J. L. Harvey, R. Prat, E. Burgess, H. Gilmore, L. Webster.

Wolfville people attended in April 1884 a "big Quadrille Party" at Windsor, and in February 1885 the Quadrille Band of Wolfville played when the Cricket Club held a benefit at the rink, clearing $14. Then the *Acadian* of February 1896 reported that the Quadrille Club was organized in January of that year and that thirty members had driven to Kentville to dance. At Wolfville the club used the large residence recently built by Professor D. M. Welton.

The club might not have met regularly but did hold a dance in 1900, eighty-five present, and again in January 1904, meeting at the home of Mrs. Jean Collins, with Bishop and Ward of Canning providing the music. The group held an "at home" in April 1907 in R. E. Harris's fruit house, and a dance two years later at the Harris fruit building. The group seems to have gone out of existence within the next fifteen years. The *Acadian* of July 1923 listed dancing every Thursday night at the Wolfville Community Hall under the auspices of the Wolfville Band.

13. Athletic Associations

After the Acadia Amateur Athletic Association held their third annual field-day of sports, in May 1893, the townspeople talked in 1908 of obtaining a suitable playground for the young people, and J. F. Herbin, R. W. Starr, W. F. Ford, I. B. Oakes, Reverend R. F. Dixon, and O. D. Harris were appointed to consider a public athletic ground for the community. No action appears to have been taken until 1920 when the Wolfville Amateur Athletic Association organized, with H. W. Phinney as president, and Dr. W. A. Coit as general manager.

The athletic grounds were finally available in August 1937 when Dr. Lalia Chase donated land on the east of Main Street for an athletic field, but action was delayed. In 1946 a Playground Board meeting was held, presided over by Mayor C. W. Fairn, and a new Amateur Athletic Association had Harry Von Zoost as president. Later, a Wolfville Youth Association elected officers: President, Alan Reynolds; Secretary, Clara Nowlan; Treasurer, Donald Machum; Advisors, Barbara Smith, Ralph Mosher. The group was known as WO-YA. The association reformed in 1950, and in 1962 they reorganized under President, Herbert Sullivan; Secretary-Treasurer, Hugh Fairn; Vice-President, Jack Herbin.

The general rise in student population set council thinking about increased recreational facilities, and the need for a recreation commission was discussed in 1965. The commission would be composed of five to seven members appointed by council, with one chosen from the council and another from the School Board. Discussion continued in 1966 when the provincial government showed interest in the plan. Council learned that any town wishing to establish a recreation commission would receive a $300 initial grant, with additional matching grants up to $1,000 a year on a dollar-for-dollar basis for salaries.

Many towns established commissions. Because as late as January 1967 provincial legislation still had taken no action, Wolfville began its own plan. Council got considerable satisfaction from its recreation and community service. The hockey program was so successful by 1973 that the town considered construction of a new rink with artificial ice. The town's first full-time recreation director was hired in 1974. As one of his first actions, Terry Moore expanded the facilities at Willow Park, submitted plans to construct a "creative playground" for children. In March he suggested a "farm market" for the summer months, providing local farmers and craftspeople with an outlet for their products. The market operated on Central Avenue Saturday mornings and proved popular enough to become an annual event. Moore resigned during the next spring for further study.

New tennis courts had been planned, and the Rotary Club approached council, offering to help maintain and improve Rotary Field. An existing building was renovated and winterized to become a recreation centre. With the aid of LIP funds, an extensive study began about Wolfville's present recreation resources and its projected needs. Meanwhile, the town had lost the senior grades of the high school, which meant absence of after-school programs for teenagers, and a growing number of young students started to loiter on Main Street. Council turned to the Recreation Commission for suggestions.

In February 1977 George Taylor of the Recreation Department announced grants available to clubs and organizations for recreation purposes, and the Rotary Club applied under the Canada Works Program to improve Stile Park and the Playing Field. The department engaged Cliff Redman and Jude Daguerre, both graduates of Acadia, to assist in the recreation program.

The Recreation Department conducted a variety of programs, including a Santa Claus Parade in 1978, and took a leading part in August 1980 in celebrating Wolfville's 150th Anniversary. After George Taylor resigned in the fall, Margaret (Peg) McInnis of Halifax was engaged as recreation director.

XVII.

CULTURAL DEVELOPMENT

1. Architecture

During the strenuous early years of the settlement of Horton, conditions were not favourable for a flourishing of the arts. The Planters managed to find or build shelters for their families but none of these earliest buildings has survived. It was only with the growth of security and economic prosperity that the village produced any architecture of significance. In the early and mid-1800s along the Post Road, now Main Street, stood a few houses which have survived. These are mostly one and a half storey houses, examples of the New England colonial style of Connecticut and Massachusetts. They were all of wood, with chimneys of brick and foundations of local stone. The roofs were steeply pitched, with two or more dormer windows. Doorways were emphasized, often with fan-light windows. Sometimes a triangular window was placed over the doorway. An occasional two-storey house appeared, with well-spaced windows. At times decorative details carved in wood were arranged around windows, fireplaces or stairways. Panelling doors continued the colonial tradition.

Several of these houses were described in a booklet by Watson Kirkconnell and B. C. Silver in 1967. There is no record of a professional architect working in the township but there were excellent carpenters, no doubt trained in shipbuilding, and a good tradition behind them. It was not uncommon for a settler to dismantle his house in the older colony, load the beams, boards and shingles on a ship bound for Nova Scotia and there reconstruct it on a new foundation. Such a house, built between 1789 and 1806, may be seen, not in Wolfville but in Cornwallis Town Plot across the river. It is still occupied, known as "Edgemere".

Of the few early homes remaining in the town, four are of special interest. The house occupied by Graham Whidden and family is the only building left standing on the actual site of the first settlement, near the harbour and wharves. It is the second house built on the site, erected in 1840. Of the several houses built by the DeWolf family, one survived until 1947 when it was first moved, then demolished for the expansion of a merchant's storage yard. It was noted for the scenic wallpaper, reportedly presented by the Duke of Kent to Elisha DeWolf, Sr. as a wedding gift for the 1817 wedding of his son Thomas Andrew Strange DeWolf. A sample from a panel of this paper is in the Randall House Museum which is a fine two-storey house built in 1815 and makes a suitable home for collections representing the early history and growth of the town.

A house stands on the Elderkin farm, on land granted in 1760 and now occupied by Ruth Elderkin, a seventh generation descendant. It was built in 1832, and though some furnishings are modern it illustrates well the gracious and hospitable appearance of that earlier day.

During the later 19th century several large houses were built by wealthy merchants who prospered in trade with the West Indies. In the elaborate style of the Victorian period two of them are presently in commercial use as tourist homes or apartments: the Chase house, now Historic Inn, and the Burgess house, now Blomidon Inn. Another, more modest in size, is used as the Acadia University president's home.

The town centre was formerly marked by three substantial public buildings — two banks and an impressive post office of red sandstone in neo-classic style. The latter was demolished because of a flaw in the foundation. In its place was erected in 1970 a one-storey building of utility but little aesthetic appeal. A small but well-kept lawn in front makes a welcome open space, and on one side stands a bronze memorial statue erected after the First World War. The only other sculpture is the war memorial record on stone in front of the Memorial Gymnasium on the Acadia campus.

The community has been fortunate to have resident architects. Leslie R. Fairn advertised in the *Acadian* as early as 1904, the construction of the present University Hall his major work in Wolfville. Ronald M. Peck was born in Wolfville, set up his architectural practice in 1948, and specialized in the reconstruction of early Maritime buildings. His son Andrew Peck is also an architect living in Wolfville.

Thomas Andrew Strange DeWolf house, built in 1817, which became Wolfville's first museum. About 1942, an Edson Graham photo of panelled Wallpaper. Left corner saved and displayed in Randall House Museum.

2. Music

Living in a university town, Wolfville citizens find it difficult to separate the artistic and cultural lives of Town and Gown. The townspeople and the collegians have been closely associated with one another. For instance, the Choral Society has been composed of university staff and students, and also those who live within and near the community. The lives of the town residents have been enriched by hearing the famous artists from all corners of the world.

Early records provided many references to music as a cultural pastime in Wolfville. Witter's Hall, owned by Burpee Witter, was a centre for musical gatherings. He started a local music society in the winter of 1885. The Music Hall had been artistically decorated during the fall and was redone a year later.

One of the first musical groups, a string band or orchestra, played in the rink. Members included George and D. R. Munro, first violins; A. J. Woodman, 2nd violin; C. H. Borden, cornet; B. G. Bishop, violoncello; and Mrs. A. Murray, organist. In 1899 the Wolfville Orchestra had as members: Mrs. Wallace, Miss Cohoon, Mr. Thompson, Mr. Borden, and Mr. Gillmore.

A high school orchestra formed in 1926, was conducted by Principal B. C. Silver. Beatrice Langley of Acadia, coached the string section, and young trumpeters were helped by Harold Phinney. This group broadcast over C.H.N.S. in 1928, the first school to do so in the Maritimes. Jessie Bishop was pianist. Many townspeople have enjoyed playing in the Acadia University Orchestra throughout the years.

Bands were mentioned as early as 1892 when one was organized by the firemen and later called the "Wolfville Harmony Band". They gave concerts every Friday night. J. W. Bigelow presented a bandstand, located where now is the corner of Acadia Street and Highland Avenue; electric lights were soon installed on it. Later bandstands were stationed on centre Main Street and on the school grounds.

The band also enjoyed themselves socially. They arranged excursions to Parrsboro and Partridge Island in September on the steamer *Hiawatha*, departing from Horton Landing. In February 1893 they travelled in two double-horse sleighs for a turkey supper at McLeod's Hotel in Kentville. Officers at the time were: President, J. F. Herbin; Secretary Treasurer, G. W. Munro; and Band Director, C. H. Borden.

The band changed leadership frequently. Professor Adams took charge in 1897, then W. W. Robson led during the following year. In 1899 O. D. Harris presented the members with caps, and the *Acadian* supported the idea of maintaining the band for summer concerts. In 1908 there was talk of re-organizing the band, which was done in 1912. In 1918 the Boy Scouts formed a band, with Mr. McAvoy as instructor, and played at the rink.

A Wolfville band played concerts in the 1920s, with the following players: J. Crowell; Percy Porter; Grant Porter; the Rand brothers — Theodore, Gilbert, Fred, and Val.; Carl Perry; Arthur Brown; Bill Johnson; Cecil Langille; George Prat; Bill Taylor; and Rex Porter. Leaders were: Professor Raugh(?), Reverend Mr. MacAvoy, Maurice Haycock, and H. W. Phinney. All were uniformed in blue coats and white trousers and presented programs as far away as Bear River for the Cherry Carnival, and at Parrsboro when transported there by *M.V. Kipawo*.

John Sproul
Merritt Gibson
Dean Gertridge
Lyall Swansburg

Sam Stanford
Paul Harris
Geo. Kennie
Larry Machum

Harold Parker
David Ross

Maurice Frank
O. R. Porter
Director
Roger Erskine

Bill Parker
Dave Richards

Hugh Fairn
Eric Murphy
Doug Spidle
Arthur Murphy

Garth Bishop
Ronald Coldwell
Tony Erskine
Ray Swansburg

Organized and directed by school Supervisor O. Rex Porter, the School Band was formed in the fall of 1936. With a membership of seventeen boys, they appeared publicly on Coronation Day, March 12, 1937. In 1942 the band became the Cadet Corps Band #268, with twenty-eight members, and in 1962 it changed from a brass to a trumpet band. From 1936 to 1968 more than 300 boys were members of this group.

The band was self-supporting, helped by a Board of Management who staged yearly skating carnivals to raise money to defray expenses and to purchase new instruments. Since 1974, through the cooperation of the Acadia School of Music, Dr. Peter Riddle and a few of the department's students headed a program of band instruction for pupils in the elementary school.

In 1884 Burpee Witter organized a Music Society, and this choral singing entertained many of the villagers. The "Kings County Annual Sing" was held during the summer of 1887 on the college grounds, with George V. Rand as secretary of the committee. The people also received pleasure from an informal outdoor concert in September. The December *Acadian* recorded a Parlour Concert, presumably vocal, given by the "Pleasant Evening Club", with participants: Mrs. Hutchins, Dr. and Mrs. Bowles and Master Ted, Mrs. Fletcher, Mrs. Pineo, and Misses Buttrick, Vaughan, Haliburton, Godfrey, and Wallace.

The community enjoyed musical treats of variety. Music festivals began in 1903, an outstanding event for the Maritimes. A considerable interest was shown in the organ grinder who attracted an appreciative and generous audience. Organ recitals were popular also, and in 1907 a first appearance of a Kinder Symphony, with toy instruments and led by Mrs. W. H. Emery, delighted the music lovers of the town. They liked the playing by the twenty-three children of the Primary Department.

Around 1904 a town and college group formed a committee to establish the Acadia Choral Club. Although this lapsed in the war years, it was reorganized in 1919, with an executive: Honorary President, Dr. Simeon Spidle; 1st Vice-President, Isobel Murray; 2nd Vice-President, Doris Crandall; Secretary, Paul Cross; Treasurer, E. C. Prime; Librarian, Claude Richardson; and Director, Winnifred Stephens of the seminary.

In 1904 town musicians shared in an organ recital given by Geo. O. Pratt Maxim. Solists were: Jennie Eaton, Agnes Johnson, Annie Murray, and violinist Margaret Evelyn Starr. Evelyn became well known internationally, performing a full schedule of concerts in Europe, United States and Canada. In 1910 a command performance for King Edward VII had to be cancelled because of his death.

Also in this time period Edith Mae Woodman graduated from the seminary in piano at the age of fourteen, and in voice at the age of sixteen. She became a teacher at Acacia Villa School at Grand Pre, at Kings Collegiate School, and later studied at New England Conservatory of Music.

A real novelty appeared in 1904 when an advertisement informed the public that Columbia Records and Graphophone could be purchased at Rand's Drug Store. The price of a good machine was $12.50. Percy Porter provided a phonograph concert, with his fine outfit and generous supply of records, entertaining the Temperance Division.

Students enjoyed other forms of music. An academy student recalled Wolfville of 1910, particularly the muddy streets. But he wrote that above Godfrey's Hardware Store was the Academy of Music, popularly known as "Keith's Nickel", the only refreshing oasis for the pleasure-starved public. When the burned depot was replaced by an excellent building the community now heard "the whir of motor, the rattle of wheels, the clatter of hoofs on a firm pavement." Worried at first that the place would be utterly holy, he concluded: "Wolfville, you are all right!"

During the last years of World War I a person who was to become a guiding

Rand's Drug Store

light in the town came to the ladies seminary. Mme. Cora Pierce Richmond, a leading pupil of Arthur Hubbard of Boston, was brought to the seminary by Principal Dr. H. T. DeWolfe. In 1917 she established her own studio in the town for voice, and people came from a number of places to study with her. Evelyn Duncanson was one of her pupils, became a noted church soloist and returned home in 1944 to give a recital in the University Fine Arts Series. Her sister Vivian Duncanson was an accompanist for the Music Department and taught piano for many years. Lewis Pick was also prominent at that time as a soloist.

Many musicals and operettas were presented during the next few years. When "H.M.S. Pinafore" was performed, among the cast were: Lewis Pick, Evelyn Neiley, Marie Wilson, Phil Hudson, Arch. Mason, Margaret Murray, Fred Rand, Eunice Curry, three Stackhouse sisters, and Mona Parsons. A three-day May festival, arranged by Mrs. Richmond, was acclaimed "the most important musical enterprise in Nova Scotia," and many of her students became special soloists in and around the town.

In April 1920 Ruth Blaisdell MacDonald, daughter of Col. John H. MacDonald, gave a recital in University Hall, assisted by O. Marie McC. Wilson (contralto). The Boston *Transcript* had previously written that "Miss MacDonald was a brilliant soprano with a bright future." In 1937 she was chosen by Sir Ernest MacMillan to sing at the coronation of King George VI.

Also in 1920 the town's first Chautauqua was held. This musical and literary six-day variety program generated wide interest at that particular time and

1926. School orchestra. Top row, L-R: Harold Perry, John Eaton, Glen Porter, Leon Shaw, Vernon Brown, Ron. Smith, Gordon Wheelock, Marshall Hennigar; middle row: Rose Cohen, Ron. Peck, Marguerite Fowler, Lloyd Shaw, Florence Jodrey, Bernard Hennigar, Helen Young, B.C. Silver (conductor); bottom row: Sydney Wheelock, Margaret Fullerton, Helen Perry, Lloyd Macpherson, Hilda Peck, Ruth Ingraham, Rex Porter, Jessie Bishop. On floor: Soley Roop, Keith Forbes.

was performed in the Opera House. Originally intending to give religious instruction, the Chautauqua educational movement began in 1874 in New York State, and conducted summer schools, home study courses, evening and college extension programs. Radio replaced Chautauqua by 1935.

Following Mrs. Richmond's musical leadership, school principal B. C. Silver inspired both young and old to participate in musical endeavors. With Nat Evans, Fred Bishop, Mrs. W. D. Withrow, A. J. Mason, Evelyn Duncanson, and Director A. J. Mann, Principal Silver helped stage in 1922 "The Chimes of Normandy" at the Opera House.

Music became a "special" subject at the high school. For Christmas competitions all grades were taught choruses of their choosing, as well as songs to accompany artistic scenes. Groups from all grades were encouraged to enter the Massed Choirs of the Apple Blossom Festivals. B. C. Silver gave his time and talent in other ways as he served as organist of the Baptist church, later in the Church of England, and pianist at the weekly Rotary meetings. In May 1935 school students entered five events at the first annual Maritime Music Festival at Halifax, winning two silver cups and a shield.

From 1956 to 1971 Wolfville had a full-time music teacher, Mrs. Robert Bishop, who had a special talent for helping all pupils to appreciate and participate in both vocal and instrumental music. Among her proteges was Walter Delahunt, son of Mr. and Mrs. Harold Delahunt, who became a concert pianist.

In 1953 eight townsmen formed a double quartet which continued for thirty years, though more recently as a single quartet. The men continued to sing together for pleasure and as a service for others, calling themselves "The Minus Four". The members were: Gordon Hansford, bass; Kenneth Cavanagh, lead; Chester Murphy, baritone; Roddie Crowe, tenor. The other original members were: Burton Bowlby, Allen Reynolds, Allen Crowe, and Eddie Crowe. Myron Johnson was a part-time helper.

From 1967 to 1971 a Women's Ensemble met weekly at the home of their director, Mrs. Ethel Morton. Members were: Mrs. Marietta Silver, Mrs. Betty Mercer, Mrs. Ruth Elderkin, Mrs. Evelyn Fairn, Mrs. Audrey Martin, Mrs. Jean DeWolfe, Mrs. Cheryl MacKay, Mrs. Mary Evelyn Merrick, with Mrs. Gladys Bishop and Mrs. Sybil Morse as pianists.

Town graduates from Acadia University with a Bachelor of Music have included: Hilda Peck Williams (violin), Frances Patterson Macphail (piano, violin), Phylis K. Anderson (piano), Douglas F. Dahlgren (piano), Helen Kirkconnell Murray (piano), Eric G. Tennant (piano), Sylvia R. Hiltz, Robert Rushton, Elise Vasileski, Peter H. Cameron, Laurel A. Nesdoly, Diane Jane MacCrae, Joanna L. Bishop, and Paul A. Collins (violin, composition).

To live in Wolfville is to have access to as much and as many types of music as one might wish, both through the university's Fine Arts Series and Faculty Recitals during the winter, and programs by Music Camp students in the summer. The community has enjoyed, and continues to experience, a rich musical heritage.

3. Literature

A young man had an outstanding literary beginning in the village of Wolfville. Leslie Loring Davison was born at Wolfville in April 1871, attending school, and working one summer in a grocery store before he joined the *Acadian* staff. He wrote in his scribbling book, "The Book of Wonders", his essays, stories, and poems. His health failed during the next year after working on the paper, and in April 1889 he died, at the age of eighteen.

Literary clubs provided a favourite pastime for some citizens in the 1800s. From 1893 to 1898 a Tennysonian Club flourished, with the names of Mrs. Crandall and Miss Burgess prominent as hostesses for the meetings. From 1895 to 1909 a Browning Club was active, having yearly picnics and meetings at the homes of Mrs. Laura H. Moore at Kent Lodge, Mrs. W. H. Chase, Mrs. Wm. Chipman, and Miss Higgins. Most members were of the fair sex.

A "Book Lovers' Club" began in 1904 when Flo M. Harris offered to secure, through her book store, the best reading materials at a cheap rate. In 1907 books used by the club were donated to the public school.

In 1902 Mrs. deBlois opened at Central House the "Strathcona Circulating Library" of 900 volumes. Five years later there was reference to a new public library. Then, in 1949 Wolfville joined other valley towns in establishing a unit of the Annapolis Valley Regional Library system. This arrangement has continued to the present.

At the turn of the century Daisy Elizabeth Sleep was the first seminary student to receive a diploma in elocution. This subject was studied by many students, and Mrs. I. S. Boates donated a gold medal for a prize. In 1908 Trevor Mitchell, a talented elocutionist, presented Tennyson's poem "Enoch Arden" at College Hall. In 1912 Reverend R. F. Dixon lectured in Temperance Hall on "The Writings of Shakespeare".

Wolfville residents have written and published books of literary merit. In 1907 John Frederic Herbin, for long the only local descendant of the exiled people who lived in the Grand Pre of the Acadians, published a new and improved edition of his *History of Grand Pre*. Other books by him included *The Heir of Grand Pre*, *The Marshlands*, and *Jen of the Marshes*. This last volume was published in 1921 and sold for $2.50 per copy. In the 1920s Arthur Hunt Chute wrote a novel, *For Gold*. In 1926 Gregory Doane Haliburton Hatfield had two of his plays included in a book published by the Canadian Authors Association, and George E. Levy, editor of *The Maritime Baptist*, published *With The Pioneer Baptists of Nova Scotia* (1959) and *Baptists of The Maritime Provinces* (1946).

In 1980 renowned ornithologist Dr. Robie Tufts celebrated his ninety-sixth birthday. He had lived in Wolfville for sixty years. He began his career in 1916 when he learned taxidermy from his older brother Harold. After he retired in 1947 he wrote six books, the best known being *The Birds of Nova Scotia* (1962) which went through two editions. He guided many students into careers as ornithologists, including Austin Rand and Earl Godfrey who became leading authorities. Earl W. Godfrey, a curator at the National Museum of Canada, wrote *Birds of Canada* (1965) which was published by the Queen's Printer.

Dr. Esther Clark Wright, native of New Brunswick but a long-time resident of Wolfville, wrote extensively on the pioneer life of New Brunswick and Nova Scotia in her *Loyalists of New Brunswick* (1955) and her *Planters and Pioneers, 1749-1775* (1978). These two books were well received, as was her popular historical narrative *Blomidon Rose* (1957), illustrated by Helen D. Beals. An energetic eighty-five in 1980, Dr. Wright is working on a similar book, to be entitled *Bay of Fundy*.

Wolfville's Historic Homes, by Watson Kirkconnell and B. C. Silver, was published in 1967, and in 1970 Dr. Kirkconnell wrote *The Streets of Wolfville, 1650-1970*. Through a special grant from the town in 1980 the Historical Society was able to have these volumes re-issued under one cover. Publications by Mrs. Marietta MacDonald Silver included *The Wolfville Historical Society and Museum, 1949-1966, A Short History of the Home and School Movement, 1895-1949,* numerous other histories, also prize-winning poetry, and writings on English drama.

Dr. M. Allen Gibson was a writer of note through the years. In 1973 he gave glimpses of his life at Wolfville in his *Train Time* and continued to interest the readers of his column "Churches by the Sea" and "Interlude" in the Halifax *Chronicle-Herald.* A brother, Dr. Merritt A. Gibson, Professor of Biology at Acadia University, wrote *Winter Nature Notes* (1980). These brothers grew up in Wolfville, sons of Dr. and Mrs. Alexander Gibson.

Alice of Grand Pre (Seminary) was the first full-length book by James Doyle Davison, President of the Wolfville Historical Society. It was completed at the end of 1980 for Acadia University Print Shop's first printing of a book. Davison had plans for a *History of Wolfville* and had also begun a sequel to *Alice* in an account of Eliza Ann Chipman (1807-1853) of Chipman Corner and Pleasant Valley (Berwick).

In 1979 Charles (Chuck) E. Eaton published 2,000 copies of his *Nova Scotia Eaton Family History.* He plans to publish the story of the Porter family. In 1980 former resident Shirley Elliott produced her *Nova Scotia Book of Days,* a historical diary of events. Mary Ann Monnon, wife of Ernest Monnon, entered the literary field as a young woman, with stories and magazine publications. Her first book, *Miracles and Mysteries*, was published in 1977. It comprised tales of the Halifax Explosion of 1917 and was written especially for the schools of the province. In 1980 former resident, Donald H. Oliver, had published his *Men Can Cook Too!*, the product of his keen interest and training in culinary skills.

Certainly, the community of Wolfville is indebted to those who have spent time and effort to record details and impressions of the past and present which otherwise would not be chronicled.

4. Picture and Opera Houses

Wolfville has its own identity in the realm of filmed entertainment and in theatre. The early citizens were well aware that "man does not live by bread alone".

February 1907 heralded an era in the cultural life of the town with an exhibition of moving pictures at College Hall. Films depicting the San Francisco earthquake and fire of 1906, and the Olympic games held at Athens in that year were shown to a large and incredulous audience.

By 1909, according to the *Acadian*, the town had its own moving picture Nicklet, when the Temperance Hall was made over to accommodate the new art form. Pictures were shown every Thursday and Friday evenings, admission five cents, later doubled to ten. The first manager was a Mr. Fielding.

Marshall Black bought the Nicklet in January 1911 and established an Opera House in the T. E. Hutchinson building on Main Street, which could seat from 500 to 700 people. The structure possessed steam heat, special exit doors, electric lights, a telephone connecting the box office to the stage, and two projection machines, one held in reserve in case of a breakdown. The stage had moveable scenery which could be used both for moving pictures and live theatre. Back stage had space for dressing rooms, while in front were footlights. A pianist accompanied the silent pictures with suitable music, sometimes provided by Minnie (Pink) Godfrey, later by Sara Eye.

The first opera was presented July 1911, "At The Old Crossroads". A gala musical evening soon followed, with young women participants: Minnie Godfrey, Stella Bleakney, Edith Thompson, Rita Boates, Marguerite Elderkin, Ada Johnson, Evelyn Johnson, Ora Woodman, Evelyn Woodman, Violet Sleep, Ferne Woodman, Gladys Elderkin, Ruth Elderkin, Vesta Pick, and Hilda West. The pianist was Mrs. Moore (Laura Haliburton?).

Weekly entertainment continued at the Opera House until the spring of 1912, when nightly movies were presented, interspersed with live entertainment and community meetings. Men and boys met on a Sunday afternoon in May to hear the Reverend G. D. Webber, and the Boy Scouts presented an entertainment later in the same month.

The highly respected Pathe News reels of current events were presented weekly in 1912. In August 1914 a direct wire from Halifax Headquarters provided the latest flashes of war news.

In July 1917 A. J. Mason became the new manager of the Opera House, he and his family also active in musical circles. Val Rand described Mason as having "the sweetest voice ever heard." The Masons left Wolfville in 1923 and moved to Springhill.

During Mason's tenure an unprecedented event occurred when in September 1920 a film on sex education, "Enlighten Your Daughters", was shown at the Opera House. Though the picture was highly recommended by leading doctors, religious leaders, and statesmen, the public viewed this presentation with mixed emotions.

Nat Evans, formerly of Halifax, purchased the Opera House in 1923, made improvements, and changed the name to the Orpheum. Early in 1924 he had a new electric sign in the shape of a "T" installed over the entrance. To all children who attended the Saturday morning matinees Evans was a warm friend and a comforting presence, especially when the weekly "Cliff-Hanger" serial proved too scary for the young patrons.

Under the direction of school principal B. C. Silver, the high school presented a yearly extravaganza at the Orpheum, usually during the Christmas season. These were considered much more ambitious than the usual concerts, and many of Silver's students had their first heady theatrical experiences at the Orpheum. Robert Hatfield and Leon Shaw went on to professional careers in American theatre.

As early as 1923 the first sound film had been shown in New York City but not until July 1930 were Wolfville patrons treated to their first talkie, the immortal Al Jolson in the memorable classic "The Jazz Singer". Some felt that talking pictures would be "a flash in the pan", and the management of the theatre doubted the wisdom of installing new equipment.

In April 1947 Orpheum Theatre closed, replaced by a cinema, and by October the Acadia Theatre opened, the first movie house in Canada to have radiant heating.

Al Whittle came to Wolfville in 1953 as Manager of the Acadia Theatre. In addition to his duties at the theatre, he acted as a checker at Wheelock Dining Hall for twenty-four years, helped in the annual Winter Carnival, was actively involved in Theatre Arts Festival International, in the Business Development Corporation, and as an executive member of the Atlantic Branch of the Association of Motion Pictures Exhibitors.

One year after Whittle took over the Acadia, Cinemascope was installed and provided a wide screen with greater depth. Some patrons were overwhelmed by the innovation; "It seemed so close and intimate." In 1967 the Acadia underwent major remodelling, with new equipment installed, the "new look" now acceptable.

5. Drama

The *Acadian* of December 1925 stated that Wolfville had the distinction of possessing the first Little Theatre Guild in the Maritime Provinces. Organized by five Acadia students, the guild presented its first production in November 1924.

Early in 1934 the Playmakers Dramatic Club was organized with the following members: Lalia Piers, Fred M. Parker, Evelyn Withrow, E. H. Freeman, Margaret Fullerton, Marietta Silver, J. R. Northover, S. C. Gordon, and Marion Eaton. During the summer of 1935 the Playmakers, directed by Harold Fritz Sipprell, staged "The Trojan Women", on the south portico of University Hall.

Recognizing the need for community-based drama, the Wolfville Players, an amateur theatre company, came into being in 1957 and presented their first offering: "Bell, Book and Candle", in Badminton Hall. In the cast were: Peggy Cornell, Tony Sheppard, Rex Lucas, Mamie Hudson, with Beth Rand as Director. Others who were prominent at that time were: Barbara Sheppard, Jean Marsh, Frances Cosman, Joan Eaton, Margaret Godfrey, and Irene Bissett.

In July 1958 the Players, directed by Beth Rand, put on a spoof on Greek tragedy, "The Nation of Ephesus", acted on the south portico of University Hall. Spurred on by the success of its first two productions, in March 1959 the Players entered their "Glass Menagerie" in the N.S. Regional Finals of the Dominion Drama Festival, with a cast of Joyce Cook, Charles Haliburton, Margaret Godfrey, and Jack Sheriff who also directed the play. The Halifax entry, directed by Wolfvillian Murray Porter, won the Best Play award.

Wolfville Players performed in the Gaspereau Barn Theatre in November 1959, and the same month the Wolfville and Gaspereau theatre groups hosted the N.S. Drama League's tenth anniversary. The Wolfville entry was directed by Jeannette Ruffee, and the cast members were Jean Marsh, Irma Cook, and Sally Blake.

In 1960 the Players staged "The Corn Is Green", in the dining room of Evangeline Inn, soon to be demolished. During that year they took part in the Planters' 200th anniversary and presented Agatha Ganong's original work that depicted the landing at Horton. This play was taken later to the N.S. Festival of the Arts at Tatamagouche.

In 1960 Murray Porter completed his term as president and was succeeded by Margaret Godfrey. Beth Rand was awarded for playacting, and became editor of the Drama League's publication, holding this position until her death in 1963.

Professor Jack Sheriff led the Acadia Summer Playhouse in 1961, replacing the Wolfville Players, and until 1971 presented about seven productions every summer in University Hall. This program attracted stage, opera, and T.V. personalities, and some local players began successful careers in the theatre and performing arts, including Steve Smith (Steve McHattie), Lenore Zann, and Bob Martyn.

In 1970 Jack Sheriff and other citizens initiated the Theatre Arts Festival International (TAFI). This ambitious series brought international artists, Joan Baez, Lillian Gish, the McGarrigle Sisters, the Bolshoi Ballet, the Red Army Chorus, pianist Roger Williams, dancer Maya Plisets Kraija, and others, to appreciative audiences.

Jack Sheriff had a dream, and in 1972 began a campaign to have *M.V. Kipawo* returned from Newfoundland to Minas Basin and to be made into a floating theatre and arts centre, moored at Wolfville. In anticipation, he founded the Kipawo Showboat Theatre, first located in the Curling Club, and later in the vacated Steadman Store building. The Theatre has provided year-round performances.

In 1972 Evelyn Garbary founded Mermaid Theatre. Mrs. Garbary's long and considerable professional experience, particularly in the British Isles, qualified her for featuring puppetry. The theatre, with Tom Miller as designer, Sara Lee Lewis as administrator, and directed by Evelyn Garbary, toured Canada, the United States, and overseas with a rich repertoire of folklore, fancy tales, and historical material. Mermaid Theatre was Atlantic Canada's first professional touring theatre for family audiences. Assisted financially by federal and provincial agencies, the theatre won awards for its distinguished presentations.

In 1954 Wolfville received television programs from Saint John, and during the 1950s and 1960s the Ed Sullivan Show (shew) and the "sitcoms" attracted much attention. Cable television came to Wolfville in 1974 when Hugh Fairn opened Kings Kable which allowed a greater selection of programs, including projects of local interest.

6. Painting

The development of the art of painting in the Planter settlement was slower than that of architecture and handicrafts. The first artist of note was Frederick S. Crawley, brother of Dr. A. E. Crawley, first president of Acadia College. Around 1868 he taught painting at Acadia Ladies Seminary, succeeding Anne Fowler, a teacher there from 1863 to 1868. His paintings were watercolour landscapes of scenes surrounding Wolfville, with pleasing misty tones of browns and blues. Classes at the seminary were open to townspeople. Frederick Crawley later moved to Halifax.

The next teachers were E. Morse, Marie Woodworth, Eliza Harding, Elinor Uphap, Minnie Chipman, and Isa Belle Andrew, all before the early 1900s. Annie Prat, of Wolfville in the late 19th century, was noted for a series of water-colours of Nova Scotia flowers. These are now in the Nova Scotia Archives collection. She also painted miniature portraits on ivory. Albert E. Barrett, a well-known painter about 1897, spent his boyhood in Wolfville.

An Art Association was formed in the town in 1898. The officers were: President, Minnie Chipman; Vice-President, Mrs. Blair; Secretary, Mrs. G. L. Weeks; Treasurer, Mrs. J. Herbin. Regular meetings were held at the homes of Miss Richardson, Mrs. G. E. Weeks, and Mrs. Chipman.

A new impetus was given to art activities in the town and university in 1927 by a grant to the university from the Carnegie Corporation. This grant made possible an Art Department at Acadia, the support of Professor Walter H. Abell, an extensive library of art books and reproductions, as well as numerous artifacts useful in teaching. Abell organized an Art Club and Picture Loan Society for the town. In 1943 he left Wolfville to take a post at the National Gallery in Ottawa.

Helen Beals had assisted Abell in the university art department and became the director, also continuing the program of travelling art exhibitions until her retirement in 1963, when Ian James became head of the department. Classes and exhibitions were open to townspeople.

Several painters made Wolfville their home. Among them were Dr. Alex Colville, Chancellor of Acadia University; Wallace Turner, Frances Bayne, Helen Beals, Jean Hancock, and George Walford. Gwen Hales, a fine water-colour painter, died in 1979; Sandy Spencer has shown paintings in the National Gallery, Ottawa; he had spent his early years at Wolfville where his family now lives. James D. Davison is among several amateur artists in the town.

An exhibition gallery attached to the Beveridge Arts Centre is open to town visitors, as well as to local artists. A small commercial gallery, "The Carriage House Gallery", managed by Marilyn Kuhn, adds to the town's artistic resources.

7. Crafts

The household crafts of the Planter families were doubtless well developed and included weaving, spinning, quilting, and mat-hooking. Surviving examples at the local museum show a high degree of knowledge and skill. Tools for wood-carving and furniture-making were an important part of their equipment as householders and builders. Examples of these delight visitors to the Wolfville Randall House Museum.

A Fancy Work and Embroidery Club were active from 1907 to 1910. There has been a revival of the pioneer crafts, especially weaving and pottery. Two Wolfville women were particularly active: Mary Black and Sally Starr. Mary Black's work was chiefly centered in Halifax where she was employed by the government as head of the Division of Handcrafts. Her textbook, *Key to Weaving*, has been widely used in the United States and Canada and has gone through twenty editions. Retired, she lives with her sister Violet at Tideways, also a weaver.

Sally Starr, a descendant of the Planter Samuel Starr, was a skilled weaver but chiefly remembered as proprietor of a small but important center for teaching and the exchange of ideas and the setting of high standards in all crafts. Charlotte (Sally) Starr is now retired.

Pottery-making was not so much revival of an old craft as the introduction of one new to Wolfville, a local resource of clay so abundant around Minas Basin. Mrs. Ruby Bleakney and Acadia instructor Helen Beals were connected with this craft which is now active under Jean Leung as president.

Woodworking was practised recently with a high degree of skill by David Burton, and George Arthur Hillier, while Edward Stewart was proficient as a gunsmith.

In 1942 John L. Bradford helped organize the Woodcarvers Guild, becoming president in April 1943. Other officers were: Vice-Presidents, Gwendolyn Hales, T. D. A. Purves; Secretary, Helen Beals; Treasurer, D. Ross Cochrane; Executive, Evelyn J. Everett, Christine Cavanagh, and L. Vye MacPherson.

The Artisan Gallery opened in the fall of 1979, located in the former Cavanagh hardware building on Main Street, displaying the creations of nine craft-oriented businesses. Across the tracks from R. W. DeWolfe's apple exporting establishment Kenneth Cavanagh began making fibreglass boats, pickling tubs, kayaks, counter tops. These and other crafts people displayed their works at the two annual fairs at Wolfville which provided a helpful sales outlet for the craftsmen.

XVIII.

ORGANIZATIONS

Wolfville has been a town of many organizations. Over the years, societies have appeared, disappeared, reappeared, and sometimes died, with the constant changes in public taste and enthusiasms.

This section of the history was not able to consider every organization that has existed in Wolfville. It is hoped that it has included most of the principal ones, along with some lesser groups of historical interest. The accounts of these groups are not of uniform length. In some cases, this is simply because material was more accessible for one society than another. Then in other cases, references were found which were particularly interesting in throwing light on attitudes in Wolfville or in showing the way that outsiders might view the town.

As the year 1980 was the cutoff date for this history, informants were asked to name the executives in office at the end of 1980. Thus if John Smith is listed as President for 1980, it means that he was President in December of that year.

1. Temperance Societies

Liquor consumption was heavy in the early days of Nova Scotia settlement. Dr. Stiles of Boston, visiting Halifax in 1760, reported that the town contained only 1000 houses, but of these 100 were licensed places and there were perhaps as many more selling liquor without a licence. The problem was not an easy one to combat. The wine merchant was often a leader in society and politics. Citizens came to taverns not only to drink but also to hear and read about the news of the world. In 1800, King's County Sesssion issued twenty-one licences for the sale of liquor.

As early as 1828, two temperance societies were formed in Nova Scotia, one in Beaver River, Yarmouth County, and one in West River, Pictou County. The Beaver River group is believed to be the earliest temperance society formed in the British colonies.

The Horton area was not far behind. The Horton Temperance Society was organized November 11, 1829 at a meeting in Wolfville chaired by the Rev. T. Harding. The first officers were: Pres.- Rev. T.S. Harding; Vice-Pres. - Rev. R. Crane, Dr. E.T. Harding, Simon Fitch; Sec. - Ashael Chapin; Treas. - William T. Fitch. Additional committee: David Coaldwell, John Clarke, Sam. Witter, James Calkin, John Armstrong, and Michael Davison. There were sixteen members from the town and eight Horton Seminary (Academy) students.

According to an interview with James R. DeWolfe (in *The Halifax Herald* of November 10, 1896), the impetus to form this group came from a certain

Captain Card of Avonport who brought a number of temperance papers from Boston. "These were freely circulated in Horton and aroused the attention of the leading men of the place. A meeting was convened in the old yellow schoolhouse at 'Mud Bridge' .. in the autumn of 1828 and a society was organized."

Members of this Society were called upon to abstain from the use of ardent spirits and also not to administer them to family, friends or others except when recommended "by a temperate physician." A difference of opinion existed as to whether this should exclude the use of wine. In 1834 a new article was introduced forbidding the use of wine "on all occasions but those held sacred and when recommended by a temperate physician." Members who chose not to sign this article would still retain their membership.

A number of expulsions took place in these early years — though some of those expelled were readmitted after they had expressed repentance. At one meeting in 1833 nine persons came forward to join the society and seven were expelled "for transgressing the rules of the society." At the same meeting it was voted that New Canaan, Beech Hill and Kentville "including as far down as Mr. Payzant's" should be a branch of the Horton Temperance Society." As far back as 1830, meetings were being held alternately in Wolfville and Gaspereau and later some meetings were held at Canaan Road. These meetings were sometimes at private houses, sometimes in meeting houses and schoolrooms.

This society lasted into the 1840s. But by 1847 the U.S. - based Sons of Temperance had begun to extend their work into New Brunswick and Nova Scotia. In 1848 a division of the Sons of Temperance, Minas No. 42, was set up in Wolfville. For some reason this did not last long. In 1853 Wolfville Division No. 112 was organized. Among the chief founders were Dr. John M. Cramp, second President of Acadia University, and W.H. Troop, a Wolfville resident whose two daughters conducted a Female School. The first officers installed were W.H. Troop, J. Chase, W.A. Rockwell, L.H. Johnson, E. DeWolf, Watson Eaton, J. Rounsefell, Stephen Shatford, Jas. Rankin, John Meagher, and Simon Fitch.

Besides promoting the cause of temperance, the Society was interested in the cultural life of the community. At its meetings essays were read on politics, farming methods, surveying, mathematics. At one meeting a debate was held as to whether the single life or married life is happier (decided in favour of the former) and at another, a debate on whether the male or female had the more influence in society. It was decided "beyond doubt" that the female had the greater influence.

In time women visitors were admitted. In April 1859 "an investigating committee" was set up consisting of Mrs. Fisk, Mrs. G.V. Rand and Mrs. W. Eagles to pass on the suitability of applicants being admitted as lady visitors. In 1868 women were admitted to full membership of the Nova Scotia Temperance Society.

However, the women later had a group of their own. The Wolfville Branch of the Women's Christian Temperance Union was organized in 1892 with sixty charter members. Officers chosen were: Pres.- Mrs. W.H. Young; Vice-Pres. - Mrs. R.D. Ross, Mrs. J.B. Hemmeon, Mrs. Charles H. Borden; Recording Sec. - Mrs. McLean; Corresponding Sec. - Minnie Fitch; Treas.

- Mrs. J.W. Coldwell, Auditor - Mrs. A.E. Coldwell. Mrs. Irene Fitch was credited with being largely responsible for the formation of this group.

Temperance societies from the different Valley towns joined from time to time to put on special events. No doubt Wolfville took part in the mammoth temperance rally held at Cornwallis in September 1865. There were said to be some 7000 people and 1500 carriages at this rally, the procession being about eight miles long.

The "Crystal" Band of Hope was organized in the Temperance Division in 1891. The officers were: Stanley Jones, Clarence Hemmeon, Tira Coldwell, Grace Patriquin, Gordon Witter, Minnie Woodman, Harold Witter, Richard Starr. School Principal Brown was supervisor of the group. In 1932 the "Amethyst" Band of Hope was organized, with Jean Duncanson as President. Other officers were Vice-Pres. - Donald Bowlby; Sec. - Lois Porter; Treas. - Reginald Scott; Guide - Eugene Burgher; Conductress - Shirley Duncanson; Sentinel - Donald Burgher. By 1940, this was one of only two Bands of Hope functioning in Kings County. (The other one was in New Minas.)

A Temperance Hall was erected shortly after the Society was founded and was dedicated in October 1858. Women supporters were active in raising money to pay off the debt incurred. In 1881 this hall and all its contents burned when J.B. Davidson was Chairman and W.H. Evans was the Secretary. A new building was erected in 1890. Dedication of the new hall took place January 29, 1892. G.V. Rand, who had been a member for thirty-five years, conducted the service. Mamie Fitch played a violin solo, Edward Blackadder read an original poem and Burpee Wallace sang. This second hall was sold in 1916, and from then to 1942 the Division met in a room above a local store. On December 15, 1941, the 88th anniversary of the Division's founding, a new hall was officially opened. This was sold to the Odd Fellows in June 1967.

A prominent member of the Wolfville Division was Jonathan F.L. Parsons who was Grand Worthy Patriarch in 1872 and Grand Scribe from 1873 to 1881. He gave the historical address on the Sons of Temperance in Nova Scotia when they held their Jubilee meeting in 1897. Another prominent figure was B.O. Davidson who was elected G.W.P. in 1915. He was Vice-President of the Kings County Termperance Alliance, and a member of its executive for many years. He received a 50-year jewel for membership.

In the early days of the temperance movement, membership was quite large. The Temperance Almanack for 1837, published in Halifax, listed Wolfville Temperance Society as having 429 members. But early in 1888 the Wolfville Division of the Sons of Temperance had only 66 members, although this had risen to 91 before the end of the year.

After World War II the numbers and influence of the temperance groups in Wolfville declined and all were dormant at the time this history was written.

2. Masonic Lodge, and Order of the Eastern Star

The Masonic Lodge had its beginnings in the 18th century. The original founder of Masons in the area was a Loyalist lawyer from New York, Benjamin Hilton, who came to the township of Cornwallis in 1779. He had been a Master Mason in his native colony and desired to attend a lodge in his new home. So he with four others — Dr. William Baxter, Samuel Wilson,

John Smith, and John North — met to discuss this matter November 22, 1784 at the home of William Allen Chipman at Chipman Corner. This meeting resulted in the formation of a group which in June 1785 became Lodge No. 11.

Interest in the new Lodge fluctuated. The membership was brought up to sixteen, but no new members were added from 1786 to 1796. In the latter year Dr. Joseph Prescott and Reverend William Twining provided fresh leadership. In 1811 the Reverend Theodore Seth Harding of Horton received three degrees.

In April 1813 the Lodge moved from Cornwallis to Horton. It purchased a hearse in 1818, but sold this six years later. The Lodge moved to Kentville in 1830 but returned to Horton and then to Cornwallis in 1832. After 1858 it went to Lower Horton. Finally in 1862 it moved to Wolfville and in 1869 became Lodge No. 20 under the registry of the Grand Lodge of Nova Scotia, located in the Eaton Block after 1897, and later in the McKenna Block.

Officers in 1869 were: Worshipful Master - James A. Cutten; Senior Warden - James Wilson; Junior Warden - Launzo Sangster; Treas. - John Strong; Sec. - Elias N. Payzant. Officers in the year 1980 were: Worshipful Master - James Amos; Senior Warden - Jerry Atwater; Junior Warden - Ronald C.W. MacNeill; Treas. - Wm. Nathaniel Parker; Sec. - Edwin Fraser. The cornerstone of the Masonic Hall on Gaspereau Avenue was laid October 26, 1961. The building was completed in January, 1962. One of Wolfville's most prominent Masons was Seymour Gordon, who after holding many offices in the Lodge, was installed as Eminent Prior by a special conclave of the Masonic Order in 1977.

The Wolfville Chapter of the Eastern Star (Blomidon Chapter No. 68) was instituted March 6, 1965 and constituted October 16 of the same year. The first Worthy Matron was Mrs. Orfie Ryan (Margaret Ryan) and the first Secretary was Miss Kathleen Smith. In 1980 Mrs. William Bevan (Lena Bevan) was elected Worthy Matron, and Mrs. Fred Blakeney was elected Secretary.

3. Odd Fellows and Rebekahs

An Independent Order of Odd Fellows Lodge was first organized in Wolfville in February 1878. This was known as Orpheus Lodge No. 31. The first officers were: Noble Grand - John W. Fullerton; Vice-Grand - W.H. Chisholm; Sec. - E. Boulter; Treas. - E. Bishop.

During the year 1880 the Lodge suffered a loss when their building just east of the Wolfville Hotel burned. The Lodge carried on and later built and furnished its own hall. Grand Master John Richards visited Wolfville in January 1881 and later wrote in his annual report that he found the new lodge building second to none in his territory. In 1883 J.P. Smith, Deputy Grand Master, stated that on his visit to Orpheus Lodge No. 31 he found their regalia and robes superior to anything he had ever seen. Next year the Lodge had its first representative in the office of Deputy Grand Master. This was C.E. Vaughan.

Misfortune came in 1885. The I.O.O.F. hall burned and the Lodge lost all its possessions. The Odd Fellows then ceased to function in Wolfville until 1904, almost twenty years later. In March of that year a new lodge was instituted, to be known as Orpheus Lodge No. 92, meeting in the Harris Block.

The principal officers of this lodge in 1904 were: Noble Grand - J. Elliott Smith; Vice-Grand - Charles A. Campbell; Recording Sec. - Clarence H. Borden; Financial Sec. - Ernest Elliott; Treas. - D.B. Shaw; Past Grand - J.M. Shaw.

Orpheus Lodge has produced a number of District Deputy Grand Masters: G.W. Abbott, 1905/06; W.M. Black, 1907/08; E.E. Wallace, 1912/13; J.W. Williams, 1915/16; L.B. Fielding, 1920/21; H.H. Jackson, 1934/35; and C.R. Connor, 1949/50.

In 1936 Past Grand Master D.G. Whidden was presented with a sixty-year jewel. On October 28, 1969, Athlone Lodge No. 39 of Canning consolidated with Orpheus Lodge No. 92.

Officers in 1980 were: Noble Grand - Percy Saltzman; Vice-Grand - Ernie Morine; Recording Sec. - Wendell Hennigar; Financial Sec. - Churchill Connor; Treas. - Lawrence Westcott.

The *Acadian* of November 1939 reported the organization of a Rebekah Lodge, claiming that the Lodge had been in existence for forty-three years. The officers were: Noble Grand - Minnie Eye; Vice-Grand - Mrs. Ruby Whitman; Sec. - H.H Jackson; Treas. - John R. Trenholm.

Officers of the Horton Rebekah Lodge in 1980 were: Noble Grand - Mrs. Ruth Coldwell; Vice-Grand - Mrs. Geraldine Cross; Recording Sec. - Mrs. Thelma Duncanson; Financial Sec. - Mrs. Elizabeth Allen; Treas. - Mrs. Georgina Morine.

4. Society for The Prevention of Cruelty

A Wolfville branch of the society for the Prevention of Cruelty was operating in 1889, as the March 29 issue of the *Acadian* that year recorded its meeting. Officers were listed: Pres.- F.W. Caldwell; Vice-Pres. - J.W. Wallace; Sec. - J.A. Woodman; Treas. - J.D. Chambers. A letter in the March 1891 issue of the *Acadian* explained that the Wolfville group had omitted the letter ''A'' from the initials as members were concerned with all victims of cruelty, including humans.

Apparently the Wolfville society died out before too long, as the *Acadian* of January 1910 reported a possibility of forming such a Society in Wolfville.

5. Bible Society

The British and Foreign Bible Society is said to be the oldest ecumenical organization in the world. It was founded in 1804 to ''encourage the wider circulation of the Holy Scripture without note and comment.'' It not only published Bibles in various languages but offered versions in English as well as foreign languages at little or no charge to those who desired them.

This was a welcome service to early settlements where books were not readily available, and the Nova Scotia Bible Society (an auxiliary of the British) was formed in 1813. Activity in the Wolfville area began at an early date. In its 1822 report the N.S. Bible Society quoted a letter from Elihu Woodworth stating that on 6th April 1818 ''the inhabitants of Horton met and revived the Bible Society which had lain dormant for some years prior to the date.'' At this meeting it was agreed to assemble on the first Monday of each April annually, to pay the amount of their subscriptions and commence anew for the ensuing year — but Woodworth added that the members subscribed for only one year and had not met since then. However, the annual report stated that the Horton branch had been revived on February 11, 1822.

The branch had a long history of ups and downs. In 1824 some opposition to the conversion of the heathen was encountered. "A few were of the opinion that the heathen are sufficiently happy in their present condition."

In 1836 it was reported that the branch had resumed its "wonted activity" and that in former years few societies had contributed more generously. But by 1874 the Society's travelling agent, Isaac Smith, reported that he had tried but failed that year to have a branch reorganized in Wolfville. In 1885 the agent John Toland collected in Wolfville the sum of only seventy-three cents!

There was apparently some interchurch dissension which hampered the Society's progress. Then in an extraordinary burst of metaphors, "Let Wolfville bury the hatchet, boom the Bible, and open her mouth wide to receive the blessing from the windows of heaven." These appeals seem to have had some effect. In 1888 Wolfville's contributions doubled, and by 1890 a branch was again organized. In 1894 still another "new committee" was formed.

Difficulties in collecting money persisted. In 1901 the agent wrote, "Wolfville is a lovely town and doubtless a charming place in which to live; the flowers and fruitage of its gardens and orchards, the numerous goodly villas and the famous Academy and College are all expressive of prosperity. It is therefore to me all the more disheartening to be refused a kindly response from about nine out of ten persons to whom I annually appeal for contributions." In 1904 larger contributions were reported than in any previous year but this was attributed chiefly to the gifts of a few faithful supporters. "From the doors of many palatial dwellings I retired with an unaugmented subscription list, but a heavy heart."

In spite of these problems, interest in the society never died out completely. Certain loyal supporters devoted time and energy to the cause, such as Dr. J.A. Glendinning, Eric Balcom and Robert W. Cooley. In 1963 the President of the N.S. Bible Society paid a special tribute to Mr. Cooley, who had served as Secretary, Treasurer, Vice-President and a member of the N.S. Board, besides being a member of the national Board.

Still a low profile group, the orgnization has continued into the present, when it is known as a branch of the Canadian Bible Society. In 1980 the President was Professor Allison Trites, and the Secretary Dr. G.M. Haliburton.

6. Board of Trade and Similar Organizations

After he attended a convention at Halifax in 1894 Mayor Bowles motivated formation of a local Board. It appears that a Board was operating by 1895 but it did not hold its first meeting until May 1898. Officers were: Pres.- W.H. Chase; Vice-Pres. - B.O. Davison; Sec. Treas. - G.L. Starr; Auditors - C.C. Morris and J.F. Herbin.

The first meeting discussed the possiblity of a new hotel, the preservation of the Grand Pre historic site, the bringing of telephone lines into Wolfville, and the building of a street from the foot of Central Avenue to the railway station. In this same year, the Board erected signs to identify nearby historic sites.

In 1899 the Board recommended widening Gaspereau Avenue between Main and Front Streets, and wanted an old barn near the railway crossing to be removed. W.H. Chase suggested that during the tourist season a small steamer might be put on duty between the town and Blomidon. In 1900 they recommended widening Mud Bridge, building a Town Hall, and publishing a small booklet to advertise the attractions of the town. In 1901 they asked the Town Council for help in publishing the tourist booklet.

The Board met in February 1902 at the People's Bank in what appeared to be a significant meeting. Present were: F.P. Rockwell, C.R.H. Starr, B.O. Davison, W.H. Chase, R.R. Duncan, J.F. Herbin, C.A. Patriquin, Geo. L. Starr, Geo. D. Ellis, Geo. W. Munro, and J.E. Hales. In 1910, they urged the cleanup of the old cemetery on Main Street.

Meanwhile, other groups with a view to town improvement were being formed. A Town Improvement Association was set up in 1895, with the following officers: Pres.- C.A. Patriquin; Vice-Pres. - F.P. Rockwell and C.W. Vaughan; Sec. Treas. - J.W. Heales. Then in March 1919 a Citizens Association was formed to improve the town through greater unity and public spirit. Officers were: Pres.- Dr. M.R. Elliott; Vice-Pres. - Dr. G.B. Cutten and Mrs. A.V. Rand; Sec. Treas. - H.Y. Bishop. In 1937 the merchants organized a Retail Association with President Tom Weaver, and Secretary George Waterbury.

The Chamber of Commerce received publicity in 1928 when they honored former mayors of the town at a banquet, and when C.H. Wright was killed, the Chamber declared war on level railway crossings. They also declared against children coasting on streets. In 1930 they professed interest in the possibility of Wolfville having an airport.

The Board of Trade had a history of ups and downs. For a time it was known as the Wolfville Chamber of Commerce. It was reorganized in 1939 with the principal officers as follows: Pres.- G.C. Nowlan; Vice-Pres. - Dr. M.R. Elliott; Sec. Treas. - B.W. Wallace; Counsellors: Edson Graham, J.H. Baltzer, C.H. Hansford, Dr. Leslie Eaton, A.R. Smith, W.J. Regan, J.G. Waterbury, and Eric Balcom. In spite of this reorganization, it seems to have been relatively inactive during the early years of the War, but in 1944 nearly forty Board of Trade members met and discussed such issues as the resumption of the Minas Basin Ferry service and the improvement or replacement of the Orpheum Theatre.

The group became more active in the 1950s and recommended that a special committee be appointed to study the town's assets and potential. This committee would consider industries available to Wolfville, advertise the town's attractions for industry, and consider tax concessions which the Council might make as inducements to business. The town minutes indicated cooperation with the Wolfville Board of Trade, also with the Retail Merchants Association and the Annapolis Valley Affiliated Board of Trade. The Council resolved in 1961 to "encourage the establishment of new business and the renovation or expansion of old business." A new Retail Merchants Association had been formed in 1956, with George Frank as President, Frank Regan as Vice-President, and Lawrence Davis as Secretary-Treasurer. This was a cooperative organization to benefit local merchants.

In 1965 the Board of Trade reorganized once more. Then in 1969 it amalgamated with the Merchants Association. But it was reactivated in 1978, with Douglas Cochrane as President. Finally it ceased to function in 1980. The officers at that time were: Pres.- Dave Chisling; Vice-Pres. - Henry Hicks; Sec. - S.L. Lewis; Treas. - J.E. Muggah; Directors - Douglas Cochrane, E.J. Jarvis, H. Austin, E. DeMont, D.G. Canfield.

In the meantime, the Merchants Assocation, with Jack Herbin as President, was still active. In 1980 it was making plans to improve store-fronts and make street developments, benefiting from a provincially-funded program and Paul Taylor became President. But it was largely replaced during the year by the Wolfville Business Development Corporation. The first President of this group was Peter Herbin; Vice-President was Paul Taylor; Treasurer was Ian Porter; and the Secretary, Jim Dewar. Robert Wrye was Chairman. The Corporation engaged Murdock MacLeod to co-ordinate plans.

7. Horticultural and Garden Clubs

Horticulture received early attention from the Fruit Growers Association and from the N.S. Government. The provincial School of Horticulture, for six months having been controlled by the Nova Scotia F.G. Association, held in 1894 its second summer school at Wolfville, and the Government assisted financially. From this School arose in 1895 a Science Club, with twenty members, and with officers: Pres. - Prof. Fairville; Vice-Pres. - J.W. Bigelow; Sec. - W.S. Blair; Treas. - C.A. Patriquin.

A local Horticultural Club also began in February 1902 when A.H. Johnson delivered a paper. Later that month the Club discussed why apple trees did not bear fruit at times, considered the cultivation of orchards and the methods of spraying. The Club met fortnightly at their Club Room where they held lively debates.

A different kind of group appeared in January 1935 when a Garden Club was organized, working during the next summer on the Post Office grounds. At their second annual meeting, in 1937, they chose officers: Hon. Pres. - Mrs. B.O. Davidson; Pres. -Mrs. G.R. Forbes; Vice-Pres. - Mrs. D.R. Munro; Sec. Treas. - Mrs. W.B. Davidson; Directors - Mrs. F.H. Beals, Mrs. A.A. Elderkin, Mrs. W.C.B. Harris, Mrs. A.C. Cox, Mrs. J.W. Smith, Mrs. M.R. Elliott. In 1938 the Club placed memorial trees on the Federal Building grounds, noting names of townsmen who died in World War I.

The Club was given the responsiblity of landscaping the Post Office grounds. The Chinese Laundry building at the west of the property was removed, as were the apple trees at the rear. The members celebrated their achievement at a special ceremony in May 1938. Caretaker Alfred Lake had assisted considerably in the work on the grounds.

The Garden Club proudly commemorated their fifteenth anniversary in 1950 but the Club discontinued meetings in 1957, when they contributed the balance of their funds to the Wolfville Historical Society. Though flower exhibits had been held previously *The Acadian* reported in 1965 that at St. Andrew's United Church Hall the town's first flower show was held.

8. The Foresters

The Independent Order of Foresters attracted a large membership around the turn of the century but lost support to other organizations. Court Blomidon, a flourishing group, had 105 members in 1899. They held their usual church parade, led by the band. The Order met in February 1902 at Temperance Hall, their regular place for their gatherings.

9. Red Cross Society

The Canadian Red Cross Society was founded in 1896, doing valuable works of mercy during the South African War and all wars since then. When the Boer War began the Society had eight provincial branches, and 1,303 when the War ended, all engaged in a world-wide program of mercy and relief. The Wolfville branch of the Canadian Red Cross received its charter in 1915, with 129 members.

During World War I it operated a tea room, rolled bandages for overseas, held sewing meetings at various residences in town, and sent Christmas stocking to soldiers overseas. With the coming of peace, its attention was directed more to needs at home. In 1933 the Society handled the sending of Christmas parcels to 160 children in Wolfville and vicinity.

In October 1939 the branch was reorganized, with Mrs. B.C. Silver as President. It was very active in World War II, raising money for wartime needs, sending clothing and bedding overseas, and arranging blood donor clinics. At this time it was using the "Old DeWolfe House" as headquarters.

In 1980 the following were voted into office: Retiring Pres. - John Vaillancourt; Pres. -Raymond Jefferson; Vice-Pres. - Rev. Douglas Hergett; Sec. - Doris Bishop; Treas. - Arnold Feener; Blood Donor - Lions Club and Acadia University Students' Union; Financial Campaign - Marjorie Dowe; Emergency Aid - Donald Mosher; Sickroom Loan - Earl Murphy; Women's Work - Mrs. D. Gesner; Publicity - Rev. James Davison.

10. Boy Scouts, Girl Guides

The Boy Scout movement in Wolfville began in 1911 - only four years after Lt. Gen. Lord Baden-Powell launched his world-wide organization. A group of eight boys met in April at the home of Percy Brown, who became a prominent figure in the organization and served as Scoutmaster for many years.

The movement seems to have grown very rapidly. By 1912 the Scouts put on an entertainment at the Opera House to raise funds. They had an outing at Starr's Point for twenty-five boys, and they later camped at Chester, having raised money for the trip by picking berries and selling ice cream. When the Duke of Connaught visited Wolfville in August of that year the Scouts provided a guard of honour.

By 1913 the Scouts had their own meeting place in a building donated by J.D. Chambers to the rear of his store. In November 1922 the *Acadian* stated that nearly every boy of Scout age in the town was a member. Percy Brown had obtained land in 1921 for a campsite at Sunken Lake where the Scouts had tented previously. In 1960 the E.P. Brown Lodge at Sunken lake was named in his honor.

1912. Boy Scouts on parade to honor the Duke of Connaught.

In 1922 the first two Cub Packs were formed, with James Northover as Cubmaster.

The *Advertiser* of March 1971 reviewed the previous sixty years of Scouting in Wolfville. This account mentioned several well-known Scoutmasters — Roy Steeves, Lloyd Shaw, O. Rex Porter, Hugh Fairn, Glen Hancock, Henry Watson, K.D.C. Haley, Lem. Morine, and Charles Strong. In 1977 S.M. Barry Moody and fourteen boys attended the Canadian Jamboree on Prince Edward Island.

The Boy Scouts Group Committee in 1980 consisted of the following: Chairman - Keith Stewart; Treas. - Gerald Porter; Assist. Treas. - Robbin MacLeod; Sec. - Rev. Douglas Hergett; Public Relations - Kenneth Campbell; "A" Cub Pack leaders - Mrs. Marilyn Van Buskirk and Donald Mosher; 'B" Cub Pack leaders - William Berryman and David Adlington; Scout Troop - Dr. Darryl Grund; Venturers - Dr. John Roscoe; Rovers - James Amos; Beavers - Mrs. Jay Bourne, Mrs. Gilchrist and Mrs. Goodwin; Committee Members - Brian Isenor, John Spencer, Graham Cheeseman.

The Girl Guides began in 1919. The principal founders were Mrs. Percy Brown and Jennie Tamplin (later Mrs. A.R. Stirling). There were three patrols at first, with Miriam Chisholm (later Mrs. G.C. Nowlan) as Captain, and Marion Grant, Helen Schurman, and Arlene Bishop as Lieutenants.

Marjorie Haley (later Mrs. Merle Bancroft) became Captain in 1921. She held that post until 1927, and during that time was credited with making her Company one of the best in the province. Other outstanding leaders have been Marjorie Wickwire (who succeeded Miss Haley), Ruth Ingraham (later Mrs. O. Rex Porter and Mrs. E.P. Linton), and in more recent years, Mrs. Florence Ogden, Mrs. F.S. Chesley, and Margaret Godfrey.

A Brownie Pack was first formed in 1925 and was reorganized by Mrs. J. Forsythe-Smith in 1933. Sally Starr led in 1946. Leah Patterson was Brown Owl from 1962 to 1968, was Pack holiday adviser for the local division and was active in camp inspections and training until 1971.

In 1980 there was one Girl Guide Company active in Wolfville, known as the 2nd Wolfville Girl Guides and led by Linda Mullen, Diane McMullen, and Sherri Goodwin. There were two Wolfville Brownie Packs: 1st Wolfville Brownies with Brown Owl Eleanor Mason and Tawny Owls Marilyn Jolley and Susan Bisset, and 3rd Wolfville Brownies with Brown Owl Lorraine Salsman, and Tawny Owls Anna Dearman and Gladys Veinott. The 1st Wolfville Pathfinders were led by Pathfinder Builders Alice Parson, Katherine MacKay, and Nan McCaffrey. M. Joan Crowe was District Commissioner for Kings I East (Wolfville-Gaspereau-Grand Pre).

Through the years, the organization has had the support of a large group of Wolfville women.

11. Camp Fire Girls

The American-based Camp Fire Girls organized at Wolfville in 1912, became for about two years a lively interest for several girls before the introduction of Girl Guides. In 1912 Reverend W.T. Stackhouse and his wife (formerly Waittie Glencrosa McKeen of Pereau, N.S.) moved to Wolfville from Winnipeg. They lived in a large house built by Elisha DeWolf, Jr. (369 Main St.) which later was made into apartments by ''Pope'' Borden, now the Douglas Apartments.

Mrs. Stackhouse had a large family of three boys and five girls. She met an American tourist, learned of the Camp Fire Girls, corresponded with the New York office, was made a Guardian and organized a branch. Members of this group and of a second group formed later under the Guardianship of Helen Moore and Mary Black were: Marion and Greta Harvey, Gladys and Ruth Elderkin, Stella Bleakney, Barbara, Frances and Margaret Stackhouse, Mary and Violet Black, Lillian Taylor, Edith Thompson, Helen Moore, Marguerita Cutten, Felice Herbin, Nina Wickwire, Marcia Calkin, Gwendolyn Hales, Marjorie Sheehy, Harriet Haley, and Mona Parsons. The girls met in a first-floor room of the Stackhouse residence.

Violet M. Black (Trugo) belonged to Gluscap Sisterhood, and Helen W. Moore (Monita) was Guardian of the Camp Fire. All were tested for Health, Crafts, Business, and Patriotism. The first meeting was held April 1914, and the Camp Fire decided on Gluskap as their name. Those late to meetings were required to pay one cent. The Camp members made outfits for Belgian babies in 1916. The last council meeting was held in February 1916 at the home of Mrs. J.F. Herbin and the Pro-Tem Guardian at that time was Mary E. Black.

These girls became in 1917 the nucleus of the Give Service Girls, a group organized to aid the War effort. In May 1919 their final money-raising effort was an entertainment in the form of a play, "Mrs. Wiggs of The Cabbage Patch," staged at the Opera House. The cast of characters were: Bert Schurman, Marjorie Chute, Arthur Tingley, Lorna Prat, Horace Brown, Carrie Baker, Arthur Brown, George Waterbury, Beth Ritchie, Blanche Fullerton, Clara Chisholm, Jean Archibald, Doane Hatfield, John Crowell, Alice Stairs, Gladdie Redden, Nell Wood, and Bryce Hatfield.

12. I.O.D.E. (Imperial Order of the Daughters of the Empire)

The Sir Robert Borden Chapter of the IODE was organized in Wolfville in 1915. Original plans were to name it "King Albert Chapter" in honour of the King of Belgium, but before the charter was issued in November of that year it was decided to change the name to "Sir Robert Borden" in honour of the wartime Prime Minister, native of Kings County. The first Regent was Mrs. Charles Fitch, wife of the Wolfville Mayor.

Besides its work in World Wars I and II, the organization has supported many local and patriotic causes. The custom has been for the Chapter to sponsor the Wolfville Princess Tea, held each year in connection with the Apple Blossom Festival. The plot of flowers in front of the town cenotaph is maintained by the Chapter.

It is worth noting that as of 1980, Mrs. A.T. Levy and Mrs. Rupert MacNeill together had served as Regent for a total of thirteen out of the preceding eighteen years, Mrs. Levy having held the office six years and Mrs. MacNeill seven. In 1980/81, the principal officers were: Regent - Mrs. David Holland; 1st Vice-Regent - Mrs. A.T. Levy; 2nd Vice-Regent - Mrs. Donald Sheehan; Sec. - Mrs. Vincent Palmer; Treas. - Mrs. Charles Fry.

A history of the Sir Robert Borden Chapter from its beginning to 1962 was written by Vera Eaton Longley; another, covering the period from 1963 to 1980, was compiled by Agatha C. Ganong and Ruth Porter Linton. Copies of both are in the Vaughan Memorial Library, Acadia University.

13. Business Girls' Club

The Business Girls' Club began in October 1930, when twenty girls met at the home of Jean Stewart, who had suggested the Club. At first they called themsleves "Odds and Ends", but later the present name was chosen. Meetings originally were held each week and weekly dues of five cents apiece were paid. The first officers were: Pres. - Maxine Williams; Vice-Pres. - Jean Stewart; Sec. Treas. - Sabra Wetmore.

During their first Christmas season, the members packed boxes for the needy. Later on, Maxine Williams designed a ring for the Club in colors of white and green.

On December 1, 1932 the Club held a fashion show which was reported in the *Acadian;* "The Business Girls Club is fast becoming an institution of which the town may well be proud. Instead of slipping behind during these months of depression, they are moving forward and are rapidly making themselves felt in the community."

During the Second World War the girls were busy with knitting, sewing, and war donations of about $150, no small sum in those days. They also adopted a girl in 1939, providing her clothing and personal needs. The group raised money for the Queen's Fund in 1942, and Cathy Beveridge and Edith Bowlby joined the CWACS.

Throughout its existence, the club has raised money for several different local organizations and charities.

The officers in 1980 were: Pres. - Ruth Smith; Vice-Pres. - Edith King; Treas. - Jessie Farris; Sec. - Helen Wilson.

14. Rotary Club

In the winter of 1934/35, Burpee Wallace, Cliff Fairn and Scott Eaton (all of whom had been Rotarians elsewhere) met to discuss the formation of a Rotary Club in Wolfville. By spring the Club was ready for its first meeting, which took place in the Acadia Villa Hotel May 14, 1935, with thirteen charter members. The orginal executive was as follows: Pres. - Burpee Wallace; Vice-Pres. - Scott Eaton; Sec. - Jimmy Williams; Treas. - Harlan Davidson; Directors - Edson Graham, Ernest Robinson, Frank Welch.

The Club has grown through the years and has been active in many projects, such as work with crippled children, scholarships for local students, and maintenance of a Rotary playing Field. One of its earliest undertakings was a programme of assistance to unemployed youth during the Great Depression. From 1957 to 1979 the Club maintained a park on the Wolfville Ridge. For many years the group had conducted an Auction to raise money.

In 1963 the Club entered upon an unusual project when it presented a beef calf to Ed Kennie of Lower Wolfville (who was top member of the Cornwallis Calf Club that year) and a Holstein dairy calf to Bryan Kenny of Gaspereau (who was grand champion showman of the Horton Club that year). A condition of the presentation to Bryan Kenny was that the first heifer calf produced by the animal would go to the champion herdman of that year. Rotary members Dr. Herman Olsen and Don Mosher purchased the 1963 dairy calf for $100 but its descendants rated at a much higher value.

There have been two Paul Harris fellows from the club — Seymour C. Gordon and Dr. Herman C. Olsen. In 1977 one of the club's members, Rupert H. MacNeill, was selected as district governor of District 782.

In 1980 Gordon MacDonald was President, and Leonard Smith was Vice-President, Gordon Woodman was Secretary, and the Treasurer was Jay Rathbone.

15. Wolfville Ridge Club

The Wolfville Ridge Club was organized at the home of Mrs. R.K. Hennigar February 20, 1936. The first officers were: Pres. - Mrs. R.K. Hennigar; Vice-Pres. - Mrs. Annie Burgher; Treas. - Mrs. N.E. Ward; Sec. - Mrs. W.A. Porter. The group was formed "for the purpose of helping others" and has worked for a great variety of good causes over the years. Support of the Eastern Kings Memorial Hospital has always been a high priority. The Club has frequently catered at wedding receptions and other special occasions.

The years 1939-1945 were especially busy. A great deal of sewing and knitting was done for the Red Cross, and donations were made to many wartime funds. In 1946 the Club held a dance at the Wolfville Curling Rink for boys newly returned from the war.

Originally, most members lived on the Wolfville Ridge but as time passed, the membership came to include a great many Wolfville residents. Officers in 1980 were: Pres. - Mrs. William (Mary) Wallace; Vice-Pres. - Mrs. Mildred (Harris) Bishop; Sec. - Mrs. Bruce (Louise) Spencer; Treas. - Mrs. Elmer (Blanche) Kennie.

16. The University Women's Club

A group of Wolfville women met in April 1938 to consider forming a University Women's Club. Mrs. C.P. Wright (Dr. Esther Clark Wright) was in the chair. Dr. Muriel Roscoe, who had recently attended a meeting of the Canadian Federation of University Women, addressed the meeting.

A Club was established and met for the first time October 14, 1938. The officers were: Pres. - Mrs. H.F.S. Thomas; Vice-Pres. - Mrs. George Chase; Sec. - Charlotte Coombs; Treas. - Katherine McLeod; Federation Representative - Mrs. F.S. Dingee, and as additional members of the executive - Mrs. Beatrice Harris and Mrs. C.P. Wright. Mrs. Wright resigned from her post and was replaced by Marion Grant.

Dr. Marion Grant became an outstanding member not only of the Wolfville Club but also of the National Federation. She represented the CFUW at conferences of the International Federation of University Women in Zurich and Helsinki, and served as National President 1949/52.

Non-members have sometimes been confused by the name "University Women's Club," assuming that the Club must have some affiliation with Acadia University. No such affiliation exists, the Club being an organization of women university graduates who support a variety of causes (particularly in education) on the local, national, and international levels. In recent years the Club is often referred to as the Wolfville branch of the Canadian Federation of University Women.

In 1969 some members of the Club tried to raise the town's collective consciousness by asking for female representation on the School Board, but the town failed to cooperate. However, Jean Marsh is the current Deputy Mayor, has been on Council since 1970.

In 1980 the Club's principal officers were: Past Pres. - Dr. Marion Grant; Pres. - Thelma Potter; Vice-Pres. - Elizabeth Logan; Treas. - Jean Vernon; Recording Sec. - Anna Hennigar; Corresp. Sec. - Connie Barss; Membership Convenor - Carol Armstrong; Additional member and Parliamentarian - Isobel Horton.

17. Celtic Club

The Celtic Club began meetings in 1939, founded through the keen desire of Dr. McGregor Fraser, Theology Professor at Acadia, to stress the importance of the Celtic people, such as the Scots, Irish, Welsh, and Bretons, especially through music, literature, folklore, and customs of the Scottish Highlands and Islands.

The Club received support from faculty, students, and town folk. The first officers were: Hon. Pres. - Dr. McGregor Fraser, Pres. - Victor Fraser, Sec. - Mary MacKay. Mrs. W.D. Withrow and S.C. Gordon were regular members of the executive. Blair Campbell of Kentville recalled his position in the Club as Piper. The last meeting of the Club was held in January 1973, and later a small bank balance was turned over to the Wolfville Historical Society.

18. Wolfville Historical Society

An early attempt was made in 1846 by Acadia College Professor Isaac Chipman to begin a Historical Society to record the county's past. Then, during the summer of 1898 the suggestion was made that a society be formed — to record the removal of the old drug store from the Main Street to Linden Avenue to make room for Dr. McKenna's new building. The community took no action but the Acadia Historical Society organized, in 1922, with officers: Pres. - Dr. George B. Cutten; Vice-Pres. - J.F. Herbin, W.H. Phinney; Sec.-Treas. - Dr. W.A. Coit.

The Wolfville Historical Society came into being in 1941, largely because of the felt need for a Museum. First officers of the Society were: Pres. - Mayor W.K. Fraser; Sec. - Rosamond Archibald; Vice-Pres. - Edson Graham; Treas. - Professor J.I. Mosher; Executive - Miss D.A. West, Rev. C.H. Johnson, Dr. R.S. Longley, and H.P. Davidson.

The Society assumed management of the "Old DeWolf House," originally the home of Thomas Andrew Strange DeWolf near the corner of Main and Gaspereau. This house served as a museum for six years. Then the Wolfville Fruit Company, which owned the property, required the use of the land but offered to give the house to the Society provided it was moved from the site. At first, the Society planned to accept this offer but later changed its mind due to the costs involved, and instead procured the Randall House on Main Street, through the aid of the Nova Scotia Government. The Society was incorporated in 1947.

Randall House was opened to the public in May 1949 and has served the public as a Town Museum ever since. The house had been bought originally from Aaron Cleaveland, youngest son of Deacon Benjamin Cleaveland who had come in 1780 with his wife and twelve children. He was a farmer and cabinet maker.

In addition to managing the Museum, the Society sponsors the publication of local historical material and holds several meetings each year, with programs that deal with the history of the area.

In the fall of 1979 the Society celebrated the Museum's thirty-eighth anniversary. At that meeting four charter members were present: Dr. Esther Clark Wright, Helen Beals, Harry Van Zoost, and Dalton MacKinnon.

Officers in 1980 were: Pres. - James D. Davison; Vice-Pres. - Harold T. Stultz; Sec. - Margaret Elliott; Treas. - Jeannette Ruffee; Mrs. Ella Hanright was Curator of Randall House Museum. Other officers were: Clarence Burton, Ernest Eaton, Agatha Ganong, George Moody, Harold Dewis, Allan Nickerson, Esther Clark Wright, Hope Kirkconnell, Rhoda Colville, Robert Starr, Adeline Bayne, Patricia Townsend, Ruby Thompson, and Trenna Turner.

19. Lions Club

The Lions Club organized in June 1950 with fifteen members. A membership of at least twenty-five was required for a charter, which they received in September. The first President was Kenneth M. Dunfield, and first Secretary Donald Williams. Allan Bertelsen was Treasurer.

In addition to supporting the national and international goals of the Lions, the Club has had many local projects. It has been especially active in supporting the Eastern Kings Memorial Hospital and has provided tents for cystic fibrosis patients and for other patients having breathing problems. The Club assisted annually at the Red Cross Blood Donor Clinic.

One of the Club's members, Buster Woodworth, served as District Governor for the Province of Nova Scotia 1973-74, and in 1974-75 he was Council Chairman for the Maritimes and the State of Maine, and was voted Lion of The Year in 1977. In 1980 Donald Lightfoot was President, and Buster Woodworth was Secretary of the Club.

In 1974 a Leo Club was formed, sponsored by the Lions Club. The first President was Donald Harrington, and Buster Woodworth served as Adviser. The *Acadian* of November 1976 reported the Leo Club in Wolfville rated first among the twenty-five provincial Clubs, recognized because of community services. In 1978 a charter member of the Leo Club, Michael Woodworth, was elected Governor for one year by the Nova Scotia Leos.

In spite of its activity, the Leo Club was unable to keep up its membership and closed out in 1979/80. The Club's last President was Tim Arsenault, and Gaye Coolen was Secretary-Treasurer. There were two Advisers - Buster and Michael Woodworth.

20. Canadian Cancer Society

Wolfville was originally part of a combined Kentville-Wolfville unit of the Canadian Cancer Society organized in 1951 but separated from Kentville in March 1962.

First officers of the new Wolfville and district unit were: Pres. - B.C. Silver; Vice-Pres. - Mrs. C.B. Lumsden; Treas. - John W. Arnold; Sec. - Mrs. Austin E. Brownell; Welfare Chairman - Ethel E. Ingraham; Education Chairman - Mrs. B.C. Silver; Medical Advisory Chairman - Dr. Clive MacDonald; Education Committee - Mrs. Watson Kirkconnell, Mrs. Bruce Trenholm, Mrs. C. Lumsden; Campaign Chairman - Prof. Rupert H. MacNeill.

The unit shared in the Society's usual educational programs and welfare services and joined in the annual fund-raising campaigns. The officers in 1980 were: Pres. - Dr. Ian Macdonald; Vice-Pres. - William Parker; Sec. - Rhoda Colville; Treas. - Jeannette Ruffee; Publicity - Helen Buckler; Educational Sec. - Elizabeth Logan; Patients' Services - Ethel Ingraham and Mrs. Margaret McCarthy; Campaign - Mrs. Ruth Linton and Mrs. Lloyd Dobson; Medical Adviser - Dr. G. Milton; Member-At-Large - Mrs. Ralph Pick.

In 1980 the Nova Scotia Division of the Society made a gold pin award to Ethel Ingraham who had joined the executive of the combined Kentville-Wolfville unit in 1957 and became a member of the Services Comittee. In 1962 she became Chairman of the Services Committee of the Wolfville and District unit, and still held that post in 1980.

21. Silver and Gold Club

The Silver and Gold Club of senior citizens was formed in Wolfville in May 1976. One of its principal founders was a retired clergyman, the Reverend Kenneth Wainwright who became the first Secretary and (on a temporary basis) first Treasurer. His wife Mabel was the first President, and Winnifred Rockwell was Vice-president.

As a social organization, the Club arranged for potluck suppers, tours, picnic outings, etc. among its members — a busy program of activities. In 1980 the President was Phyllis Miner; the Vice-President was Barbara Shepherd; the Secretary was Mabel Gray, and the Treasurer was Josie Price.

A family party.

XIX.

PEOPLE AND HAPPENINGS

Every community has people whose sayings and doings create notable impressions on their contemporaries, and are worth recording. To portray them and their times, a sample has been assembled to introduce those selected. To begin, a former resident, Graham Patriquin, wrote of some of the folk that he knew about:

"Colin Munroe's grandfather was a pioneer in several enterprises in town, while his father also was innovative as all get out, and an unusual character, even for Wolfville, which had more than a fair share of colourful personalities."

Graham Patriquin also sent a weekly edition of the October 8, 1879 Wolfville *Star* and commented on some of the names in that issue.

I find many names that my Dad often mentioned: S. P. Chute, C. L. Dodge, P. Innes, F. G. Currie, A. E. Calkin(s), and members of the Wolfville Division, Sons of Temperance — William Evans, William Fitch, J. Alfred Elderkin, Miss Belle Pick, and A. C. Borden. . . . Most familiar of Wolfville names is, oddly, that of Burpee Witter. He must have been a particular friend of Dad; he often spoke of him. S. P. Chute was still a power in business when I was a small boy. Will Evans had an ice business in addition to his farm at Scott's Corner, now occupied by the Kenny family. His son Harold — 'Cousin Trout' — was employed by Hugh E. Calkin, druggist, for a long time before establishing his own druggist business in Kentville. Trout also played right field for the town baseball team. People used to quote fellow townsmen (and women) frequently, and Alfred Elderkin (father of Angus Elderkin) was a favourite source of verbal illustrations.

Previously, Graham Patriquin had written of his parents who lived in the Randall House from 1927 to 1947. He commented on the property, also described the elderly Randall brother and sister who were regarded with foreboding by youngsters as they passed the house.

Until 1927, the property was totally unkempt, half-mysterious tanglewood of neglected fruit and ornamental trees, with shoulder-high grasses and thistles making it even more ill-defined by midsummer. The house, equally neglected, displayed virtually no signs of habitation save from occasional smoke from the chimney (the eastern one only) and a rare appearance of Eardley Randall at the door, answering a neighbour's knock for admission. This, incidentally, was mainly refused, and only a few more devoted or socially conscientious persons were able to visit the invalided 'Sister Annie,' as the hermit, Eardley, always called her. If any property in Wolfville was unproductive, it was the Randall house. It had a spooky reputation among the young fry, and was a symbol of chronic inertia to the mature inhabitants of the town. . . . I helped with the final stages of clearing out the house to make it fit for human habitation, but I had been out of town when Dad first attacked the debris and accumulated dirt of several decades. For example, he wheeled eleven barrel loads of ashes from the kitchen floor.

1. The 1800s

Now the reader is invited to consider the potpourri that has been prepared. The editor has included material at hand and acknowledges that many other people and events merited recognition.

John L. Brown left his mercantile business at Grand Pre in 1847 and moved to Wolfville to the west half of a surgery of his brother Dr. E. L. Brown. After five years he bought the so-called Graham property on Main Street where he died in January 1887. In 1852 he built the store on the south-west corner of Main Street and the present Highland Avenue, occupied in 1887 by Johnson H. Bishop and sold after ten years by Brown to his brother Frederick Brown. He soon became partner with George Forsythe, Dr. Hea and John Rounsefell as general dealers. For a time he joined J. W. Caldwell under the firm name of J. L. Brown and Company, and afterwards with his son as F. L. Brown and Company. He then returned to farming. He contested for the Liberals in the township of Horton in 1859 against his brother, Dr. Brown, and won, holding office until 1863.

The Acadia university president's house of today was built in 1852 for John L. Brown. It had Ionic pilasters on the front and twin pillars facing a spiral staircase in the front hall, emulating the four Ionic pillars fronting the first college hall and made by Edmund and Lewis Davison of Greenwich.

Dr. George DeWitt bought the house in 1892 and added a sun porch. He employed Frank Angus to build a stone wall across the front of the property, with stone from White Rock. At the age of eighty-two, George DeWitt died in 1924, having resided in Wolfville for thirty-five years. He had been mayor for three terms. In his medical practice he campaigned against tuberculosis.

1880's Left: Sawyer house; left centre: West house; centre, on nearer side of Main Street: the Eliza Harris house.

At the junction of the first college hall centre path and the Main Street, in about 1850, Elijah Harris ran a business in a building at the location. It was sold in 1862 to Henry B. Witter who came to Wolfville about 1853; he ran a flour and feed store in that building. I. B. Oakes recalled the 1860s: "A small old cottage . . . just a little south-east of the site of the present Manual Training hall and near the street. It was burned about 1869." Witter had previously advertised in the 1864-1865 Hutchinson's Directory as "Birmingham House," selling hardware, stoves, groceries, cutlery. He was listed in the Church map of about 1870 as a flour merchant. The burned building appears to have been the earlier Graham farmhouse used first by Horton academy in 1829. Previously it might have been lived in by Lucy Peake and afterwards by the Christie family. An 1876 photo showed a three-storey structure that Elijah Harris had built. In 1874 Burpee Witter began business in the Borden Block on Main Street. Presumably, he sold the old property.

The Elijah Harris building fronting the college property reportedly was later occupied by the Misses Tamar (1856-1947) and Sabina (1841-1940) Butler, whose parents Philip and Mary I. Butler lived later on Main Street, near the present Esso station. Mrs. Butler was a widow by 1893. A daughter Mary was also alive at that time. Sabina and Tamar were remembered later by older citizens as "taking in washing" and doing housework for others by the day. A W. E. Butler lived at Wolfville in 1891, belonged to the bicycle club. In 1912 this house on the campus was known as "The Butler House." It housed male students in 1915 when the Student Council heard a complaint that two fuse plugs had been taken from "Butt Inn," the name apparently coined by the inmates. Later in the 1920s other families lived there: the Blesedells, the Harry Mollins, the Roy Steeves. In March 1925 the Acadia Board of Governors considered the fate of "the building known as Butt Inn." They apparently had it torn down soon afterwards.

William Oliver was the first of five generations of that Wolfville family. He came of a distinctive family line, in that he descended from American slaves who came to Nova Scotia in 1816. William Oliver was born in Lucasville, Nova Scotia, learned to care for livestock as he had charge of a farm belonging to Dalhousie University Professor Lawson. After eleven years he began about 1875 to work at Wolfville where for four years he took care of the Ladies Seminary when Acadia president Dr. Cutten was a student. In 1898 he advanced to a larger work, to superintend the college buildings and grounds. He and his family lived in a small house south of the seminary building.

William Oliver was described as a unique character, willing to oblige his favourites with warm affection and to tolerate others. The *Athenaeum* paid tribute in 1915 to him as adept at coining words and phrases. He did more than sweep floors; he was "a real teacher, although he never received a degree from any college, nor set an examination for any student. The faithfulness with which he performed his daily task, the readiness with which he responded to every request, and the cheerfulness and optimism of his nature may well be copied by any student of life in his preparation for the final exam."

Oliver served under five presidents and died in 1934 at the age of 84. His son Clifford followed in his father's footsteps, employed also at the university, manager of the farm and caretaker of buildings and driver of the truck. He did his work without fuss, ever congenial. His first wife was Dorothy Moore of Halifax, and his second wife, a musician and now an efficient seamstress, was Helena White of Halifax, daughter of Captain White, pastor of Cornwallis Baptist Church and Canada's only black chaplain in the First World War. Clifford died in 1966, aged 85. He had always stressed the importance of education, and five of his six children graduated from Acadia.

William Oliver (II), the son of Clifford and his first wife, graduated from Acadia in 1936 with a Bachelor of Divinity after schooling at Wolfville where he captained both the high school hockey and football teams. In 1927 and 1928 he placed first in the seven-mile race, setting a record. He was ordained in 1936 into the Baptist ministry, served as pastor of the Cornwallis Church at Halifax from 1937 to 1962, was president of the United Baptist Convention in 1960, and later received honorary degrees from King's and Acadia universities. He was an armed forces chaplain during World War II and engaged in the work of adult education. In 1962 he resigned his pastorate and became regional representative of Continuing Education in Nova Scotia Department of Education for the area in and about Halifax, especially aiding blacks. He retired in 1977, voluntarily assisting churches, and now resides with his wife, the former Pearleen Borden of New Glasgow, at Lucasville, the birthplace of his grandfather William. Three of their five sons graduated from Acadia.

Donald H. Oliver, William, Jr.'s half-brother, son of Clifford and Helena, graduated from Acadia in 1960, studied law and became a Q.C., married

The Seminary and the Oliver family.

Linda MacLellan of Halifax, and wrote a popular cook book. Others of the Oliver family have also made worthy contributions towards an improved Canadian society.

The Butlers were another black family, with Tamar and Sabina recalled by older residents as living in a small yellow and white cottage close to the highwater mark of east Main Street. These capable women gave professional laundering service. Their custom was to walk in a dignified manner along the sidewalk, one always about ten feet in front of the other, and at the Methodist church there was always considerable walking and sitting distance between them.

Alice Johnson was also a member of the black community, servant of the Starr family all her life. In recent years she has lived at the home of Mrs. George Boggs. Dorothy Gibson lived here as a domestic with the Creighton family. She now resides with Mrs. Anne Annand.

From 1883 to the end of this account the editors of the *Acadian* walked and talked with Wolfville citizens, knew them well, and from that publication readers are invited to learn about these people. The story is presented mostly chronologically as the pages of the *Acadian* provided the news of the day.

The account includes a minor disaster. J. R. Bishop and J. B. Davison drove on the back road near Charles Murphy's. When the horse stumbled, it and the waggon went partly over the bank, with the men headlong into the gulley. P. H. Murphy and Samuel Morse rescued them. The *Acadian* accompanied that story with information that D. W. Patterson shipped sixty bushels of plums weekly.

In the 1880s the community took seriously the Queen's birthday celebration of May 24, but when the paper proposed recognition of the Queen's Jubilee of 1887 no action was taken. However, Arbor Day got considerable attention on June 1, 1888, with a programme by school pupils. Taking part were: Hattie Day, Carrie Blair, Teddie Bowles, Tira Caldwell, Avard Davison, Edith Johnson, Minnie Brown, and Grace Patriquin. Sixteen new trees were planted by: Florence Vaughan, Harold Gillmore, Frank Wortman, Lola Bishop, Lina Burgess, Archie Murphy, Amy Prat, Etta Cook, Stanley Jones, May Prat, Nellie Murphy, Aubrey Benjamin, Everett Brown, Carrie Caldwell, Ella Wallace, Addie Minard, Clifford Jones, Harold Witter, Bell Patriquin, Amanda Caldwell, May Henderson, Stella Rogers, Archie Minard, John Caldwell, Reginald Gillmore, Louise Cowan, and Kate Murphy.

The village heard from John Rounsefell who had done well in Vancouver; one of his sons had recently attended Acacia Villa Seminary at Grand Pre. John Rounsefell came to Nova Scotia from Cornwall, England, became a tailor at Wolfville. He was a Methodist class leader and local preacher, was also strong for temperance, a charter member of the Division. He died in September 1891, was buried at Lower Horton in the Methodist cemetery. His wife died in October 1890.

Late in 1893 young Jack McGinty died. His mother's memorial in verse form was published in the *Canning Gazette*, printed in Kentville in January 1894. The thoughtful lines read:

The autumn leaves were whirling past, The autumn winds were sighing.
Nature put on her sombre robes For little Jack was dying.
He called his mama to his side. His parent fond and true
Bent lowly o'er the dying lad, And wept as mamas do.
Oh Jack, my son, my precious son, How can I lose you now?
Just when you have begun to wear Bright laurels on your brow.
To think that when I sadly stand Above your lowly bed,
The local press will tell the world That Jack McGinty's dead.

Later, Jack's aunt explained what happened, that the boy walked on the railroad track the day after a big snowstorm. A special express came through from Ottawa, apparently preceded by a snowplough which struck Jack on the head, hurling him twenty feet. His mother was away at the time and failed to see her boy alive gain. She retained a lawyer as she threatened a lawsuit against the railroad company.

D. R. Munro was Wolfville's adventurous spirit. He launched his new yacht in August 1884 but it got caught in the mud. During September of the next year five or six vessels were tied up at the same time at the wharf. While building boats and yachts Munro shaped a lead keel on his *Petrel*. "He purchased 1,100 pounds of tea lead, placed it in a bushel pot, and after erecting a mud furnace around it he melted the whole mass and ran a 1,000 pounds of lead into the keel of the yacht after preparing a receptacle for it." Munro again made news in 1896 when he announced plans to build a vessel even larger than his naphtha gasoline launch. In 1900 the Munro Brothers and Company sold their naphtha launch to a company in Bridgewater; the boat was the only one of its kind in the province. He also possessed a one-man skiff which had oars on hinges and arranged so that the rower faced the prow.

Dr. Harris Otis McClatchey, for thirty years a medical practitioner at Wolfville, died in July 1887 at the age of fifty-eight. He was a native of Windsor, attended Horton Academy and graduated from Acadia in 1848, then from Jefferson Medical College, Philadelphia. He came to Wolfville in 1856 to begin his practice.

John W. Barss, born in 1812 at Liverpool, Nova Scotia, came to Wolfville when five years old. He removed to Halifax in 1836 for fourteen years but failing health required his return to Wolfville. He was described as a wealthy man and he devoted himself to Acadia College, giving generously. After becoming treasurer in 1861 the college finances improved considerably. When a businessman in his forties he refused to have anything to do with the sale of liquor. In his generosity he also provided half of the capital needed to erect Wolfville Baptist church and parsonage. He was a deacon of the church and superintendent of the Sunday School. He died in May 1902.

Mrs. J. W. Barss died in 1894 at the age of seventy-nine. She was a daughter of Simon Fitch and was born at Fitchdale, Wallbrook. She married in 1838 and returned from Halifax with Mr. Barss in 1851. She was a useful member of the Baptist Church.

Runaways were a common nuisance. One took place in 1894 when Frank Gertridge stood on his sled in front of Charles Strong's store and a boy with a whip frightened the horse which broke the reins, throwing the driver. When the horse turned the corner of Main and Chapel a pile of lumber separated from the sled. The horse was caught on Chapel Street; no great damage was done.

The *Western Chronicle* noted in April 1895 that Joseph Edwards was a brakeman on a gravel train and became one of the most popular conductors in America. When a boy he had carried chain when the railway was built. He admired Longfellow for his "Evangeline" and sent him a cane from an apple tree. He got in return a costly conductor's cap. The writeup, in three consecutive issues of the paper, credited "Foss Blood Purifier" for curing Edwards of his rheumatism.

In June 1897 Queen Victoria's Diamond Jubilee created considerable interest but Wolfville residents went mainly to Canning, and the No. 9 Company of the militia also attended. Sports events included sprints, shot put, bicycle racing. During the battle between warring companies one soldier was injured by a doughnut thrown by the besieged. The Wolfville baseball team won at Annapolis, 25—18. Some people went fishing.

In 1898 the Beaver Mills flour business was operated by Arthur L. Calhoun, who had graduated from Acadia in 1882 and from Harvard in 1885. He married Margaret Ellis, whose father was editor of the *St. John Globe*. After being a newspaper reporter, editor, and teacher in the United States, he set up business at St. John, then became proprietor of the flour mill at Wolfville early in 1898. He had purchased the "Skoda" building, then moved it to the waterfront where he had a well-equipped mill and a superior product. When a vessel from Boston arrived with a large cargo for his mill, Calhoun, standing at the end of the platform, was struck by one of the tubs and thrown about thirty feet to the wharf below. He was killed instantly from a skull fracture. After a brief service in Wolfville he was buried in St. John.

Hallowe'en was referred to in 1898, seemingly for the first time. Previously, the date was observed as Cabbage Night, with a similar purpose.

About 1900. Skoda building at left, and entrance to Mud Creek inlet.

2. The First Decade of the 20th Century

In 1904 J. Clarence Hemmeon won a scholarship for $350 at Harvard University, and in 1908 Dr. Theodore Boggs received honours at Yale University. J. F. Herbin received publicity when he suffered a fall on his way to the American House fire as he struck a wire across the foot of Church Hill.

The editors of the *Acadian* were apparently so impressed by the big snow of February 1905 that they commissioned editor-in-chief Margaret Barss, and sub-editors Louise Mears and Rosamond Archibald to put out *A Snowball* on March 8 — "Lest We Forget."

Repeated snowstorms blocked the tracks and closed in the community for several weeks. Relief was beginning as the special edition was composed in recognition of the worst storm since 1865. The D.A.R. secured more men, the churches gave pulpit announcements requesting volunteer shovellers, at Mayor DeWitt's request. Though blizzards continued, 250 men cleared the tracks from Grand Pre to Hantsport. Wolfville people and 150 Acadia students and professors completed their portion to Grand Pre, and on the next Sabbath all churches, except the Presbyterians, closed from lack of coal. When working through to Windsor, the students were served preserved horsemeat and hardtack.

But the worst was over, the train whistle was heard and the mail came through, delayed only by ice on the rails and trains off the tracks. However, from Kentville to Digby no train ran all this time. Only ferries and teams could take the mail through to Annapolis and Middleton. Schools were closed everywhere. Coal had given out. Mail had stopped.

In her story of the D.A.R. and the storm, Marguerite Woodworth wrote in 1936: "The first train to go through was crowded, not with regular passengers, but hundreds of students who had been given free passes for their work and who had made up parties to celebrate the occasion." The cost to the D.A.R. was over $100,000 for snow clearance alone.

Wolfville's rink suffered with the churches and the schools. The tremendous weight of snow crushed the structure on February 25 and sank the roof flat to the ground. The seminary students had skated happily that afternoon, though they had heard crackling sounds. They and manager Heales left before six, planning to return. While the students awaited the manager's arrival and entry to the rink, the crash came — just as the door was being opened. Thousands of tons of snow lowered with a thunderous roar. Hundreds of young people could have died and thousands of homes saddened had not Providence determined the time of the disaster, according to the young editors who also had a sense of humour. They filled in the paper with selected poems by Longfellow, Spencer, Emerson, Rossetti, and Watson, all extolling snow.

In Nova Scotia Edgar S. Archibald joined the teaching staff at the Agricultural College at Truro, and Reverend F. W. Waring, of the Anglican Church, gave a lecture on "Sex and Sociology." In the summer of 1909 W. Karl Wortman won the Standard Empire free trip to England, sailing on the "Empress of Britain," and Waldo Davison won three prizes showing Brown Leghorn poultry at Middleton. At the same time, Mrs. Sarah Spencer died at the age of 102, and Sophia Bishop, descended from the first Bishops who came from Massachusetts, died at the age of 85.

In 1914, H. E. Calkin, a member of the Pharmaceutical Society since 1894, moved his drug business from Springhill to Wolfville. This was discontinued about 1930. Previously, G. S. Parker conducted a drug business from 1900 to 1905, and Fred Churchill was registered in Wolfville from 1903 to 1909. In 1924 D. Ross Cochrane opened a new store, now operated by his son Douglas.

George V. Rand died in December 1908. He had lived on what is now Linden Avenue, was one of the first of three non-medical druggists in the province. In his store on Main Street he conducted both the drug store and post office, and operated the telegraph. He was one of the town's most public-spirited men. Deeply interested in music, he had charge of the Baptist choir for many years, beginning in 1884, also assisting other church choirs of the village. He worked assiduously to improve the town water system and he was an advocate of temperance; supporters of the liquor interests burned his barn. In 1896 his son Aubrey was associated with him until his father died, continuing until 1929 when the business was taken over by Dalton R. MacKinnon. The store burned in 1937 and a new structure was erected. MacKinnon was succeeded by Robert L. Bearne's Drug Ltd.

3. 1910 — 1919

In 1910 the community attended a memorial service at St. John's church at the death of King Edward. Some of the locals made news: Kate Mitchell was employed in the public schools at Slocum City, British Columbia; Gordon Bill became assistant professor at Dartmouth College; Ernest Porter was paid ten dollars for removing the weather vane on the Baptist church steeple; W. M. Black saved a Windsor girl from drowning at Evangeline Beach; Victor Woodworth was now school principal at Duncan, British Columbia, with an annual salary of $1,200.

The community observed Victoria Day in 1911, this time to travel on the "Prince Albert" to Parrsboro for a ball game. Politics was a lively issue that summer as the Union Reform candidate, Campbell Eaton, held a meeting at Black's Opera House, and R. H. Phinney defeated A. L. Davison by nine votes to represent the Federal Liberal Conservatives. Frank Toney, Chief of the Kings County Indians, was proficient in manufacturing hockey sticks.

In February 1912 the community's oldest citizen died at the age of 105. Robert Chisholm, of County Tyrone in Ireland, came to St. John when ten, to Annapolis when thirty, and retired at Wolfville with his son R. D. Chisholm. He recalled the early years in this country when nearly all farmers lived in log houses with pole floors.

The big event that summer was Lord Connaught's visit. For the Governor-General the town put on gala attire on a beautiful day, displaying flags and evergreen arches of "Welcome" and "One Empire." The Duke, the Duchess and Princess Patricia arrived at the local train station, were met by the mayor and councillors, and the Boy Scouts formed a guard of honour. On the platform were: Councillors Hales, Sleep, Haycock, Harris, Regan, and Bishop, and ladies; President Cutten, Dean Tufts and daughter, Dean and Mrs. Chute, Dean and Mrs. Haley, Dr. and Mrs. Manning, A. E. Coldwell and wife, Reverend Mr. and Mrs. Miller, Reverend Mr. and Mrs. Rackham. Mayor Chambers read the address and the Misses Bernice Hales and Jean

Creighton presented the Duchess and Princess with bouquets.

The reception committee was: The Mayor, Recorder and Town Clerk; in charge of decorations were Councillor Bishop, J. F. Herbin, J. W. Williams, Frank Bishop, Herbert Johnson, Chas. H. Porter, Arthur Young; the band; councillors Regan, Grant Porter; Boy Scouts: Morgan, Templin, E. Percy Brown. The regal party travelled by automobile about the town, viewed the valley from the ridge, went to the old church at Grand Pre, to the Old Willow and Evangeline Beach, to Acadia grounds, Greenwich, Port Williams, Starr's

1912. Duke and Duchess of Connaught and Princess Patricia arrived at the train station.

A parade to honor the Duke of Connaught.

214

Point, Canard, Upper Dyke, and Kentville. The Wolfville Museum has pictures of the group on the college grounds.

Graham Patriquin reminisced about his early years at Wolfville. He recalled when he was six years old that his mother entrusted him to take two post cards to the post office where he dropped them into the slot without postage. T. L. Harvey, owner of Crystal Palace grocery, responded to the boy's sobbing, provided four pennies and instructed Brighton Fielding to stamp the cards. Then there was the season when his mother, from a disturbed conscience, invited the two young Chinese laundrymen to eat with the family on Christmas day. However, she had to report that her invitation was not accepted, and the family found it difficult to understand the explanation: "We don't celebrate Christmas."

Patriquin also wrote that the popular practice for some lads was to attend two Sunday Schools, in the Methodist at the 10 a.m. time, and at the Baptist in the afternoon. The week's reading from the libraries at each church provided the incentive, and the works of Henty, Alger and other approved writers got considerable use. Because church attendance was required in the morning the Baptist boys would have to dash from the Methodist Sunday School, then rush for the morning service to the gallery seats at the Baptist church, considerably out of breath.

Scoutmaster E. Percy Brown, a benevolent despot, believed that Boy Scouts must never swear. At the Sunken Lake campfires Val Rand's trumpet encouraged the singing. However, the scoutmaster shuddered at "How dry I am," and exploded with wrath at the line, "God only knows how dry I am." That was too much. Gordon Kennedy, Cecil Langille and the other boys wisely adjusted, sang the next verse, "Nobody knows how dry I am."

The first attempt to hold a Thanksgiving Service under civic direction proved a success in 1913. Mayor Chambers presided at the Opera House and addressed the meeting. Also in that year the town celebrated Mothers' Day.

On Canada's entry into the Great War Kenneth D. Dixon joined the fifty Canadians at the White City in London, under canvas. In 1915 a steamer from Victoria, British Columbia, commanded by Captain F. C. Eagles, was captured by the German navy, though it was United States command.

Dissension arose during the First World War when Judson (Juddie) Harris arranged an unique display. Late in 1917 some Long Island residents reported a dirigible, supporting the rumour that the Germans were planning to bomb Nova Scotia. The junior members of R. E. Harris and Sons responded ingeniously and aroused the ire of Long Islanders. In the window they hung a four-foot green zucchini with a cardboard gondola below it, painted rudder and elevator vanes, and an electric fan blowing to revolve the propellor. Also, the "zeppelin" was clearly marked with an iron cross. The offensive part of the display was the lettering strung between the two supporting ropes: LONG ISLAND ZEPPELIN.

In May of 1917 the flags hung half mast on the death of W. Marshall Black but the place cheered when Scout Terrance Hagen received a Silver Cross for saving a woman in a sleigh pulled by a runaway horse, and Clyde West received a Military Medal in 1918 for repairing telephone wires while exposed overseas to shell and gas fire.

F. J. Woodman was blessed with a strong, true bass voice which he used as choir master of the Methodist Church on Gaspereau Avenue. Mrs. Harold Bowlby, the former LaVaughan F. Woodworth, a talented musician and a 1911 graduate in music from Acadia Seminary, played the church organ. She remembered when Woodman's mastery of choir music stood him in good stead. One Easter Sunday around 1918, when the choir presented Handel's Messiah, a sudden, stiff breeze through an open window blew off the organist's music. Woodman was close to the organ, and the organist knew that he could carry on without his music score. Scarcely missing a beat, she snatched the needed page from his hands and continued the accompaniment. Woodman kept on singing.

The war over, Lieutenant Stuart Graham, son of Edson Graham, made the first long-distance airplane flight in Canada. Accompanied by his wife and mechanic, he left Halifax at 2.15 p.m. Thursday in his Curtis seaplane and arrived at Saint John at 4.33 p.m. In two more flights he reached his destination of Trois Rivieres, Quebec. The first airplane appeared a year later at Wolfville, piloted by Lieutenant I. Logan Barnhill, with mechanic E. C. Atkinson, son of Mrs. E. G. Atkinson of Wolfville.

4. 1920 — 1929

In a more serious vein in 1920, Gladys Vaughan, daughter of Mr. and Mrs. C. M. Vaughan, with a Polish mission at Warsaw, led 2,300 terrified refugees to safety in small boats across the Dneister River. In December the Duke of Devonshire, Governor-General of Canada, visited the town, and in August 1922 the Governor-General, Lord Byng of Vimy and Lady Byng, visited Wolfville. Led by H. S. Boates, about ninety excursionists went to Parrsboro on the "Prince Albert" to spend Dominion Day. A group of Theo Rand, Fred Herbin, Clarence Coldwell, John Sheehey, Budd Cook, Harold Beattie, and Robert Stewart left to join the Harvesters' Excursion for the West.

In 1923 H. W. Phinney held office as mayor. However, his business concerns caused him to seek release for his duties that removed him too often from the town. He completed his term but left Wolfville in 1925. He died in 1966, at the age of eighty-six.

The death of a valued citizen occurred in December 1923. John F. Herbin died enroute home from a shooting trip. Of Acadian descent, he was born at Windsor, Nova Scotia, in 1860. When a young man he came to Wolfville in 1885, having previously lived in western United States and New Mexico. Here, he set up a jewellery business. He graduated from Acadia in 1890 and in 1895 built the store that still houses Herbins Ltd. He married Minnie Rounsefell Simson of Grand Pre in 1896, and also became mayor of Wolfville. Herbin achieved renown as a poet, portraying the Evangeline country and the Acadians. At the age of twenty-two his son Frederick George Herbin succeeded his father in business and improved the efficiency of the store. Upon his death in 1951 he was followed by his son John who joined the firm in 1950. His son Peter trained in Toronto in watchmaking and became a member of the firm in 1975.

Inhabitants received awards in 1924. Wolf Cub Bryce Hatfield received the Gilt Cross for rescuing his young brother from drowning, and Wolf Cub Jason Coldwell finished runner-up (by one point) in the National Marble

Championship at Toronto. Also, Paul R. Tingley received his degree in medicine from Edinburgh University and continued work at the Royal Edinburgh Infirmary.

In 1923 Stephen MacIntosh returned to town and bought the old Hardwick place at the corner of Highland Avenue and Pleasant Street. He had been born at Grand Pre before 1830 and he first came to Wolfville when he was three years old, lived in the "old red house" at the rear of the site occupied later by St. Andrew's church, on Stephen B. DeWolf's farm. Young MacIntosh attended a boys' school at "Scott's Corner." DeWolf's house was where now stands the fire station, was burned in the spring of 1915, and L. W. Sleep's hardware store was just east of the house. When a boy, MacIntosh worked for Sleep, also took the cows to pasture and kept in repair the fences that prevented the geese from wandering. Stephen MacIntosh died in 1925. His father, William MacIntosh (1783-1881), had worked in Wolfville as an undertaker and cabinet maker.

Stephen P. Heales was born at St. John in 1841, died March 1926, nearly eighty-five years old. For a time he had a store here, later built the skating rink on Front Street; it was destroyed in 1905 by the excessive weight of snow.

Prime Minister W. L. MacKenzie King visited the town in 1925. Kentville held a summer carnival in 1926, with beauty contest representatives from Wolfville: Greta Eagles, Mildred Eye, Margaret Johnson, Mona Parsons, Flora Patriquin, Frances Sanford, Zelma Tretheway. Mildred Eye was chosen to represent Wolfville. Varied other activities took place as Wolfville Fruit Company won four first prizes at the Imperial Fruit Show, and for the first time a "Father and Son Week" was observed.

Arthur Tingley won the Ralph M. Hunt Oratorical contest at the university in 1927 and later became Junior Canadian Trade Commissioner in Scotland and Ireland. The town celebrated that year the Diamond Jubilee of Confederation as throngs of visitors gathered for three days. Mayor J. T. Roach presided at the programme which included historical pageants directed by G. D. H. Hatfield and Rosamond Archibald, sports events, and an orchestra and chorus of 500 voices. B. C. Silver directed the music, with Beatrice Rockwell and Nita Tretheway as pianists, and Grace Perry the concert master.

E. Sydney Crawley was born in December 1830, died in May 1927 at his Elm Street home. He was town solicitor and stipendiary magistrate from the incorporation of the town until he retired in 1922. He became postmaster in 1909 and earlier had learned photography. He studied law at Halifax, was admitted to the Bar in January 1847, after which he returned to Wolfville in 1878.

Vernon Eville's prowess attracted attention in 1928 as he accumulated highest individual scores at the Maritime track meet. He repeated his success at the next year's Maritime junior meet, set three new records and was selected to the Canadian team for the British Empire Games. Eville later became one of Acadia's greatest athletes. He was crippled in 1929 by polio but graduated from the university and worked at the maintenance department under superintendent Robie Roscoe, another member of the class of 1932. At his graduation Acadia president Dr. F. W. Patterson said of Eville: "I regret that I am not empowered to confer upon you an M.A. at this moment, because you have shown us how to master the art of living." Eville died at Halifax in 1974.

Gertrude Phinney Beattie was another outstanding athlete of the 1920s. She was born in Lawrencetown but received much of her early education at Wolfville. Following high school, she became a member of Dalhousie University's basketball team that went as far as the Dominion finals. She specialized in track events, winning medals in the sprints, hurdles, standing and running broad jumps, and at the 1928 Saint John meet she won the High Aggregate and the Halifax *Chronicle* trophy for the second time. At the 1928 Olympics at Halifax she came first in the 220 and placed second in the 60- and 100-yard dashes. In 1929 she established record runs in some of the dashes, her 50-yard an indoor record of world calibre.

Hon. R. B. Bennett, leader of the Federal Conservative Party, visited the town in 1928, and Charles H. Wright was awarded a contract to build the Digby Neck hydro extension transmission lines. He had numerous large contracts and building projects. In the fall Eunice Whidden left for Edmonton to become general secretary of the Y.W.C.A., and Canadian poet Bliss Carman visited Wolfville.

The coal business divided the community socially. Others ranked as leading citizens, while the blackened shovellers were of a different class. Two brothers poked fun at their dirtiness and, according to an apocryphal story, argued and bet twenty-five cents which was the dirtier. At Brown's Creek they stripped, evaluated one another's condition, and Elisha won. In response, Bill growled: "Hell, you ought to be; you're older'n I am."

5. 1930 — 1939

The Chamber of Commerce promoted the idea of celebrating the Centennial anniversary of the naming of Wolfville but the solicitor ruled that council "had no authority to expend money for such a purpose." Regardless, the council appointed a committee to help with the festivities. The successful celebration took place in August 1930, with a full day's programme of parades, contests, sports, and pageants. Dr. J. H. MacDonald wrote a hymn for the occasion, B. C. Silver composing the music. L. E. Shaw chaired the celebration, with G. S. Stairs as secretary. Ten pageants and plays were presented, of which Ethel L. Hemmeon directed eight, and Mrs. George Boggs and Dr. MacDonald directed one each. Other chairmen included Dr. Leslie Eaton, J. A. Macpherson, Dr. J. A. M. Hemmeon, H. P. Davidson, J. D. Chambers, and Mary MacMillan.

Jack Harris made the news in 1931 when he shot seventy-one over eighteen holes at the Ken-Wo club, a new amateur record. He won the Nova Scotia championship in 1932 at Ken-Wo.

Early in 1932 the *Acadian* suggested an Apple Blossom festival, an idea proposed years before. In August the usual Nova Scotia beauty contest was held at the Orpheum Theatre. Joan Marriott represented the town at the Provincial Exhibition at Halifax; the town voted not to make a small grant to cover her expenses. Young men got publicity also as Frank Chipman Higgins was in charge of the air force in the Maritimes, and Austin Rand led an expedition into the unexplored jungles of New Guinea.

The first Apple Blossom festival was held in 1933, and Wolfville's Maie

DeWitt was crowned Queen of the May by Margaret Shaffner who had been selected Miss Evangeline at the Halifax Exhibition the previous year. Mary Armour of Middleton was chosen Queen of the Festival, and for the Festival B. C. Silver trained a chorus of 1,000 school children. The town had additional excitement when Governor-General Lord Bessborough and his wife visited, and Sydney H. Wheelock was selected Rhodes Scholar for Nova Scotia.

The Wolfville *Acadian* of August 1930 reported the career of William Hardwick: "It is certain that no one now living has been so long a continuous resident of Wolfville, who at the age of nearly ninety-seven years is hale and hearty and enjoying an optimistic outlook on life." Born in January 1834, he came from Annapolis to Wolfville when he was twenty-one.

The *Canning Gazette* reported in 1893 that William Hardwick was made Superintendent of Streets and Waterworks, the first to occupy that office in the newly incorporated Town of Wolfville. Unfortunately, while making pipe repairs, superintendent Hardwick broke the large plate glass window in T. A. Munro's store.

Bill Hardwick's second wife was Mrs. Carrie Kinsman Bishop and they lived where the Esso station now stands. During his closing years he stayed with his eldest daughter, Mrs. Frank K. Trenholm at Grand Pre. Hardwick died in July 1933 at the age of ninety-nine.

Early one summer morning in 1933 Graham Patriquin, Harold "Trout" Evans, Wallace Barteaux, and Colin Munro concluded their nickel and dime poker game, left the Cornwallis Inn and in Colin's yellow sports roadster headed east. Said one: "We're coming home, Wolfville." Added another: "A town to live in." With a large pride swelling within, Graham Patriquin recorded through the years his memory of the people and the happenings of the past, glad that good fortune allowed him to live in and to enjoy his home town of Wolfville.

Deaths continued, and old-time citizen Margaret Frances Arnold died at the age of 102. Three other deaths were noted in the September 28 issue of the *Acadian*. Bessie B. Saxton began her successful millinery business in 1903. She had read widely, possessed a cultured mind and was much interested in community affairs. Aubrey V. Rand was born at Wolfville and lived to be sixty-four. After he sold his pharmacy to D. R. MacKinnon he became a chemist at the Nova Scotia Sanatorium, at Kentville. For six years he was a member of the town council and was on the school board, also a member of the Masonic Order. He died in 1933.

Charles R. H. Starr came to Wolfville in 1887 or 1888, carried on farming and orcharding, and was one of the first apple shippers to Great Britain. He exhibited at London's Crystal Palace. He had moved to Wolfville to handle better his overseas apple business. He was a charter member of the Board of Trade and led in the publication of an elaborate tourist booklet.

A member of the town council, he served as promoter and president of the Acadia Dairy Company. He held the office of secretary in the Nova Scotia Fruit Growers Association and helped establish at Wolfville the Nova Scotia School of Horticulture. He was a member of the Baptist Church and on the executive of the Acadia University Board of Governors. When Starr first came to Wolfville he bought the J. W. Johnson estate of about eight acres and opened up a road from Main Street through the centre of his land. Another cut was made from this to Chipman Hall Street (University Avenue).

An outstanding leader in the apple business, William H. Chase died in November 1933 in his eighty-second year. He had also distinguished himself as a financier, and inaugurated an improved apple shipping overseas. He gained part of his education at Acacia Villa school, and when seventeen began work at a general store at Port Williams where he developed a large trade selling potatoes and apples. He moved to Wolfville in 1896 and erected a fine residence, now "Historic Inn." He promoted the Board of Trade and became its first president. He served as an elder in the Presbyterian church, assisted in establishing Eastern Kings Memorial Hospital, and was director of several financial groups.

Another loss came in 1934 when Fred J. Porter died in March. Porter had come to Wolfville in the spring of 1883 and opened a grocery business with his cousin, George Porter, in a brief partnership. He continued in business until he removed to Kentville in 1915. He was a pioneer in automobiles, selling Fords. He held several public positions, became a Justice of the Peace in 1888, a Commissioner of the Supreme Court in 1935. He managed the Kings-Hants Exhibition at Wolfville in 1904.

A royal event occurred in 1935 when the town celebrated King George V's Silver Jubilee. The local Boy Scouts joined other troops in the Valley to shoot off rockets and set bonfires from a series of hilltops from Windsor to Digby. The council allocated funds the next year to mark the coronation of the King's successor, Edward VIII. Scoutmaster E. Percy Brown was made a member of the Order of the British Empire.

Clifford Oliver was succeeded in the care of University Hall by Henry Baines who also was devoted to his work. He assiduously discouraged students and faculty from walking where he was sweeping. The editor recalls Henry's shrill cry, "Get off them steps," a stern challenge to all alike.

In December 1935 Mr. and Mrs. George A. Prat celebrated their seventy-first wedding anniversary but Mr. Prat failed by a few weeks to reach his century, dying August 1936. Born in Gloucester, England, he resided in Wolfville since 1878, coming at the age of ten. Prat was prominent in civic

July 1936. Stuart Graham and his hydroplane.

offices, a member of the town council for some years. As an architect he remodelled the St. John's Anglican church nearly fifty years before his death. During more than half his life he served as a vestry clerk. He had married Euphemia Leonard of Paradise.

Happy reports were read in 1937. Murray Wannamaker was selected as one of the Valley high school students to attend the coronation of George VI, and the town celebrated in May, with the King's portrait unveiled and trees planted on the post office grounds, and bonfires and fireworks as part of the celebration. In the same month Gwladys "Babsie" Harris, daughter of Mr. and Mrs. J. D. Harris, was chosen Queen Annapolisa and represented Nova Scotia in the Shenandoah Valley Apple Blossom Festival at Winchester, Virginia, in 1938.

Carmelita Kinley, daughter of Reverend and Mrs. E. A. Kinley, became in 1938 Wolfville's second Queen Annapolisa, and Frances Patterson sat in cap and gown on the town's float. Ron Peck, third year student at McGill, won an architectual engineering prize. He had won in 1937 the high jump event in Toronto. The year ended with W. Earl Godfrey tutoring the young son of Cyrus Eaton at Cleveland before he became curator of ornithology at the National Museum at Ottawa. He and Ronald Smith had first been encouraged and instructed by Robie Tufts of Wolfville.

6. 1940 — 1949

The year 1940 began with Margaret A. Godfrey graduating from the Saint John General Hospital, and in May the Queen Annapolisa honours fell upon Audrey Clarke, daughter of Mr. and Mrs. W. A. Clarke. The 1941 Festival took on a military atmosphere, war having begun in the fall of 1939. A modified festival was held in 1942, and the returns of $700 were turned over to the Red Cross. Aldershot troops took part in Army Week during July, with a programme of sports and band music.

Son of David Hutchinson and Abbie MacDonald, Thomas E. Hutchinson died in February 1940 at the age of seventy. He left Wolfville early for the "Boston States" to work, and then for ten years in New York as an expressman with a single horse and waggon. He purchased the livery stable equipment of W. J. Balcom of Wolfville when Balcom retired. When the automobile came into general use he changed from horses to motors and established a bus service about 1922 between Wolfville and Kentville and later to Berwick. This he discontinued in 1935 but he carried on a taxi and express business until his retirement. He belonged to the Odd Fellows and the Masonic Order.

Rupert E. Harris, son of J. D. Harris and Sophia A. Eaton, was born at Belcher Street in 1863, died in November 1940. He married Nancy Bill and moved in 1891 to Wolfville where he and T. L. Harvey took over the grocery business at the corner of Main and Gaspereau Avenue. Harris later bought out his partner, and his sons W. C. B. and J. D. Harris continued the business. R. E. Harris exported apples to England and potatoes to the West Indies, using both sailing and steam vessels. One of the first full cargoes of apples travelled on the barquentine "Skoda" in 1904. He served on the town council and was active on the Board of Trade, and managed Willow Bank cemetery.

Boxing Day was first observed in the community in 1942, and people wondered about its meaning. In January 1943 Reverend Lydia E. Gurchy, first woman ordained in the United Church of Canada, visited Wolfville, and for the first time in many years May 24 was observed as a holiday. Because of the war, only a brief ceremony on the post office grounds celebrated the fiftieth anniversary of the town's incorporation.

J. Edward Hales died June 1943 at age seventy-four. When he was young the family moved from Horton Town Plot to Wolfville where he began his business career in the Western Book and News Company. He later joined the dry goods store of his uncle O. D. Harris and afterwards took over the business. Town councillor and mayor for fifteen years, he was chairman of the Streets Committee when the streets were first paved. He was past master of the Masons, an early member of the Board of Trade, and helped establish Ken-Wo country club. His wife was the former Laura Borden.

The 1944 Apple Blossom festival was stripped of much of its pomp and pageantry but Wolfville women received recognition as in 1945 Sub-Lieutenant Irene Fraser, R.N., daughter of Mr. and Mrs. W. L. Fraser, was chosen Queen Annapolisa, Mrs. Evelyn S. Tufts, correspondent for the Halifax *Herald,* was the first woman of the elected members of the Board of Directors of the Parliamentary Press at Ottawa.

Son of J. D. Harris, R.E. Harris retired in June 1944 and sold his grocery business to Robert L. Hancock. He had been a member of the town council for many years, a past grand master of the I.O.O.F., director of Ken-Wo golf club, and a charter member of the curling club. Mona Parsons, daughter of Colonel and Mrs. N. A. Parsons, made news early in 1945 when she escaped from the Gestapo who had imprisoned her while she worked for the Dutch underground.

The *Acadian* reported the death of Harlan P. Davidson, editor of the paper. He died in November, ending a long career. The eldest son of B. O. and Mrs. Davidson, he received his schooling at Wolfville and studied at Acadia. About 1920 he and his brother Waldo B. Davidson took over from their father. Harlan had other local interests, serving as elder of St. Andrew's United Church and for a considerable time as organist. He was a member of the Masonic Order and of the Board of Trade, and in the First World War was secretary of the Victory Loans campaign. In 1923 he had married Clairie Lamb, of Boston.

In April 1946 Burpee W. Wallace died at the age of seventy-seven, survived by his wife, the former Mary Fitch of Wolfville. He studied at Acadia and McMaster universities. As an educator, he served mostly in Western Canada, coming in 1934 to Wolfville where he was a charter member and the first president of the Rotary Club. He was also a charter member and president for a term of the Curling Club, as well as a member of the Ken-Wo Golf Club. He served for his last nine years as chairman of the school board and took part in several service groups and projects, also being coroner for the county and stipendiary magistrate for the town.

Lady Baden-Powell visited the town in June 1946 and inspected the Girl Guides. The town's first taxi driver, James Bruce Spencer, died at the age of seventy-five. A community Christmas tree stood in December in front of the park.

Charles A. Patriquin died in April 1947. In his tribute, Reverend F. H. Eaton, pastor of the Baptist Church, recounted Patriquin's concerns as a naturalist and as a lover of people, particularly for the welfare of youths who grew up and served their country overseas. Patriquin was born at Wolfville in 1864, oldest son of James G. and Matilda (Pick) Patriquin. While yet a boy he took over his father's harness-making business. With F. P. Rockwell, he began the Evangeline Beach development in 1896, selling the property in 1908, and returning to Wolfville in 1909. After the town's incorporation he was one of the early council members. He was active in the Division, Sons of Temperance, and for about sixty years served as inspector under the Canada Temperance Act. With others, he pioneered in small fruit growing and was an expert market gardener. He participated in the Children's Aid Society, the Cemetery Corporation, the Boy Scout movement, and he promoted Tabernacle services. He had married Sarah Craig of Cambridge, Kings County.

Dr, I. B. Oakes, highly esteemed citizen and Acadia's oldest graduate, died in June 1948, a few months short of one hundred. Educated at Horton Academy and Acadia University, Ingram Burpee Oakes devoted his life to education, first in New Brunswick as Inspector of Schools from 1879 to 1889. For ten years he was principal of Horton Academy and was chief census officer for Nova Scotia and Prince Edward Island in 1901, and agent for Nova Scotia and the Canadian government in England and Scotland in 1907. He was provincial examiner in geometry for many years and was elected a governor of Acadia in 1904. For ten years previous to 1926 he was Prothonotary of the Supreme Court, clerk of the County Court, and county clerk of the Crown. He served as an official in the Baptist Church, was an officer of the Masonic Order, a member of the town council and school board and the local Board of Trade. In 1878 he had married Elizabeth Jardine Smith of Richibucto, New Brunswick.

Honours came to Wolfville when in December 1948 George C. Nowlan won the federal election for Digby-Annapolis-Kings riding. Next year Wolfville had another Queen Annapolisa in the person of Jean Cochrane, daughter of Mr. and Mrs. D. Ross Cochrane.

In 1949 Wolfville lost other senior citizens. At the age of seventy-nine, James Lake, veteran of the Boer War and World War I, died in August. He had married Emily Gilbert in 1895, and moved to Wolfville from England in 1912 to begin farming. He was a member of the Legion and of the Church of England.

John D. Chambers, former mayor, died in December at the age of eighty-eight. He came to Wolfville in 1882 and clerked in the Caldwell and Murray dry goods establishment, then became a partner of Caldwell, Chambers and Company. From 1871 to 1879 he resided at Yarmouth but returned to Wolfville to take over the business at the corner of Main Street and Central Avenue where he continued for twenty-two years, selling to C. H. Porter. He served on the town council and for three terms as mayor. The Main Street was first paved during his later term of office, between 1912 and 1926, the first town in the Valley to have street paving. The sidewalks were paved during his later term in office. He was a member of the Presbyterian Church, later the United Church. He was a Past Master of the Masonic Lodge, the first president of the Boy Scout association, a member of the Board of Trade, and for some years the president of the Victorian Order of Nurses. He promoted improvement of the "Mud Bridge" area and the old cemetery. He married Frances M. Woodman of Wolfville.

Former school principal and town clerk and treasurer, Robie W. Ford died in December 1949 at the age of ninety. He was principal for twenty-four years and was at the town hall for twenty-one years. At the town office he also was secretary of the School Board, secretary of the Electric Commission, and later was appointed County Stipendiary. He was treasurer of the Baptist Church, and Past Master of the Masons. He married in 1899 Sadie Jamieson of Truro. In April of the following year George C. Nowlan unveiled at the Munro school building a portrait honoring Mr. Ford.

7. 1950 — 1959

Paul Collins, violinist son of Dean and Mrs. Collins of the university, won distinction for his long-distance running. The town gave him a "rousing welcome" in 1950 for representing Canada well at the British Empire Games in New Zealand. He later placed eighth in the Boston Marathon, and in 1952 won the Canadian Marathon championship, also represented Canada at the Olympic Games at Helsinki, Finland. C. W. Fairn headed the Apple Blossom festival, and the Sunday afternoon service was held at University Hall, instead of at Grand Pre park. In 1951 the Wolfville Curling Club held a three-day bonspiel at University Rink as part of the festivities. A near tragedy took place when Private Sheldon Henshaw fell 250 feet near Whirlpool Rapids at Niagara Falls. He was rescued.

King George VI died early in 1952 and the town held a "civic" day of mourning. Later, on the playing field on Victoria Avenue the Scouts, Guides and Cubs helped celebrate Queen Elizabeth's coronation.

Rosamond M. DeWolfe Archibald died in May 1953 at the age of seventy-one. She received schooling at Windsor and Acadia, then got further degrees at Smith College. She was instructor at Horton Academy and librarian of the university. Then from 1913 to 1925 she became head of the Seminary's English department. She taught English at Horton Academy, 1925-1946, during which time she campaigned for "Better English," and wrote *The King's English Drill* which was published in several editions. She contributed much to Wolfville also as she sparked the founding of the Historical Society in 1941, and was its first secretary, serving for many years. She strove to preserve the historic DeWolf House. The Historical Society honoured her memory in 1980 by naming one of the Randall House museum's rooms after her.

Rosamond Archibald frequently corrected the English usage of the Gibson boys next door. Either because or in spite of this display of her interest, Allen Gibson painted for Miss Archibald a sign "Toad Hall" over the entry of the arbour of white poles over which grew her cucumber vines.

Allen Gibson had other memories. He recalled amusing incidents, such as when Santa's tummy slipped disastrously, and a youngster replied to Santa, "You mean you don't know" when the old man asked the lad if he had been good. Gibson particularly recalled the Grade XI concert of 1936, headed by principal B. C. Silver and teachers O. Rex Porter and A. E. Crowdis. Those taking part in the comedy were: Esther Fitch, Annette Merriott, Bella Cohen, Eugene Merry, Stuart Roach, Norman Fowlow, Barbara Harris, Gerald Hughes, K. MacDonald, Lawrence Johnson, Jim Stairs, Stuart Kenney, Marion Keith, Robbins Elliott, Donald Burgher, Jean Duncanson, and Allen Gibson.

In another Christmas drama, those participating were: David Waterbury, George Fraser, Glen Hancock, Jeannette Ruffee, Geraldine Clark, Jim MacLauchlan, George Ruffee, Max Forsythe-Smith, Pauline Fraser, Murray Wannamaker, Shirley Duncanson, Milton Gregg, Florence Gates, John Merry, and Murray Tupper.

Prime Minister Louis St. Laurent visited Wolfville in July 1953, and Ashton M. Wheaton, aged eighty-two died in October. He came to Wolfville from Upper Sackville, New Brunswick, as a young man and became manager of the town's first co-operative, the Acadia Dairy Company. He later bought and sold the business. He was a town councillor for several years, holding the office of mayor for ten years. Also, he was president of the Board of Trade, president of Kings County Conservative Association, and chief assessor of the town. He was a Past Master of the Masonic Lodge and prominent in the United Church.

A stir was caused when in April 1954 Robin Rideout, aged thirteen, got locked into the old vault of the town hall while clearing the records; town clerk Fowler was able to release him. Perhaps the worst wind storm to visit Wolfville, Hurricane Edna, hit the Valley in September, damaging the apple crop.

Former editor of the Wolfville *Acadian* Bowman O. Davidson died in January 1955 at the age of ninety-two. He was the son of Joseph B. and Margaret A. Davidson and had married in 1889 Ella M. Taylor of Billtown. He received his education in Wolfville and through experience. He and his brother Arthur S. founded the paper in 1883 and he continued in active service until he lost his sight in 1945. He was an Elder of the Presbyterian Church for many years, also active in temperance since 1881. He was a charter member of the Board of Trade of which he was president for some years, and he helped organize the County Children's Aid Society and the Wolfville branch of the Victorian Order of Nurses.

Death came to Dr. John B. Eaton in October 1955. Son of Dr. and Mrs. Eugene Eaton, John came to Canada from India when he was four, was educated at Wolfville, at Acadia and Harvard. He and his wife, the former Joan Templeman, lived in India for about seven years, returning to Wolfville in 1946 to continue dentistry. He led the Wolf Cubs here for several years and was prominent in the Rotary Club.

Edson Graham died in December 1956. He was well known for his portraits and scenic views of beauty spots in the province. In the community he was a town councillor, a Boy Scout enthusiast, president of the Board of Trade for several years, and a member of the Baptist Church.

In May 1957 Governor-General Vincent Massey visited Wolfville. During the next year Daisy West retired from town hall as assistant clerk and was given a testimonial dinner by the council. She had earlier substituted as town clerk in 1908, served as a bookkeeper and business manager of Sleep's tinsmith, plumbing, and hardware store. She was the oldest daughter of Mr. and Mrs. Samuel West, died in March 1963 at the age of seventy-seven.

Her youngest sister Hilda was also a bookkeeper, employed at T. E. Hales dry goods store. From the mezzanine she surveyed the business below, handled the cash sales propelled to her in metal boxes by the speedily moving cord. Another sister, Gladys, taught in the local school, with a no-nonsense approach, always fair. The fourth sister, Gertrude, had her R.N. and was a public health nurse in New York city.

John W. Williams died in October 1958. He had been born and educated at Charlottetown, Prince Edward Island, and clerked in a drug store before coming to Kentville and then to Waltham, Massachusetts, to work in the watch factory there. He opened his own jewellery business at Wolfville in 1911 and served in the 85th Battalion when in 1917 he was wounded, losing a leg at Ypres. He was prominent in sports, including hockey and curling. He was a member of the United Church and charter member of the Rotary Club, being secretary for twenty-one years, and also a member of the Masonic Lodge and the Canadian Legion.

Margaret Godfrey McCarthy recalled that J. W. Williams' given name was John Wallace; by mistake he acquired the name of "Jimmy" because at the time there was a well-known hockey player by that name. When Williams came to Wolfville he showed an interest in hockey and it was assumed he was Jimmy, and the name stayed with him. He was Wally to his family.

Aubrey S. Dakin completed fifty years in 1959 as Superintendent of Works. He began working for the town when aged seventeen. He died in 1964 and the town passed legislation so that his widow would receive a modest pension.

8. 1960 — 1969

R. C. Vanwart celebrated in March 1960 his fiftieth year in the hardware business. He began clerking at Fredericton, New Brunswick, served in the armed forces from 1915 to 1919 and returned to Fredericton. After 1925 he worked at New Glasgow, then moved to Bridgetown until 1938 when he came to Wolfville. Here he acted as a town councillor, was president of the Board of Trade, and served for eight years as treasurer of the Masonic Lodge where he was a Master. He was on the session of the United Church. He had married the former Minnie M. Burpee of Fredericton.

E. Percy Brown died in July at the age of eighty-seven. He had been educated at R.M.C., Kingston, Ontario, and at Massachusetts Institute of Technology. He moved to Wolfville in 1910 and became the first Scoutmaster early in 1911. His contribution to Scouting was recognized in November 1958 when 175 attended a testimonial banquet. He was made a member of the Order of the British Empire in 1935 and received the Silver Wolf.

Lloyd E. Shaw died at Halifax in August at the age of eighty-one. He began brickmaking at the age of seven, driving the horse at his father's small brickyard at Avonport which had equipment valued at about $100. Robert Shaw moved to Hantsport and bought a much larger brickyard where Lloyd entered the business. Lloyd was educated at Patterson School for Boys at Hortonville and in 1905 married Lillian Morse of Bridgetown where he managed a brickworks. After a business venture at Middleton and as a superintendent of the Annapolis plant, in 1914 he opened a brickyard at Avonport. The Halifax Explosion of 1917 increased his business and he bought out his rivals. Shaw's brick and tile plant turned out 20,000 bricks each day, and his relationship with his workers was fair and comfortable as they gave him respect and appreciation. He lived at Wolfville where he was deacon and Sunday School superintendent of the Baptist Church and was also a member of the town council, president of the Boy Scout Association, president of the Board of Trade. He served on Acadia's Board of Governors for many years.

Son of Thomas and Harriett Bresnan, Frank Welch Bresnan died in February 1962 at the age of sixty-six. In March 1931 he had married Elizabeth Fields of Truro, and as a master carpenter and contractor he had built many fine homes at Hantsport and Wolfville. In 1953 he suffered a stroke which forced him to discontinue his business.

In 1962 Frank C. Welch, head of Wolfville Fruit company and president of the Nova Scotia Conservative Association since 1953, was appointed to the Senate. During that same fall Mrs. Theodosia Ernest Denton died at the age of 103.

Royal W. DeWolfe died in March 1963 at the age of sixty-seven. He was described as the province's largest apple grower and shipper. He was born at Canning, Nova Scotia, son of John and Margaret (Warner) DeWolfe. He worked in a bank there after his schooling, and enlisted in 1916 with the 85th Battalion. After the war he worked with R. A. Jodrey before starting his business at Wolfville. He held many offices related to the apple industry and to finance, was director of E.K.M. Hospital and an officer of the St. Andrew's United Church. He held offices in the Rotary Club, the Masonic Order, and the Canadian Legion. He had married Emily Eaton of Canning. The *Acadian* repoted in August that R. W. DeWolfe Limited had operated the apple exporting business about fifty years, with Owen DeWolfe now in charge. The overseas apple business was not as profitable as it was in his father's years.

Lawson Brighton Fielding, for forty-four years employed with the post office, was honoured at his retirement in February 1953 by the Board of Trade, Harry Van Zoost the president. He had come with his parents to Wolfville in 1898, joined the post office staff in 1908. He was a Past Noble Grand of I.O.O.F. Lodge, a member of the Baptist Church, was unmarried. At the age of seventy-five he died in February 1963.

Dr. Perry S. Cochrane was chief of staff at E.K.M. hospital when he died February 1964. He was born in Cumberland County sixty-five years before, son of Captain and Mrs. John W. Cochrane. He graduated from Dalhousie University medical school in 1923, came to Wolfville in 1927 where he belonged to the Masonic Order, St. Andrew's United Church, and several medical societies. Keenly interested in sports, he was a member of the curling and badminton clubs. He married Constance Collins of Advocate, Nova Scotia.

In 1964 Jocelyn Cameron became the first woman to graduate from the Nova Scotia Land Survey Institute at Lawrencetown. R.A. Jodrey gave land on Cape Blomidon to the province for a park, and Frank Angus reached the age of 100.

Karl W. Borden died January 1965 at the age of seventy-two. Born at Canard, son of Lawen and Maud (Cox) Borden, he studied at Mount Allison and taught manual training in the Nova Scotia Sanatorium, Kentville, and worked later in the engineering department of Acadia University. Until 1931 he superintended maintenance of buildings, after which he owned and managed several apartment buildings and a campus restaurant. He served four years on the town council and for one term as deputy mayor, was also on the school board. He participated in Provincial and Dominion rifle competition and was chief fire warden for the town up to the time of his death.

When Karl Borden worked for the university he took over from Atwood Cohoon who for twenty-five years had promoted Acadia's finances and also superintended the property, became known as "The Pope." Karl Borden acquired the title with the job, and at his house the student lodgers dubbed themselves "The Cardinals." When he bought Cohoon's large dwelling on Prospect Street for an apartment it became "The Vatican." Borden's wife was the former Amy Wamboldt of Lunenburg.

The Honourable George C. Nowlan died May 1965 after public service in politics since 1925 in the Provincial Legislature, and as a Conservative in the House of Commons since 1948. He held several Cabinet positions, representing Digby-Annapolis-Kings. Son of Charles Nowlan, he was born in Havelock, Digby County, graduated from Acadia University, served overseas in World War I, was a Masonic Lodge member, and belonged to the Canadian Legion. He had married Miriam Chisholm in July 1923. After his father died, Patrick Nowlan assumed the Tory leadership in this constituency.

9. 1970 — 1979

Governor-General Roland Michener came to Wolfville in 1971.

Dr. Leslie R. Fairn (1875-1971) died in August. In 1902 he became principal of the E. W. Young Mechanic Science school at Horton Academy for a year, moved to Aylesford, then returned in 1927. As an experienced and recognized architect, he constructed several college buildings here and other structures about the province. At the same time, he entered into community activities as a member of the Masonic Order and of the Rotarians, and as a contributor to the Baptist Church. He helped to establish the Leslie R. Fairn Wildlife Management Laboratory in 1965 at Acadia which honoured him in 1968 with the D.C.L. degree.

In 1974 Mrs. Rex Porter was honoured for achieving high sales of *World Book* encyclopedias. During the same year Harry W. How was M.L.A. for Kings South, and Glen Hancock addressed the Rotary club for the John Howard society.

The death of O. Rex Porter in November 1975 meant a significant loss to the community. Son of Grant and Emma Porter, he had his schooling at Wolfville, from Acadia, and University of Toronto. He and Ruth Ingraham married in 1935. Having specialized in adult education, he helped administer the programme in the county, but mainly he served the local schools, concluding as supervisor from 1940 to 1970. He also organized and directed the school bands for thirty-five years and led the cadet corps. He re-established Scouting and was Scoutmaster of the Second Troop, was president of the Rotary club and the East Kings Local of the Nova Scotia Teachers Union, president of the County Home and School Association, and was a member of the Masonic Lodge. He served on many health and church groups and on professional bodies.

Mrs. Herbert D'Arcy Johnson attended Acadia Seminary in 1908, and in 1953 received a certificate of fine arts from the university. She formerly attended the Normal School at Truro, taught in Nova Scotia and in Quebec, then lived forty-five years at Wolfville. She was a charter member of the I.O.D.E. and occupied offices in several capacities. She was active in Red Cross, gave blood fifteen times. Since the E.K.M. Hospital Auxiliary first began she was a member. Mr. and Mrs. Johnson were shareholders of the Ken-Wo country club, enjoying golf. She spent much time at gardening, exhibited and was reported to be "the only lady horticulturalist in Nova Scotia." She died in the fall of 1965.

The popular deliveryman of the Halifax *Herald,* Fred Holloway retired after over thirty years at the business of calling out with his clear English accent the name of the paper. He also sold the *War Cry* for the Salvation Army, of which he was a faithful member, and he annually guarded the Army's Christmas kettle, was a writer of hymns. Holloway died early in 1966, at the age of eighty.

Guilford Douglas Jefferson ran a shoe store in 1919 where now is the Cochrane drug store. It suffered in the Depression, and he later became the town's shoe repairman. He died in 1967, over eight-five years of age.

Wolfville hosted the Apple Blossom festival in 1969. The town's floats won high honours from time to time in the past. In 1967 Ivan Pulsifer's float, designed by Mrs. Pulsifer, won the grand prize; it was built by Ivan Pulsifer, Donald Pulsifer, and Al Whittle.

Older citizens of Wolfville recall the eccentric recluse Maud Kennedy and her thirty cats, all secluded in a carelessly tended house on Acadia Street where now stands part of the university library. She was Professor Kennedy's only child who died in June 1969 after living for several years with Mr. and Mrs. Clarence Burton. For this publication Burton provided scenes, some photographed perhaps by Kennedy in 1876.

In 1976 Wolfville Princess Fredda Murray, daughter of Mr. and Mrs. Walter Murray, became Queen Annapolisa 44. Robert Jadis, fomerly of Wolfville, achieved another kind of honour when he carried the Olympic torch at Ottawa. Further recognition came to the community when Queen Elizabeth and His Royal Highness Prince Phillip toured the campus, banqueting at Wheelock dining hall. Mrs. I. Judson Levy was elected president of the Atlantic Baptist Missionary Union.

Academic recognition came in 1978 to Julie Porter, daughter of Mr. and Mrs. Gerald Porter, when awarded an $8,000 National Research Council scholarship. Donald F. Archibald ran for Kings South New Democratic Party, and Harry W. How for the Progressive Conservatives in the provincial election.

Granddaughter of Dr. and Mrs. M. R. Elliott, and daughter of Robbins, Wendy Elliott (Slipp) published her writings in the *Kentville Advertiser* during the summer of 1979. Her caricature by her husband Steven appeared early in October in the *Advertiser.* Clara Nowlan Jefferson was appointed to the Provincial Advisory Council on the Status of Women.

10. The Year 1980

Harold W. Stultz, earlier retired from the federal agricultural department, was honoured in April with a membership plaque from the Acadian Ontological Society. The past was recalled by W. D. Withrow who came to Wolfville in 1920 as a lawyer. He remembered that Tom Kelly's cobbler shop and Andrew Delahunt's blacksmith shop were then near the present Willow Park.

When reading *Historic Homes* and *Streets of Wolfville*, James D. Davison, president of the Wolfville Historical Society, realized that the 150th anniversary of the renaming of the town would occur in 1980. At the society's November 1979 meeting he announced this in the presence of new mayor William Kenny, Jr. He was there to help celebrate the group's 38th anniversary of its organization. Mayor and council arranged for a community organization and Davison became the anniversary committee chairman. With the mayor, other officers were: Vice-chairman George A. Taylor of the town's recreation department, secretary Lucille Yates, publicity chairman Donald Mosher of the Rotary club, and town councillor Jean Marsh.

The "Mud Creek Days" celebration extended from August 8 to 17 and provided a variety programme outlined in a twelve-page booklet that included greetings from the mayor, a list of all the previous mayors, described places to see, walking tours, listed historic homes open to the public, and other houses associated with the DeWolfes, and with appreciation by the DeWolfes for recognition of their name. Gordon R. Hansford won the Coat of Arms contest, his creation being officially adopted by the council.

The programme was varied and included handcraft and produce booths daily, a historical display of pictures, nightly music by bands, sports tournaments, kite-flying, mud-sliding and a soap slide, also a bake sale, a pancake breakfast, and a barbecue.

The mayor's reception on August 13, the anniversary of the day the name-change was made, honoured the DeWolfes and former mayors. Town crier Lloyd Smith of Windsor led the procession from Town Hall to Willow Park where the mayor welcomed the assembly. Federal M.P. Patrick Nowlan and Acadia acting-president James R. C. Perkin brought greetings, and James D. Davison told of the Wolfville of 1830. The mayor planted a tree to celebrate the occasion, and members of the Interchurch Council conducted a service of praise and thanksgiving at Willow Park on the final evening of the celebration. Committee chairman Davison related another story of Wolfville's beginnings and the Acadia University Gospel Team provided a special programme of song.

In November the Historical Society enacted a drama on the life of R.A. Jodrey from a biography by Harry Bruce. Taking part were: James Davison, Margaret Elliott, Ethel Ingraham, George Moody, Dr. Marion Grant, Russell MacKay, and Harold Stultz. The *Acadian's* final issue of 1980 recorded that Murdock MacLeod was busy as co-ordinator of Wolfville's Business Development Corporation.

Dr. Robie W. Tufts acquired prominence, first through his skill in taxidermy; for several years he donated one of his birds to the annual Rotary Club auction. His name was well known also through his writings. From 1917 to 1947 he administered the Migratory Bird Convention Act throughout the Maritimes, and in 1919 became the Chief Federal Migratory Bird Officer. His first wife was Evelyn S. Smith, and he later married Lillian Thompson. He graduated from Dalhousie University and received in 1973 an honorary degree from Acadia. In 1980 he was a bright and energetic ninety-six-year-old citizen who still chopped his firewood.

1979. Historical Society charter members, L to R: Dalton MacKinnon, Esther Clark Wright, Mayor William Kenny, Jr., Helen D. Beals, Harry Van Zoost.

XX.

TOWN OFFICIALS, 1893-1980

Mayors E.P. Bowles, 1893,94; James W. Bigelow, 1895,96; George Thomson, 1897-1902; J.F. Herbin, 1902-03; George E. DeWitt, 1903-05; W.M. Black, 1906-08; Thomas L. Harvey, 1909-11; J.D. Chambers, 1912-14,24,25; C.S. Fitch, 1915,16,20,21; J.E. Hales, 1917-19; Alexander Sutherland, 1922; H.W. Phinney, 1923; John T. Roach, 1926,27; A.B. Balcom, Sr., 1928-31; A.M. Wheaton, 1932-38; W.K. Fraser, 1939-43; C.W. Fairn, 1944-49; E.W. Balcom, 1950-55; R.S. Longley, 1956-62; A.B. Balcom, Jr., 1962-65; Murdock MacLeod, 1966-73; Paul Kinsman, 1974-76; Robert A. Wrye, 1977-79; William J. Kenny, Jr. 1980—.

Clerks Walter Brown, 1893; Frank Dixon, 1894-1904; A.E. Coldwell, 1905-12; W.M. Black, 1913-17; H.Y. Bishop, 1917-21; R.W. Ford, 1922-41; G. Garberry, 1941-52; G.D. Feindel, 1952-55; A. Watkins, 1955-61; B.H. Mason, 1961-68; R.A. Steeves, 1969; T.L. Allen, 1969-71; Roy Thomson, 1971—.

Councillors George Thomson, 1893,94; George W. Borden, 1893-96,98,99; Clarence H. Borden, 1893,94; E.W. Sawyer, 1893,94; A. DeW. Barss, 1893; C.R.H. Starr, 1893-95; I.B. Davison, 1894,95; Fred J. Porter, 1895-99,1902,03,13-15; Enoch L. Collins, 1895-97; R.E. Harris, 1895-97,1912; J.W. Caldwell, 1895-98; Frank Haley, 1896-98; E.P. Bowles, 1897; W.H. Chase, 1898,1902,03; Thomas L. Harvey, 1898-1901; G.E. DeWitt, 1899,1900; W.A. Chipman, 1899,1900; J.L. Franklin, 1899, 1900; J.F. Herbin, 1900,01; I.B. Oakes, 1900-03; Charles Fitch, 1901-04,06-09; G.A. Prat, 1901,02; C.A. Patriquin, 1901,02; Harold Lawrence, 1903,04; J.B. Tingley, 1903,04; W.M. Black, 1904,05; W.H. Duncan, 1904; Reuben Wallace, 1904,05; J.D. Chambers, 1905,06,09-11; Dwight Sherwood, 1905,06; J.E. Hales, 1905-16; Edward Johnson, 1905-07; George Abbott, 1906-09; William Ford, 1907,08; Abner McKenna, 1907,08; John Selfridge, 1908,09; R.F. Burgess, 1909,10; C.R.H. Starr, 1910,11; William Regan, 1910-19; Ernest Haycock, 1910-15; L.W. Sleep, 1911-14; J.C. Bishop, 1912; W.C.B. Harris, 1913-19,28,29; A.V. Rand, 1915-20; J.D. Sherwood, 1916-19; S.W. Beardsley, 1916; Thomas L. Harvey, 1917,18; C.E.A. DeWitt, 1917,18; Edson Graham, 1919,20; Alexander Sutherland, 1919-21; Charles Nowlan, 1920-22; Laura H. Moore, 1920,21; Lloyd E. Shaw, 1920,21; A.M. Wheaton, 1921,22; A.C. Cox, 1921,22; Leslie Eaton, 1922,23; A.M. Young, 1922,23; H.A. Peck, 1922-24; D.G. Whidden, 1922,23; A.B. Balcom, Sr., 1923,24; W.A. Reid, 1923,24; Freeman A. Leslie, 1924-31; John T. Roach, 1924,25; Joseph C. Mitchell, 1924,25; C.H. Porter, 1925-27; Chester Coombs, 1925,26; Joseph Macpherson, 1925; R.W. DeWolfe, 1925-28; Clarence A. Spinney, 1926-29; William Grant, 1925-27; P.W. Davidson, 1927-29; C.A. Brown, 1928-31; Frederic G. Herbin,

1929,30; J.H. Baltzer, 1930,31,39-42,44-49; H. Stairs, 1930-32; Leslie Fairn, 1930-39; W.K. Fraser, 1931-38; E.C. Bishop, 1932,33; D.R. Cochrane, 1932,33; E.R. Wickwire, 1932,33; R.M. Keirstead, 1933-36; H.Y. Bishop, 1934,35; O.H. Foshay, 1934,35; J.D. Harris, 1934,35; Cecil Hansford, 1936-38,40; Enoch Bishop, 1936,37; Merle Bancroft, 1936-39; Frank C. Welch, 1937,38,49-58,60,61; H. Jackson, 1938,39; Samuel Beardsley, 1939,40; Thomas Weaver, 1939-44; C.W. Small, 1940-43; H.L. Baird, 1940-43; R.C. VanWart, 1941,42; W.A. Clarke, 1941,43,44; A.R. Macpherson, 1942,43; E. Cameron, 1943,44; Harry VanZoost, 1944-51; Eric Balcom, 1944-49; Karl W. Borden, 1945-48; W. McCurdy, 1945,46; M.A. Welch, 1945-48; F.T. Lewis, 1947,48; A.B. Balcom, Jr., 1949,50,52,54,55; R.E. MacCluskey, 1949,50; L.C. Trites, 1950-53; Nelson Grant, 1950-55; G.R. Bromley, 1951-53; Owen DeWolfe, 1951-54; Bernard N. Cain, 1953,54; Winston Mullen, 1954-57; Austin E. Brownell, 1955-58; R.S. Longley, 1955; W.J. Kenny, Sr., 1956-59,62,63,66-68; V.H. MacKay, 1956-59; J.F. Herbin, 1956-58,62-65; C.S. Parsons, 1958; W.C. Hatt, 1959-61,64,65; Murdock MacLeod, 1959-65; Rupert MacNeill, 1959,60; A.M. Sutherland, 1959,60; S.B. Westcott, 1960,61; Erik Hansen, 1961-65; Charles Eaton, 1961-68; D.L. Davison, 1962-65; Gordon C. MacDonald, 1966-69; W.H. Mowat, 1966-71; M.V. Skerry, 1966,67; J.M. Wilson, 1966; D.O. Snow, 1967,68; R.H. Taylor, 1968-70; T.L. Allen, 1969; Murray H. Boland, 1969-71,75—; J. Glen Tillotson, 1969-72,75-78; Jean E. Marsh, 1970,71,73—; E.R. Hutchinson, 1970-74; Robert A. Wrye, 1971-76; Clarence Burton, 1972-74; Paul Kinsman, 1972,73; John W. Murphy, 1972,73; William Parker, 1973,74; Douglas Cochrane, 1975,76; Ian Fraser, 1975-77; Agar Adamson, 1976,77; Marshall Conley, 1977; Andrea Hornborg, 1977-79; William Townsend, 1978—; Eric Murphy, 1978-80; John Martens, 1979—; Garry R. Balcom, 1980—.

John W. Barss house, and Church of England house of worship.

XXI INDEX

236

244

CENTENNIAL OF HERBIN'S JEWELLERY, 1885-1985

J.F. Herbin

Reportedly, also the Post Office, 1860-1895.

The publishers of *Mud Creek* are pleased to recognize in their history the place of the Herbin family in this community. The Herbins celebrate this year their one-hundredth birthday since their business began here, and it is fitting that together the Town, and the Historical Society, and the Herbins celebrate this significant occasion.

Many of the family names of numerous New England Planters, and of the few of the American Loyalists, occur again and again in this story of *Mud Creek*. But probably alone among the ethnic groups that established and nurtured the Town of Wolfville is the Herbin family that traces back to the Acadians and has remained intact and constant in the Town records for 100 years.

The first of the Herbins to come here was the poet John Frederic Herbin, who established the jewellery business in 1885. His mother's people had been expelled from Grand Pre in 1755. For four generations they have been community leaders and remain the solitary link with the first inhabitants of the Acadian dyked lands. The centennial observance of their Main Street commerical enterprise is a tribute not only to Herbin's but to Wolfville businesses in general.